POLITICAL IDENTITY
AND SOCIAL CHANGE

SUNY series in Global Politics
James N. Rosenau, editor

POLITICAL IDENTITY AND SOCIAL CHANGE

The Remaking of the South African Social Order

JAMIE FRUEH

Foreword by Nicholas Onuf

STATE UNIVERSITY OF NEW YORK PRESS

Published by
STATE UNIVERSITY OF NEW YORK PRESS, ALBANY

© 2003 State University of New York

All rights reserved

Printed in the United States of America

No part of this book may be used or reproduced in any manner whatsoever without written permission. No part of this book may be stored in a retrieval system or transmitted in any form or by any means including electronic, electrostatic, magnetic tape, mechanical, photocopying, recording, or otherwise without the prior permission in writing of the publisher.

For information, address State University of New York Press,
90 State Street, Suite 700, Albany, NY 12207

Production, Laurie Searl
Marketing, Patrick Durocher

Library of Congress Cataloging-in-Publication Data

Frueh, Jamie, 1966–
   Political identity and social change : the remaking of the South African social order / Jamie Frueh.
     p. cm. — (SUNY series in global politics)
   Includes bibliographical references and index.
   ISBN 0-7914-5547-5 (alk. paper) — ISBN 0-7914-5548-3 (pbk. : alk. paper)
   1. Social change—South Africa. 2. Group identity—South Africa. 3. South Africa—Social conditions—1994– 4. South Africa—Politics and government—1994– 5. Constructivism (Philosophy) I. Title. II. Series.

HN801.A8 F78 2002
303.4'0968—dc21

2002017730

10 9 8 7 6 5 4 3 2 1

To my parents,
who taught me to dream big;
to Eileen,
who lets me;
and to Wren and Gavin,
the results.

Contents

Acknowledgments, ix

Foreword by Nicholas Onuf, xiii

Chapter One
INTRODUCTION, 1

Chapter Two
A THEORY OF POLITICAL IDENTITY, 9

Constructivism
Identity
Identity Labels as Units of a Constructivist Method
Conclusion

Chapter Three
SOUTH AFRICA AND IDENTITY, 39

Apartheid and Its Historical Context
Analysis of South African Politics
The Practicalities of Studying South African Identity

Chapter Four
SOWETO 1976, 65

Soweto, June 16, 1976—A Story
Competing Discourses on Soweto
The Political Identity of Soweto
Conclusion: The Beginning of the End

Chapter Five
CONSTITUTIONAL REFORM, 1983–1984, 95

Reform, Resistance, Repression
Competing Discourses on the Constitution
Constitutional Reform and Political Identity
Conclusion

Chapter Six
POST-APARTHEID CRIME, 133

Crime in South Africa
The Discourse on Crime
Crime and Political Identity
Conclusion

Chapter Seven
IDENTITY AND THE TRANSITION:
Conclusions for the Political Theory of Social Change, 169

The Argument for Constructivist Political Identity
The Argument about South Africa
Conclusions and Generalizations

Notes, 185

Bibliography, 215

Index, 231

Acknowledgments

One of the first things a wise man told me was that finishing a project like this required two things, passion and discipline. As I readily admit (and my family and friends will certainly attest), this project was finished almost in spite of the latter requirement. But I have had an abundance of the former: passion about the identity ideas, passion about the teaching career that this research helped launch, and the passion that the people of South Africa have shared with me. The tragedy about writing a book, especially an academic treatise, is that the passion that drives the original inquiry must get chopped up into words. And for those of us who are not poets, words too often mask more than they reveal. Analysis demands breaking something into pieces and sorting those pieces according to a judgment about their importance for the task at hand. That my passion for understanding South Africa got channeled into the concepts of identity and change says nothing about the rest of what the place and the people evoke in me. Perhaps this passion arose from the fact that my first visit to South Africa was also my baptism into culture shock, but I prefer to think that it was something exogenous to my personal experiences of the place.

In the flurry of activity that accompanied my attempts to meet the deadline for this book, I took an hour out to mow my lawn. At the time I had a push mower, so listening to the radio while reducing nature to a socially acceptable height was actually possible. Donald Woods, one of the better known of the millions of courageous South Africans who took a stand against apartheid, had died during the week and the commentator on NPR was remembering him. It was a very personal remembrance, with poignant and evocative stories about the White newspaper editor who came to understand Black Consciousness. At the end, Scott Simon told the story about how Mr. Woods had been received by the crowds waiting in line to vote for the first time in April 1994. It was a story, I know, and one well told by a professional storyteller. But I stood on my front lawn and cried because of what the South Africans in the story, and all South Africans, did. I know that the pages of this book do not convey those kinds of feelings, but I hope they somehow encourage readers to try to find their own appreciation of the people and their beautiful land. So my first acknowledgment is to the people of South Africa who lived the experiences that struck me as inspirational. I don't really know how to say that without sounding trite.

In particular, I want to thank the two communities that accepted me as an untrained volunteer teacher in 1989 and 1990: Impumelelo High School, in what was then the homeland of KwaZulu, and Pax High School, in the homeland of Lebowa. Thanks to my students Bhekizitha, Musa, Precious, Elvis, and all the rest, who taught me a hundred times more outside the classroom than I taught them in it. Special thanks go to my fellow teachers (and friends)—Miser and George, Connie and Erika, our dormmate Mr. Kgomo, and my principal, Brother Edwin "Mataka" Matsu. They taught me that teachers in apartheid South Africa deserved the respect and admiration they received. I also need to thank the South Africans I interviewed in 1997.

I want to thank a particular group of mentors who helped me forge these ideas, often by supplying what seemed at the time to be much more hammer and fire than gentle bending and molding. I was lucky enough to have Nick Onuf as one of my first doctoral instructors. The fact that someone could put into words the amorphous feelings of truth that I had been carrying around gave me the confidence that I might be able to do that for someone else. Simona Sharoni was unceasing in her support and gave me more than my fair share of the unbelievable energy she bestows upon those lucky enough to be her students. The highest compliment I think I can pay Mustapha Pasha is that he is a true academic, a person who took me in because he believed that I wanted to explore ideas, not because he necessarily agreed with the way I put those ideas together. Thanks seems completely inadequate for Susan Collin Marks, who asked and listened and felt my tough year with me.

This book was built during my years at American University and its School of International Service, and many people helped me there, but mostly I got through because of my cohort in the doctoral program (even Cynthia). I couldn't have survived the gauntlet in more than one piece without you all. Thanks for helping me stay confused, disjointed, and wondering. Bim! I also want to thank John Richardson for believing enough to get me off the waiting list, even if it seemed like a mistake for a while, and Louis Goodman for his support, both financial and creative. Thanks to Mary Barton for helping me navigate the program. And for their particular help with the book, thanks to Randy Persaud, without whom this would almost certainly still be a pile of paper on my office floor, and Patrick Thaddeus Jackson, whose appetite for ideas seems to be insatiable. In the same vein I would like to acknowledge Michael Rinella, Laurie Searl, and the anonymous reviewers from SUNY Press for helping me turn this book into something that people other than my family and friends might like to read.

I want to thank the people who shared my first African experiences with me, especially Kurt Weiler for his energetic embrace of Africa and his supply of fine sipping whiskey, and Derrick Nielson for making sure I didn't stumble down any koppies at three in the morning. Spencer Reisinger, Bo Martin, Alex Laskaris, Jim O'Connor, Eddie Lynch, and Steve Holman all helped me live as an American in an entirely different homeland. During my field work, the Centre for Conflict Resolution in Cape Town gave me someplace to go where people cared whether I showed up. I especially want to thank Peter Batchelor, whose hospitality was an example that I hope to live up to one day, and Derrick Nielson again for easing my transition back and introducing me to some great interviewees. To Doreen Scott and her daughter Ruth, thanks for sharing with me your home, your friends, and a surprisingly good production of "My Fair Lady."

This book is dedicated to my family, to their patience, and to their abiding belief in me. They deserve so much more than a few lines here, and now that this book is done, I will try to give that to them.

Foreword

The way of talking about global politics that we have come to call *constructivism* arose in the 1980s—before the Berlin Wall came down, the Cold War ended, and South Africans remade themselves and thrilled the world by dismantling apartheid. So dramatic were these changes, so extraordinary were they in speed and scale, that they shook the modern world to its very foundations. This familiar turn of phrase also tells us quite a bit about the study of International Relations in the few years before these events took place. Here, too, foundations shook.

On the one hand, most scholars and commentators took for granted a world whose foundations are, for better or for worse, firmly in place. Such a world has partitions. Its levels, sectors, spheres, classes, and periods form containers within which change can be isolated, explained, and manipulated. Not least of these containers are nation-states, international systems, historical epochs, and fields of study.

On the other hand, a small but vocal contingent of scholars challenged even the possibility of foundations for any world. They dismissed as unfounded any claim to universal knowledge. Instead they went about "breaking up the ordered surfaces and all the planes" that we moderns use to "tame the wild profusion of existing things" and to maintain the "age-old distinction between the Same and the Other." So Foucault (Preface, *The Order of Things*) said of Borges. So may be said of Foucault, who insisted that "we shall never succeed in defining a stable relation of container to contained." When change strikes unexpectedly and, it would seem, capriciously, then we should realize that our received categories—sedimented contrivances of some moment or another—have lulled us into a false sense of stable relations and secure foundations.

In the field of International Relations, a few scholars—constructivists, as we were soon calling ourselves—rejected both of these constructions of the world. We saw social construction everywhere, all the time, in the complex irregularities and adjustments of everyday life. In this view, changes are random, incidental, and deliberate, in varying proportions, intricate combinations, and endless permutations. Yet human beings sense their—I should say *our*—own bodies as a continuous presence. We see patterns, hear rhythms, expect recurrences, and find reasons for hope and despair in a world of change. We speak of what we feel, hear, see, expect, want. Together we impose order on our affairs, frame alternatives, form conclusions, make choices, seek foundations. We act on the world as we experience it; by doing so, we change the world even as the world, now including our actions, changes us.

Wherever we, as observers, find social activity, we will find agents and structures constituting each other. They do so simultaneously; the process is continuous and unending. It might help to unpack this rather dry but convenient formula. Individual human beings constitute the world as a social reality. Human individuals are agents only because society makes it possible for us to act on behalf of ourselves, other people, and even society in its many manifestations.

Socially situated in place and time, our actions form regular practices and durable artifacts. Institutions in the broadest sense, these routines and their accompaniments contain and constrain our actions, not least by defining the conditions of agency. Institutions actually become agents when they deploy human agents to act on behalf of other human beings. Yet these institutional features of our social reality are constantly changing because we, as agents, act on them by acting in them.

Mirroring the seemingly paradoxical conditions of agency—we are free to act within limits—are paradoxical structural conditions: our actions continuously affect institutional limits. When we stand back from the institutions that most immediately affect us as agents, we may notice regular features of society, which we may also take into account when we act. Observers become agents. Only to the extent that agents make structure institutionally relevant does it enter the process of social construction.

For human agents, speech is an indispensable method by which to achieve our goals. We tell others what acts they should perform, what acts we will perform ourselves, and why these acts are the ones that indicated agents should perform. Furthermore, speech gives rise to additional, institutionally situated normative and strategic resources for agents to use. The latter resources are rules and norms (terms that constructivists end up using more or less interchangeably). Continuously put to use, all such resources are connected, as media, in the process of social construction.

Before great changes in global politics presaged the end of an epoch, constructivist scholars grappled with the agent-structure problem, as it was called, and directed their attention to the media of social construction. For the most part, early constructivists granted less attention to the consequences of social construction. Structural consequences were easy to ignore. After all, other scholars and commentators already had a great deal to say about the distinctive structural features of relations among national societies organized as states.

Only by challenging the common view that the relations of states constitute a world apart could constructivists add very much to the discussion. Yet this would have been a challenge to the field of International Relations as an institution in its own right. Until epochal changes made it possible for scholars to talk about Global Politics as a much broader enterprise, few of them were up to the challenge. Here I count myself an exception.

If possible, early constructivists (myself among them) had even less to say about the impact of social construction on the conditions of agency. At least some of the blame goes to the liberal assumptions undergirding most social science scholarship, at least in the United States. In particular, liberals tend to assume that agency is the natural condition of human individuals. To the extent that individual human beings are separated from each other in the pursuit of ends that can only be their own, maximizing behavior is a condition of agency. Autonomous agents are rational by definition; society is the aggregate of agents' choices; structure refers to those variations in the aggregate consequences of rational choice that help or hinder agents in the pursuit of their individual ends.

Great changes in the world gave many observers, and not just constructivists, a mandate to reconsider the liberal conception of the individual in society. Confronted with the spectacle of irresistible popular movements and rejuvenated civil societies, observers as/and activists devoted themselves to issues of participation, representation, and recognition. In doing so, they had to work through the perplexities of collective agency. Furthermore, collective action turned familiar containers—nation-states, public and private spheres, fields of study—into leaky sieves. Liberal politics were local, global, and everything in between.

The issue of participation highlights the marginal(ized) status of whole groups in liberal(izing) societies. Democratization turns on the integrity of representative institutions and procedures. In language that goes back to Hegel, recognition calls for an acknowledgment of difference, thereby overcoming the "age-old distinction," to use Foucault's words, "between the Same and the Other." The last of these issues most directly bears on the global dimension of Global Politics and is the one that so many constructivists responded to, if only indirectly, when they made identity the primary focus of their inquiries.

In recent years, the resurgence of ethnicity in so many places, so often with devastating consequences, insures that no observer of Global Politics can fail to mark its importance. For liberal observers, the term *identity* opens an appropriate conceptual domain, or container, for talking about ethnic differences—and for recognizing in others what we accept in ourselves. Interest in *personal identity* goes back to Locke (he may have been first to use these two words together). Popular discourse has long linked personal identity and the normal development of the autonomous individual. At the same time, identity links the individual to society through the many sentiments, symbols, and institutions with which individuals identify themselves, individually and collectively.

Even if, in liberal terms, identity is necessarily personal, it is also always social. Conveniently ambiguous, this formulation enables scholars to contemplate the dynamics of collective identity in a world of porous containers and unsteady foundations. Obviously, recognition is an act of social construction, and collective identity, as a consequence of many such acts, is both compellingly real and capable of change—even rapid change in unforeseen directions. Ethnic identity is a striking instance of a more general phenomenon that constructivists are exceedingly well equipped to talk about.

Talk they do. The trouble is, they talk about identity in such broadly collective terms—*culture* is a particular favorite—that they lose all sight of the conditions of agency and institutional limits constituting social reality from one moment to the next. It is only possible to keep these conditions and limits in view by focusing on the process, and thus the media, of social construction. This they do not do.

And this is precisely what Jamie Frueh does focus on in this book. In conceptualizing the media of social construction, Frueh introduces a crucial conceptual innovation. *Identity labels* are the specific medium by which agents acquire identities. Individual human beings are what they are by virtue of the identity labels that society makes peculiarly available to them. As the primary structural feature of our collective social reality, overlapping clusters of identity labels join us together and keep us apart in multiple, institutionally identifiable combinations.

Frueh tells us in chapter 2 that "intricate and shifting systems of identity labels are the principal means by which agents know which social rules to translate into action, and how to do so in such a way that their behavior not only makes sense, but is coordinated with the behavior of others." Just so. "Identity labels are codes, statements that give cues for how individuals should behave and how others should behave toward them." Indeed, they are rules—the kind of rules that, by telling us who we are, also tell us what we can and should do in relation to the much larger stock of rules that make society what it is.

If rules fix identities by limiting agents' choices, nothing is fixed for long. Rules constantly change, and with them identities—here, a shorthand description of the conditions of agency, the institutional parameters of action, the very structure of society. "While social arrangements organize and control agency through identity labels, identity labels are also the medium through which agents affect the social system." Identity labels change because agents act on them, resisting what others tell them their identities are, insisting that their identities have changed.

With this powerful conceptual apparatus, Frueh is ready to talk about profound social change—change right down to the foundations of any society. His subject here is the collapse of apartheid and the reconstruction of South Africa, I might say, from the foundations up. Thanks to his familiarity with the country, thorough research, skill as an interviewer, regard for context, and strong narrative sense, it is a gripping story in its own terms. Yet, in Frueh's capable hands, the story is also an exemplary instance of social construction as the central reality of the human condition in all its astounding variety.

What changed in South Africa, and continues to change, are the identities of its people—one by one, as groups of people, as a whole. More precisely, South Africa was a large society whose most conspicuous foundations consisted of an extraordinary arrangement of collective identities. Indeed these were racial identities—extensively developed and formally defined, relentlessly imposed, notoriously instrumental in distributing privilege of all sorts, passionately defended at home, and overwhelmingly deplored everywhere else in the world. Foundations crumbled when large numbers of ordinary people rejected the identity labels that others had assigned them. As an act of resistance, they changed their identities.

They did so as agents. I think Frueh is wrong when he says that "[n]o one is an agent all of the time." The ensemble of statuses, offices, and roles that constitute our identities at any moment confer some measure of agency upon us, whether we know it or not. Agency is always "context-specific," as Frueh says, and always available for any one of us to "change some part of social or material reality in a creative way."

Constructivism helps us to identify the creative possibilities in our everyday circumstances—inextricably social and material as they are—and to alter the immediate limits of our identity labels. Constructivism reminds us that these acts may have consequences that reach far beyond any that we might imagine. Jamie Frueh's careful yet creative constructivism helps us to understand how the people of South Africa went about transforming their society with far less violence, material cost, and loss of life than most of us imagined possible. Remaking their identities, they changed our world.

NICHOLAS ONUF

Chapter One

INTRODUCTION

> One of the most significant facts about us may finally be that we all begin with the natural equipment to live a thousand kinds of life but end in the end having only lived one.
> —Clifford Geertz, *The Interpretation of Cultures*

It was autumn in the southern hemisphere when an unexpected victory in all-White national parliamentary elections swept South Africa's National Party (NP) to power in 1948. The victory signaled the consolidation of the Afrikaner ethnic identity and facilitated the implementation of a series of racist laws that became known to the world as apartheid. These laws provided the pattern for a social fabric, woven by South Africans from their everyday activities. On another autumn day twenty-eight years later, that fabric was punctured in a violent convulsion that released some of the resentment that the normality of ordinary life had effectively hidden from view. Then, in 1994, forty-six autumns after its designs were laid out and eighteen autumns after the unraveling began in earnest, another election placed the African National Congress (ANC) at the head of a government dedicated to severing the last threads that held together the apartheid way of life. In a world still hung over from the Cold War, this transformation struck many as inspirational, even miraculous. Amid the celebrations that accompanied the formal transfer of power to erstwhile rebels, a few warned of the problems that South Africa still faced, but for the most part, South Africans took the opportunity to revel in the success of their negotiated revolution. Miracle did not seem too strong a word. Even ANC leader Nelson Mandela, in his speech claiming electoral victory, referred to the birth of non-racial democracy in South Africa as "a small miracle."

While commentators are still able to find aspects of the transition worthy of being labeled a miracle, the use of the term has become problematic. Analyses published since 1997 tend to position themselves in opposition to earlier journalistic accounts that present the transition through anecdotal stories in which personalities, chance encounters, and transformative moments dominate.[1] Even academic texts published in the years immediately following the elections seem, from this "morning-after" position of "painful sobriety," to have been so caught up in the celebratory atmosphere that they overstated the successes of the transition and mythologized change while downplaying significant continuities and obstacles still to be overcome.[2] By constructing this antinomy, more recent studies are juxtaposed against once-dominant trends in South African analysis and cast as attacking, if not eliminating, the euphoric residue of this "misunderstood miracle."[3] The implication is that the transition has been neither as complete nor as deep as the term *miracle* would suggest.

Aside from apparently overstating the quality of the transformation, using the term *miracle* to describe the end of apartheid carries an implicit theory of super-human agency that deprives South African actors of their role in remaking their social order. This rhetoric of transcendental causation, even as a metaphor, is indicative of the presumption of stability that dominates both formal Political Science and everyday social discourse. We have been trained to think of change as an anomaly, as something that needs to be explained. This book argues that we can gain valuable insights by adopting a perspective in which change is always happening—to societies, to actors, and to the identities of both. Certainly some changes are more important than others. The transformation of the apartheid social order is an important change, and one that might yield valuable lessons if it is understood more fully. One way to understand it better has been to search for its causes, divine or otherwise. But rather than asking *why*, this study seeks to explain *how* the transformation of apartheid society happened. In it, I argue that understanding social change, both in the South African context and generally, depends on examining the political identities of the actors involved.

This book describes the transformation of the South African social order as seen through the window of identity. It traces the demise of apartheid by focusing a gaze on the concepts and words, the labels, that are available for South Africans to use as they struggle to make sense of themselves, their actions, and their society. The protagonists in this story are the shifting networks of ideas that mediate the relationships between South Africans and between South Africans and their social order. I am not concerned with personal identity, with the identity crises of particular individuals or the ways that they have described themselves over time. I am interested in identities as systems of meaning, as intersubjective but malleable tools that people use to build descriptions, explanations, and justifications. This is a study of the power of South Africans' identity labels and how that power ebbed and flowed over the course of broader revolutions in politics. It describes the undulating patterns that have differentiated South

Africans from each other during the last three decades, the changes in those patterns, and the relationship of those changes to the transition in governance.

This focus makes sense for a study of South Africa because apartheid life was politicized by a particular manifestation of identity. Under apartheid, South Africans organized reality (not just social life, economics, and politics, but reality as a whole) through a framework of race; today, if post-apartheid rhetoric is to be believed, they do not. From the perspective of political identity, this state of affairs produces two broad sets of questions. The first set is related to the category (or categories) of identity that has power in post-apartheid society. If race is no longer the most important thing about South Africans, what is? What is the most important type of characteristic for people in contemporary South Africa? A variety of possibilities exists—nationality, class, ethnicity. It is also possible that racial characteristics continue to dominate social relations. However, if a change in political identity has taken place, a second set of questions arises concerning the process by which that shift in categorizing schema was brought about. How did South Africans go about changing the identity structures of their social order?

My attempts to answer these questions have produced an interpretive, empirical analysis of the power of South African identity labels, the ways that they organize social activity and the changes both the labels and their power have undergone during the course of the transition away from apartheid. This is a rigorous study, but it is not an attempt to measure the causes of the South African transition. Changes to identity are neither a cause nor an effect of the move from apartheid to post-apartheid reality in the sense of variables. Large-scale social transformations are very complex phenomena. Institutions of identity influence and are influenced by larger social transformations in intricate and interesting ways. Cause, at least in this case, is not unidirectional, but multilayered and complex, and when a social order is explicitly changed in revolutionary rather than evolutionary ways, the presumption of widespread stability that roots the very idea of most traditional social science fails us. Control groups for large-scale social change are very difficult to come by. Instead, such change is best studied using an interpretative approach that is open to the possibilities of creative agency. Following the course of the transition by paying attention to questions of identity yields particular insights into the dynamics and politics of social transformation generally, just as focusing on economics or political institutions would. This, then, is a study of the process by which society makes and remakes itself.

It is difficult to fit this approach into a single disciplinary field. This book is being published in a series on Global Politics. I take this term to encompass the study of relationships that would conventionally be the purview of International Relations, those for which Comparative Politics would claim to speak, as well as those large-scale phenomena that do not fit comfortably in the analytical lens of either disciplinary tradition. For better or for worse, this book seems to fit best into the latter group. The conflicts that make up the case studies are primarily domestic South African contests, although I have done my best to embed them within larger global dynamics. What makes this book a contribution to Global

Politics is its challenge to the disciplinary boundaries of Political Science. By beginning with a very broad definition of society and providing scholars with a much more precise mechanism for representing the distribution of agency within it, the constructivist theory of political identity alters the framework within which the "level of analysis problem" makes sense. By removing agency from entities and placing it in the social environment, we can gain insights into the process of social transformation that are not limited to a single type of social arrangement or agent. Whether this will be borne out by a more expansive application of the theory has yet to be seen, but the challenge from Global Politics is that important analysis can take place across the disciplinary boundaries of International Relations and Comparative Politics. In order to differentiate these various academic disciplines from the phenomena they study, I have adopted Onuf's practice of capitalizing the names of the disciplines (International Relations) and leaving the activities themselves in lower case.

Every treatise on apartheid, it seems, begins with an obligatory disclaimer acknowledging the contested nature of the identity labels used in the text and lamenting the impracticalities of the various strategies—using quotation marks or the word *so-called*—for honoring those complexities. This purpose of this book is to deal with those complexities deeply, but there is still the matter of how to refer to the subjects of the study. One of the principal points I hope to convey is that this is a decision fraught with implications for power. To try to honor that power, I refer to people using labels that fit the immediate political context of the discussion. Often this will be *South Africans,* a label that groups people according to the globally dominant understanding of geographic boundaries and large units of governance. Apartheid, as a series of laws, took place in the context of a nation-state and often the best way to talk about the people most affected by it is by using a national term. Other times, the most practical way of referring to the group is with apartheid's racial labels. These labels—*White* or *European, Native* or *African, Indian* or *Asian,* and *Coloured*—are neither clear nor unproblematic, but they carried a kind of functional consensus in everyday apartheid life that had a solid definitional center even if they did not have well-defined boundaries. Also, following the anti-apartheid pattern, I will use *Black* to refer to Africans, Coloureds, and Indians collectively, and the more specific labels when that is necessary. As explored later, however, during the years encompassed by this study the label *Black* became a site of political struggle. Therefore, in some quotations, especially those of the government or its apologists, *Black* may be used to mean only African. Because these labels are no more natural or primary or basic than any others, even if they are sometimes more politically powerful, it only seems logical to capitalize them, to use them as formal, proper nouns rather than as a description of some natural fact about the people to whom the labels apply. The capitalization of White, Black, African, and other similar labels is intended, therefore, to convey their politicized nature. I have not, however, altered quotations from other authors.

While the use of first person singular pronouns is not standard protocol in a work like this, I have, at certain junctures, felt it necessary to refer to myself and to claim my opinions. The epistemological implication of a constructivist ontology, understood deeply, is that "truth" must be treated as contextual and interpretive. We may certainly be able to state transcendental truths about the universe, but we have no way of knowing when we do. We can, however, make claims of truth that are appropriately circumscribed by acknowledging their context. In my case, that context is a particular perspective on the intersection of identity theory, understandings of social change, and the material reality of the South African transition from apartheid. Failure to acknowledge that context would be to assert a certainty that may be highly prized, but to which I have no claim. The epistemology behind this disclaimer will, I trust, become more clear as I describe and analyze the constructivist approach to politics.

Constructivism and the theory of constructivist political identity are laid out in chapter 2. The social theory of constructivism provides a particularly useful foundation for studying social change, in part because, in contrast to the vision of reality in more mainstream social and political science, constructivist reality changes continuously. When combined with a more specific theory of the power of identity labels and how they facilitate the process by which social reality is constituted, the theory of political identity becomes a powerful tool for studying social change. While the constructivist theory of political identity precedes the empirical evidence spatially, it would be misleading to leave the reader with the impression that these more abstract parts of the analysis were clearly solidified prior to or in the absence of the case studies of South African politics that follow. Instead the relationship between the substantive text and the theoretical context is best thought of as cyclic, complex, and recursive. Not surprisingly, these same themes are at the center of the theory of social constructivism.

Chapter 3 provides the background necessary to make sense of the case studies that follow. There is a brief overview of the history of the area that is now South Africa. It is necessarily oversimplified, but it does provide some useful context for readers unfamiliar with South African politics. Also in this chapter is an examination of the academic discourse surrounding South African identity, some thoughts on methodology, and an exploration of the practical considerations of translating the constructivist theory of political identity into empirical research.

The theme of chapter 4, the uprisings in Soweto in 1976, constitutes a study in popular resistance. The instigators of the uprisings were schoolchildren, not even high school students but junior secondary students—thirteen-, fourteen-, and fifteen-year-olds—although the demographics of the participants quickly diversified. This chapter analyzes contemporary newspaper reports, student interpretations, academic analysis, government propaganda pamphlets, and ANC and popular commemorations of June 16 in order to understand how systems of identity were used to describe and explain events, how identity labels framed the understanding of actors on both sides, and how social boundaries were redrawn through action, precipitating the end of apartheid's relative stability.

The second conflict, the political debate that raged over the constitutional changes proposed in 1983, was another significant watershed in the transformation of apartheid, and the discourse that surrounded it centers chapter 5. The reforms were presented as an expansion of democracy, but failed to capture the imagination or respect of the vast majority of South Africans or the international community, primarily because Whites maintained an effective veto and Africans were still completely excluded from central power. As a result, their most significant effects were changes in how people opposed apartheid, including the coalescing of a significant internal opposition movement and the forging of a practical, mobilized, non-racial identity. Because identity was such an explicit factor in this debate, it serves as an excellent indicator of where the institutions of identity were in the mid-1980s and a prime example of how identities were mobilized for political purposes.

As one of the most important social problems in contemporary South Africa, crime forms the basis for the examination of post-apartheid identity in chapter 6. From a theoretical perspective, crime is one of the common symptoms of the loss of social order, of the dissolution of a broad social agreement on rules. This anomic violence may seem natural as South Africans search for new rules around which legitimacy can coalesce, but from the very practical perspective of living in an urban area (and especially in Johannesburg), the specter of crime influences almost every activity. It has redrawn many of the old social boundaries as the crime that has always pervaded townships extends into the traditionally insulated, traditionally White urban and suburban areas and as crime in general becomes more violent. As such, the politics of crime provides a very useful mechanism to explore dominant perceptions of social categories.

Each empirical chapter begins with an historical description of a conflict of the transition and its social and political context. This description is followed by an examination of the discourse of the conflict, presented through its artifacts. These artifacts differ from conflict to conflict, with the first two cases relying more on archival and other printed material and the third supplementing printed texts with a substantial number of interviews. In order to provide the reader with as much of the relevant texts as possible and to try to let South Africans speak for themselves, these pages often contain substantial blocks of quotations. Following each section representing the discourse, I analyze the texts for the identity labels through which participants and observers understand and explain the events of each conflict. Each chapter analyzes the power of identity labels at a different stage in the process of transformation. The chapter on the events in Soweto in 1976 demonstrates the power of agents to disrupt the dominant social order by stepping out of the identities prescribed to them by that order. In the constitutional reforms of 1983 to 1984, politics shift from resisting apartheid identities to building alternatives. Chapter 6, on contemporary crime, analyzes the role of political identity in helping to solidify a post-apartheid social order. Finally each chapter concludes with analysis of the discourse's implications for the broader process of transforming South African political identity.

The conclusion summarizes the changes to South Africa's social structures of identity and assesses the general applicability of that experience. The transition away from apartheid makes apparent the complexity of contemporary political identity, the processes of remaking a social order, and the value of a constructivist understanding of identity that can help us understand both. The argument is that labels are a valuable key to how people organize social power. The remainder of the book builds that idea into a way to mine insights from the processes of social change. My goal is to weave together a coherent story about identity and social change, to make sense of the transformation of the South African social order by focusing on one aspect of human interaction. Regardless of whether the transition from apartheid to the New South Africa has been miraculous, it certainly has been evocative. I hope that, in the process of narrowing the negotiated revolution to talk about identity, I have accentuated rather than obscured its power to make us wonder.

Chapter Two

A Theory of Political Identity

Literally, the word *context* refers to pieces of text—a word or a sentence or larger blocks like a chapter or even whole manuscripts—that surround or are related to another, presumably more important piece. It is text that is deemed important for helping to find meaning in the segment being analyzed. Each text, including this one, is surrounded by others that influence how both the author and the reader interpret its message. This chapter examines the context for this study, providing a kind of theoretical nest within which the analysis of South African identity rests. It begins in the abstract, with the meta-theory of constructivism, and moves progressively toward the concrete, exploring existing theories of identity in politics, until it concludes with an examination of the theoretical and practical implications of incorporating identity into theories of social constructivism. The result is a mid-range theory that provides a basis for examining social change in South Africa. I argue that this theory is also flexible enough to provide insights into the process of social change more generally. At its most broad, the perspective on political identity presented in this chapter demonstrates one way in which constructivism can bridge the gulf between theoretical context and empirical text.

CONSTRUCTIVISM

Social constructivism is a theory of "what makes the world hang together."[1] It is ontological—it deals with questions of what is real—and sociological—it is concerned with the relationship between individuals and their collectivities. While there is considerable agreement on the theoretical propositions that separate constructivism from other meta-theories used to study global politics, constructivism has yet to solidify into a single identifiable framework and the term *constructivism* continues to mean different things to different people. This disputed meaning makes it incumbent on those who wish to contribute to the constructivist discourse to be rather specific about what they mean. I will therefore attempt to outline briefly what I mean by constructivism, a perspective that differs in small but significant ways from the dominant image of constructivism in the field provided by Alexander Wendt in his 1999 book *Social Theory of International Politics*.[2]

Social Constructivism and Reality

Constructivism is a reaction against and an alternative to both the nihilism of postmodern deconstructivism and the certainty of positivist behavioralism and for this reason has sometimes been cast as a middle ground for the field of International Relations.[3] In opposition to deconstructivist theory, constructivism holds that humans physically interact with a real, material, phenomenal world. In opposition to philosophical realism (and the common sense view of reality dominant in the West), it posits that any order that seems to exist in that world must be considered invented by the human mind and imposed on the world through the process of cognition. The external environment is not invented, but human perception of it must be treated as impure because the human mind imposes order on phenomena as they are discerned. Whether that order exists or is a product of discernment is unknowable, making it a waste of time for constructivists to study problems of existence. Reality is better thought of as a quality that humans attribute to phenomena by noticing them, talking about them with others, and generally acting *as if* these "real" phenomena are important.

Constructivism, as I see it, does not deny material existence, but neither should it depend on it for its ontology. In our most philosophical of moments when questions arise about whether the material world exists, constructivism forces us to remain agnostic. Since constructivist epistemology asserts that it is beyond our capacity to know the world's ultimate foundations, constructivist ontology shifts the referent for the word *reality* from material existence to importance. Whether something qualifies as real depends not on whether it exists, but on whether humans treat it as important. Because assessments of importance are culturally specific, the study of politics should try to answer contextualizing questions about what is important in a society rather than universalizing questions of existence. One implication of this perspective is that it sidesteps the teleology of progress, as there is no qualitative difference between the realities of ancient Greece, Shaka Zulu, and modern physics. Each has an interlocking set of beliefs about the material world that informs its members as to what requires attention and how those aspects of reality should be interpreted. Each society has a reality made up of those aspects of the material world that are designated to be important, and while we may know the world better than we did three hundred years ago, we may just know it differently. This is not to deny the importance of material constraints on action and policy, or the value of an ontology based on scientific realism for most westerners all of the time, and for all westerners most of the time. But for constructivists, at the end of the day, scientific realism is a discourse of truth endemic to a modern, western, scientific understanding of reality.[4]

What keeps the potential for unlimited and conflicting judgments of importance from spinning out of control is society. People generally adopt standards of importance from their social environment. This shared understanding of the world, what Jurgen Habermas calls a "lifeworld," functions as reality for those enacting it.[5] As such, it is political. Understanding the process by which humans develop and share these values of importance is the crux of constructivism. As should be evident from the label, the theory suggests that this process is one of construction. What may not be evident is that for constructivists, this process flows in two directions simultaneously.

> Fundamental to constructivism is the proposition that human beings are social beings, and we would not be human but for our social relations. In other words, social relations *make* or *construct* people—*ourselves*—into the kind of beings that we are. Conversely, we *make* the world what it is, from the raw materials that nature provides, by doing what we do with each other and saying what we say to each other.[6]

This is the same process that Peter Berger and Thomas Luckmann laid out in 1966 and that Anthony Giddens called "structuration" in 1984.[7] People *construct* the rules and institutions that make up the social world and, at the same time, society *constructs* the meanings that define the reality of people. Each defines the other through assertions of importance. Human actions (including but not limited to speech acts) are based on and are themselves assertions of what is important about the world. By acting, humans advance an understanding of reality. To the degree that different people assert the same reality, society exists and a social world is defined. In this way, humans make the world what it is. Simultaneously, however, the only way people can understand themselves and those with whom they interact is in light of the accumulated assertions of importance that they inherit from the world around them. The force of those assertions defines what is important (and therefore what is real) about people in that society. The world makes humans what they are. This process of co-constitution is continuous, and its practicalities are overwhelmingly complex.

The construction in constructivism therefore refers to the process by which the meaning of behavior is established. As people go about their daily lives—working, eating, speaking, playing—both the actors themselves and the people around them think of their activities as meaningful, as done for a purpose. Most of the time, that purpose remains unstated because actions or statements make sense: they fit the patterns that people are used to and are therefore generally understandable, even if they are not always predictable.[8] Daily life in a society takes place within these mostly unspoken patterns and the more people follow these patterns, the more they seem to be the normal or even natural way to go about doing things. Patterns confront individuals with varying degrees of force, but their existence is what defines a society and the particular set of patterns is what differentiates one society from another. Because these patterns often are presented as natural or objective facts, they are often treated as reified things—structures.

As part of the social world, human beings are also defined by these social dynamics of meaning. Individuals are born into a social environment in which some personal characteristics are valued more than others. While sometimes these value hierarchies are explicitly institutionalized, such as with race in apartheid, gender in patriarchy, citizenship in nationalism, or wealth in capitalism, all characteristics that are part of the social vocabulary are part of implicit hierarchies. As Ian Burkitt argues, through the processes of social relations, humans actively internalize these hierarchies into their perceptions of what it means to be a human in society.

> Social relations are thus the mode of existence for human bodies, in which the organic structure actively realizes itself. The essence of humanity is therefore excentric; it is not to be found within the body as an essence, for it is established between individuals as social relations and then appropriated by individuals as personality. Thus there is a continuous process of elaboration in the dialectical relation between active individuals and the structure of social relations.[9]

Individuals learn what it means to be human by interacting with those around them. The same can be said of corporate entities within their societies. Normality is judged by the success in (or at least efforts at) approximating the ideals of the societies in which individuals, states, and other actors participate. The more actors behave normally, the more coherent their society and the more that society can claim to provide for all its members an ordered life in which rewards and punishments are properly distributed.

Society, Order, and Privilege

For the purposes of this discussion, I will define society very broadly, as any group whose activities link its members to a common centering theme. This makes a society out of everything from a bowling league to a nation-state to web users to the Red Cross to groups of corporate entities like OPEC or the international system. In trying to describe the complexity of these (and similar) entities, scholars often use metaphors that treat them as if they were material things that could be physically felt, measured, or counted—like a tree (Montesquieu's branches of government) or a body (Hobbes' leviathan) or a building (Marxist structure and superstructure). When studying global politics, scholars often attribute the same kind of agency to large corporate entities—governments, corporations, races, classes, genders—that psychologists and modern common sense (in the Gramscian sense) do to individuals, granting them status as legal or practical persons for the purposes of simplifying discussions of action. That individuals or corporate entities are cast as agents does not express anything about the true nature of individuals or corporate entities, but it does say something about how people organize their world, and the term *person* accurately reflects these modern western attributions of agency. A person can be said to be a member of a society when she, he, or it can demonstrate an acquaintance with the patterns of that society by using them in the appropriate context. Most actors thus participate in many societies during the course of a day. Persons can choose to associate with groups that are explicitly opposed to dominant social standards, but these groups are themselves societies, with their own rules and risks for breaking those rules. Membership in any society carries expectations that may be employed in interactions, both by the members and by those with whom they interact. Later I argue that because identity labels are used to organize societal memberships, identity can serve as a valuable tool for studying agency and social change.

Just as society is often reified for heuristic purposes, patterns of behavior often are presented as "a social order." Two meanings of the term *order* are important for the argument in this book. The first meaning is the aggregate of a society's rules, the list, if it were possible to make one, of all the things that a person should know to be considered a sane member of a society. This is order as structure or social arrangement.[10] These rules orchestrate the shared meanings and goals of the members of a society and legitimate the acceptable means to pursue those goals. A social order identifies which objects and events deserve attention and prescribes the correct way for members to approach, analyze, and act with respect to their world. By programming both the perception of reality and the patterns of behavior that people strive to actualize, the social order legitimates the normal functioning of its members and decreases the randomness of human interaction with the world, particularly with other actors. The rules of the order are embodied in the ideational and bureaucratic institutions that pressure actors to continually recreate the order. From 1948 to 1994, South Africa's dominant social order was apartheid.

The second meaning of importance here is order as result. Order exists to the degree that members of a society act according to the same set of rules. In this sense, order is the lived coherence of activity in a society. It is the antipode of disorder, chaos, or anarchy. It is, however, an ideal type, a goal whose attainment is impossible, but whose mere existence legitimates the normal functioning of those who live according to its rules. This coherence in human activity is derived from largely implicit, interwoven sets of assumptions about the world that are intersubjective, that is, shared by the members of the society. The congruence of social behavior rests upon and represents the shared understanding of reality that conditions how individual members relate to and interact with each other and their world. Over time, many of the shared ideas, beliefs, attitudes, and practices become unquestioned habit, part of the unnoticed backdrop against which life must be lived. Social arrangements function not only to synchronize behavior, but also to regulate even the perception of events and objects. This social self-orchestration produces a harmony in the perception of objects and events, and "correct" ways for members to approach, analyze, and act with respect to the world. The existence of legitimated, normal patterns of everyday life decreases the randomness of human interaction with the world, particularly with other actors. As people generally behave according to the rules, the social arrangements become the order that members reflexively impose on the material world through the process of cognition. Society exists in this overlapping of individuals' realities and it is this interwoven nature that confronts individuals as objective reality.

The power of a social order, that is, its ability to govern the discourse of actions, meanings, and explanations used by the actors that constitute it, can be described as momentum. Actors either contribute to the momentum by following the rules or implicitly try to steer the social arrangement in a new direction simply by successfully asserting different rules in their behavior. In general, however, social arrangements restrict who feels competent to even try to steer. This metaphor of momentum implies that a social order has a mass, but here that mass must be understood as continuously changing. One way to picture this is to suggest that a social order behaves something like a comet hurtling through space.[11] The body of the comet—a conglomeration of dust and ice particles—may appear as a thing but it is constantly changing. Particles are blown off to form the comet's tail, and new particles in its path become embedded in the giant snowball. If the imagination stretches far enough, the particles can be the rules that make up the social order, with some rules more central and others more liminal and transient. Rather than an entity with a clearly defined inside/outside boundary, a social order is better imagined as a cluster centered around a core that seems more coherent the closer to the center one gets. Even this center, however, is ultimately susceptible. The comet is continuously changing, swapping one particle for another, moving through space. Actions that abide by the rules reinforce the momentum along the comet's current trajectory, actions that are interpreted as not following the rules slow the momentum or even alter the comet's trajectory. This analogy assumes change while explaining the appearance of constancy from afar (Haley's comet could still be called Haley's comet even if none of its original particles remained) and allowing for the kinds of explicit changes that happened in South Africa.

All members benefit from the existence of social arrangements. Their intersubjective networks of meaning and goals allow members to coordinate actions and increase the efficiency of interaction by decreasing the amount of information that must be exchanged, by orienting all members toward the same ends and by making interactions, to a large extent, predictable.[12] However, a society's elites benefit relatively more than others because they possess qualities institutionalized by the social order as valuable, making some seem naturally more deserving of a disproportionate share of social goods. The process of governance involves the implementation of policies intended to make social reality approximate an idealized model of privilege distribution.[13] Because there is no "true" human nature against which to measure social arrangements, all privilege distribution schemes are ultimately arbitrary, making all governance institutions exploitative when viewed from outside their legitimating paradigm. By hiding the fragile nature and constructed normativity of social hierarchies, institutionalization falsely legitimizes particular asymmetries, vesting the powerful in the maintenance of existing social arrangements. The invented nature of the rules is concealed through various strategies (religion, science, ideology) that claim to know the "true" nature of reality and those at the top of hierarchies continue to enjoy the benefits of patterns of behavior that seem natural to all. Under apartheid, for example, White elites benefited from Calvinist theology, colonial anthropology, the science of eugenics, a mythology of historic conflicts, and an ideology of radical difference. While some institutions of rule may fit a particular society's value systems better than others, all do violence to the inherently fluid relationships between people and between people and their shifting definitions of importance by freezing perceptions of power and value in a world that continues to change. This freezing is necessary for society, but it is also ultimately exploitative.

At the heart of this discussion is power. Power is an orienting concept for the discipline of Political Science generally, and there is a sweeping spectrum of definitions and theories on the subject. While most mainstream scholars of Global Politics tend to reify power into either wealth or military might, constructivist power is much more fluid and diverse. Constructivism draws heavily on Michel Foucault's penetrating analyses of the link between power, knowledge, and meaning.[14] For Foucault, power is inherent in human comprehension of the world, in the attribution of significance and in the solidification of meanings. Constructivist conceptions of power are linked by the idea that power does not exist in the abstract, but only in the context of relationships and is therefore dependent on how the participants define each other and the context of their interaction. As a result, power is rather diffuse. It exists both in the momentum of social arrangements and in the ability of humans as agents to create and affect that momentum. It exists, in other words, in both structure and agency.

STRUCTURE, AGENCY, AND CHANGE

Constructivism was built, in part, as a reaction to the dichotomous cleavage of structure/agency in sociological debates about the determinants of human behavior.[15] Within this broader discourse, agency stands for the ability of persons to invent and creatively alter the progression of history. On the other hand, structures are represented as manifestations of social dynamics that are beyond the power of persons to effect. In general, theories that privilege structures stress continuity and explain social change through reference to the internal dynamics of social arrangements, while those that privilege agency stress the power of human rationality to invent institutions and solutions to the flow of social problems. In contrast, constructivism posits that agents and structures co-constitute both each other and the broader social reality. In this theory, individual agents are the ultimate source of the rules that constitute a social order; individuals make and alter structural reality. At the same time, social arrangements define what it means to be a person and erect the rules by which individuals actualize their perceptions of power; structures make and alter human reality.

Agency is the perceived ability to purposefully change some part of social or material reality in a creative way. It is concerned with the causes of behavior and is, therefore, most easily measured by changes in that behavior. However, a person can possess agency and choose not to change anything. Agency is an empowered state of consciousness, a relationship between an actor and a very specific temporal-spatial context. Even if, at a certain moment in time and space, one may be considered an agent with respect to, say, theories of political identity, that says nothing about the continuity of that relationship or about the agent's relationship to automobile transmissions or raspberry soufflés.

Action alone does not qualify an actor as an agent; acts of agency must be creative. There is a sense in which all acts are creative, but creative acts of agency are qualitatively different from acts for which a person is merely responsible. This creativity implies invention, an ownership based in a holistic understanding that is beyond knowledge or responsibility. Creation, in other words, is not rote actualization, but action that implies an intimacy that resonates from constructing for oneself the ideas and connections that make up an understanding. Michel Foucault suggests that there is a similar differentiation between someone who writes a private letter and an author.[16] This process of creation does not have to be original. It is the process of putting things together for oneself, rather than the novelty of how it is done, that qualifies an act as creative. To summarize, agency entails awareness of some reality, the belief that this reality could somehow be different, and the confidence that the agent could act to bring about such a change.

The focus here is behavior. Actions immediately become part of the existing social world, available for judgment and adoption by others. Whatever the intended purpose or ultimate effect may be, every action arises out of an understanding of both material reality and the powers and constraints inherent in social arrangements. Society is based on each member having a minimum grasp of this social reality and its rules, but each person acquires their understanding uniquely and has an individualized set of experiences, generalizations, and metaphors to use to organize it. The constructivist ontology suggests that the complexity inherent in this interface between persons and their social order makes it impossible to reduce agency to a single, transportable theoretical essence. Rather than modern social science's image of agency as possession (which is interwoven with the dominant reified conceptualization of power), for constructivism, agency exists only in the relationship between an actor and a specific part of the social/material world. While it is possible to specify some of its general qualities (creativity, for example), agency must be considered context-specific, and explanations and predictions must be rooted in an empirical social reality.[17]

Given the diversity of impacts that social arrangements have on their members, societies provide stability by institutionalizing structures and erecting rewards and sanctions tied to social rules. Actors make decisions concerning whether or not to obey a rule based on a calculus of the potential costs and benefits, weighted according to hierarchies ingrained in the social structure and processes classified by society as rational. Social rules do not dictate which choices must be made, but they do govern the construction of the situation within which choices are made intelligible and rational. Reason is culturally specific and rationality is best understood as a rhetorical device for legitimating the choice in terms of existing social arrangements. A society's dominant decision-making calculus is designed to make the outcomes that benefit existing elites appear to be the most rational, if not the only, choice for each subordinate actor. This gives existing social arrangements a large amount of practical momentum.

In practice, actors generally seem to abide by social arrangements, lending society the appearance of stability and order. From a different point of view, however, even stable institutions are far from static; social arrangements are continuously changing to account for the flow and accumulation of events. As people act and interact, they use the rules of social arrangements to help them know how to do so. In adapting the general rules to specific situations, people either reinforce or change those rules. Regardless of whether the rules are reinforced or altered, the actions are generally represented as maintaining the integrity of existing rules and social goals. Members of society normally work to maintain their social arrangements homeostatically in the face of changing circumstances, and their usually subtle adaptations are almost always framed as continuity. This continuity is generally perceived as a social good because it provides the predictability that makes social interaction efficient and worthwhile.[18] Constructivism allows scholars to adopt an analytical focus that accentuates and appreciates how individual acts of creative agency produce and maintain structures and their apparent stability.

Social change, therefore, is largely made up of the accumulation of everyday adaptations, applications of existing rules to the progression of lived events, and slight alterations in those rules to account for variations in circumstances. These adaptations take place within the context of particular interactions and relationships. Interlocutors often renegotiate the social rules that govern their interactions. As they do so, they sometimes create new and particular solutions to interactional problems, and occasionally these adaptations attract enough attention from other members of society to become widely adopted. All social actors possess the potential to challenge existing frameworks of rule simply by behaving in unexpected ways. Persons act creatively every day and each unexpected action is, in effect, a proposal for a new behavioral pattern. Such acts will only have a broader social impact if other actors notice and accede to them by fitting them into the jagged surface of their own existing understandings of the world.

It is remotely possible that any particular adaptation, invented in any particular interaction, could catch on and present a widespread challenge to existing patterns. If it becomes adopted widely enough, the adapted behavior could become normalized, the new "best" way to behave in that context. The only requirement is for some critical mass of society's members to notice and accede to the new pattern and actualize its rules in contexts they deem to be similar. Since each person's understanding is uniquely tinted by personal experiences and beliefs about the world, the ultimate success of a proposed change is fundamentally unpredictable in the abstract, especially on any large scale. This is, however, the process by which individual agents are able to change social orders; simply by inventing new ways of behaving that attain a measure of consensus in society, agents alter social arrangements. Structures are ultimately the cumulative result of creative acts of agency carried out by a variety of individuals, even though these acts of creativity are often obscured, ignored, or forgotten. Behaviors that are widely adopted may make the actors into agents with respect to some small part of the social structure, but the vast remainder will continue to confront them as natural and unchangeable.

The viability of a particular change is, to a large degree, dependent upon the perceived power of the actor who performed it. To the degree that they are perceived as legitimate, structures therefore control agency by specifying which people are empowered to act in a given situation and by delineating when action should be taken and what should be done. Structures guide how a society's actors perceive both opportunities and constraints on action.

> Agents are never free to act upon the world in all the ways that they might wish to. Many limits have a material component. We need air to breathe; we do not have wings to fly. No rule can readily make things otherwise, even though rules allow us, agents, to use resources to alter these limits, for example, by fashioning scuba gear and airplanes. Rules that give any agent an opportunity to act create limits for other agents. Rules in general limit the range of acts that other agents are free to take.[19]

Control over the distribution of agency in the political arena is one of the primary means by which the perception of order, continuity, and stability is brought to everyday life. It is also how those in power ensure that the existing methods of distributing privilege are maintained. Achieving *explicit* social change therefore requires some critical mass of a society's members to choose to switch those rules that they explicitly invoke as justifications for action.[20] In order for this to happen, actors must be convinced that the old rules are somehow bad or at least relatively worse than an alternative. For old social rules and arrangements to be under stress, actors must notice problems and believe that they are related to those rules; for change to occur, actors must believe that an alternative system is available that could solve those problems better. This is the role of resistance.

RESISTANCE

Resistance refers to an opposing force. For electricians, it is the extent to which an electrical conductor impedes the flow of current through it. In politics, resistance is attitudes and actions that oppose the momentum of and/or challenge the trajectory of existing social arrangements. To the degree that people follow the rules that make up the social order, the social order has momentum. Every action that is in line with the rules reinforces the momentum. If the actor obeys the rules unconsciously, the act will reinforce the momentum more than if the actor takes the time and energy to consider it. Acts of resistance are interpreted as not conforming to the rules and patterns of the dominant social order, and as such they present a vision of how these social patterns could be different. Acts of resistance may be unintentional, but in order to challenge existing power, they must be interpreted as a viable alternative, either by the actor or by others. The force of such acts may alter the trajectory of a social order.

For heuristic purposes, it is possible to divide resistance into four distinct and progressive levels—noticing, questioning, causing trouble, and working for a specific alternative. Resistance begins with simply noticing that people always seem to do something a certain way. Order is often based on selective ignoring and social forgetting. Noticing means that an actor has stepped out of the "brainwashing" that this is "just how things are" for a moment. Resistance at this level is often unpredictable. The next step in resistance is questioning why a thing or a process is organized the way that it is. Resistance at the first two levels produces a net decrease in forward momentum by failing to reinforce the current direction as strongly as an action might in those circumstances. If a resistor moves beyond questioning, the next step is to make trouble by forcing others to notice and perhaps even question the aspect of social reality that is being resisted. This is often when agents become designated as leaders, people who make changing the "way things are" make sense. In resistance of the third kind, acts push against the forces propelling the social order on its current trajectory, but this pushing is not necessarily organized in any particular direction. Finally, rather than just resisting what exists, actors can work for a specific alternative set of arrangements. It is only once resistance reaches the fourth level that acts can be said to be an attempt to steer the social order.

Resistance is effective if it diverts or withdraws the practical consensus upon which social order as effect depends. Social authority requires the acceptance of assertions of power by those over whom authority is sought. This acceptance can be won through rhetoric, naturalized through hegemony, or coerced through violence. Acceptance can be withdrawn, however, and subordinates may then act in unexpected and unauthorized ways. Resistance to prevailing arrangements materializes when agents actualize creative solutions in contexts normally covered by those arrangements. As these actions are noticed by others and validated, they may begin to catch on as patterns, and may even be joined with other rules to form a system of coherent ideas. Those with power derived from the dominant system may well respond with the full force of that social power to reimpose the old order on the situation. Often this power differential makes explicit challenges unwise, but socially subordinate actors can still challenge the system through those channels of action that the social arrangements make available to them. James Scott calls this "the arts of political disguise" and includes activities like rumors, gossip, linguistic tricks, metaphors, euphemisms, folk tales, and ritual gestures.[21] Most often acts of resistance become isolated as structurally subordinate individuals are subjected to the manifestations of social power available to superordinate members of society.

When resistance does survive and expand, however, conflict is often the result. Social orders are constructed in order to avoid conflict, but what constitutes a conflict is socially defined—actions that would be conflictual in some arrangements are acceptable means of settling differences in others. The spread of alternative social arrangements means there is an increase in interactions requiring negotiation. As people interact within a context of greater flux, conflicts increase because people act in unexpected ways. These conflicts often force people to justify their actions. The standards by which competing justifications will be judged—in the West, for example, by reason, rights, social standing, physical force, or politeness—are defined and maintained by the prevailing order. This process helps to solidify and organize systems of justifications, explanations, and symbols. Resistance succeeds in producing revolutions when it is no longer possible to defend very important aspects of dominant social arrangements against demonstrations of anomalies.[22]

THEORIES OF CONSTRUCTIVIST METHODOLOGY

As many scholars have noted, constructivism encompasses a variety of epistemologies.[23] Many scholars, including John Ruggie, Peter Katzenstein, Martha Finnemore, and Alexander Wendt, have contributed to the evolution of the constructivist discourse in International Relations. Across these various manifestations, however, the process at the core of constructivist ontology—the mutual constitution of agents and structures—is mediated by similar or at least related concepts. While there are important (if somewhat parochial) differences between rules, norms, institutions, and discursive practices, each refers to a social reification of ideational and behavioral patterns that attains a level of authority and power in the social realm. Condensing the diversity of constructivist theories into a single iconic manifestation is admittedly problematic in significant ways, especially with respect to epistemology. However, taking the explanation of constructivism beyond these shared principles requires selecting one of these manifestations to serve as a representative of the group as a whole. Since the methodology of political identity developed below was built largely on the model of social construction articulated by Nicholas Onuf, it seems logical to use his terminology of rules and negotiation, even if adopting this perspective will entail a more intense ontological investment than many thin, conventional, or instrumental constructivists would be willing to take.[24]

In this rule-centered approach, each direction of the two-way co-constitution process—agents making structures and structures making agents—passes through rules, which may or may not be explicitly formulated. Individual agents are the creative source of social rules, which, as an aggregate, define the social world. But this social world confronts each of its members as an intricate system of constraints and possibilities, organized as rules, and these rules define each member's identity and social power. Rules establish standards; they tell actors what they should do when confronted with a defined situation. These standards, however, are generally determined by patterns of action from past situations that seem similar in important ways to the contemporary one.

According to this theory, society and the social world are constituted by the transformation of speech and other acts into shared rules and through the institutionalization of these rules into a social arrangement. The context in which this process takes place is everyday social interaction.

> Individuals are continually confronted with the problem of locating themselves, and others, in a web of social categories that periodically confront them as salient. They have limited cognitive resources to devote to this task and, as a result, make much use of simplifying and memory-enhancing strategies. In constructivist terms, "rules" present agents with simpler ways to interpret the world and to make choices.[25]

While transcendental truth is a fiction, continuous awareness of the constructed nature of reality would present actors with so many choices as to make daily life debilitating. To provide a shared basis for action, rules function as truth in everyday social life. To the degree that truth exists, it does so only "for us" or "for all practical purposes," even if for all but the most philosophical of moments it is easier just to forget or ignore those qualifying phrases. Most often we know that we are living with people who function according to the same assumptions and expectations as we do and so it is just easier to live as if *our* truth is *the* truth. As generations change, the institutional memory of how, or even that, the rules were invented is lost and they become "just how things are done."[26]

Resistance is breaking a rule. If the violator is immediately punished, the rule is re-affirmed and social momentum continues apace. If, however, the actor is able to convince others that either the situation confronted was new, different enough in important ways to remove the actor from responsibility for disobeying the rule, or that the old rule was bad or at least worse than the rule implicit in the new action, a new rule may begin to be created. Negotiation is an excellent metaphor for the general process of rule creation. This process is not always, or even most often, conscious, but the comparison flows from treating all actions, whether acts of speech or not, as assertions.

> If I hereby state that X counts as Y, and you accept this statement as operative between us, without qualifications (which, if offered, I may accept in turn), then that statement rules our intersubjective situation a propos [sic] the relation of X and Y. We can always agree to change a rule; others can join in the agreement; it may become generally accepted. Were such to happen ... we speak of a convention emerging. ... Conventions once established in this fashion begin to substitute for new sets of agreements. ...

Eventually I feel no obligation to seek your agreement; I merely invoke the convention. We may say that conventions have become institutionalized and, in this process, acquire additional normativity, that is, they generate expectations not dependent on fresh agreement."[27]

Each member participates in the implicit negotiation through their actions (including speech acts) and by accepting or rejecting other actors' assertions. Such negotiations are, of course, influenced by the relative social power of the participants, but, as in Scott's theory, there are ways in which subordinates can influence negotiations with those upon whom the social order has bestowed relative power.

Rules, therefore, mediate both processes of co-constitution. Agents create social arrangements because their actions constitute assertions of rules. At the same time, social arrangements define not only the context within which agents act, but the agents and their abilities to act as well. Actions flow from a fluid combination of creativity by agents and the constraining force of social arrangements. In this version of constructivism, the entities that mediate this interaction, that allow social arrangements to affect human behavior and allow human creativity to impact social arrangements, are rules.

> If we start with rules, we can move in either direction—toward agents and the choices that rules give them an opportunity to make, or toward the social arrangements that emerge from the choices that agents are making all the time.... The practical problem is that, as constructivists, we want to move in both directions at the same time. Yet if we try to do so, we come up against the staggering complexity of the social reality that we want to know about. It is impossible to do everything. The practical solution is to start with rules and show how rules make agents and institutions what they are in relation to each other.[28]

The primacy of rules is, however, just an aesthetic choice; there is no real ground from whence to begin to think about these things. But for Onuf, rules are methodologically convenient. Rules (or institutions or norms or discursive activities) seem to be the best place for an inquisitive researcher to jump into the complex and flowing stream of mutual constitution.

Several prominent theorists have suggested that identity may hold another way to translate constructivism into rigorous empirical research. Yosef Lapid has claimed "culture and identity offer unmatched opportunities to sensitize the IR [International Relations] scholarly community to the research implications of the social construction of reality...."[29] Friedrich Kratochwil advocates "a more fine-grained approach for understanding the co-constitution of self (identity) and society."[30] Jeffrey Checkel suggests that if constructivism is to properly theorize the construction of agents, it will be necessary to further understand the relationship between structure and identity and the ways in which identities change.[31] Ted Hopf notes the promise of constructivism as a theory lies in its ability to "restore a kind of partial order and predictability to world politics that derives not from imposed homogeneity, but from the appreciation of difference."[32] And yet, while most constructivists stress identity, they do so merely as an intervening or intermediate variable between interests and action. Later, I argue that identity can provide a primary methodological focus that is at least as useful for the study of politics as rules or institutions or discourse in the abstract for constructivist research, and that in terms of assessing social change, it is even better. First, however, an examination of identity as a political concept is required.

IDENTITY

Theories of the Self

The everyday, common sense definition of identity used in American culture, and in the modern Western tradition generally, presents an individual as a self-contained combination of a mind, body, and core personality that is significantly atemporal. The individual's identity is "who she is."

> The view of human beings as self-contained unitary individuals who carry their uniqueness deep inside themselves, like pearls hidden in their shells, is one that is deeply ingrained in the Western tradition of thought. It is a vision captured in the idea of the person as monad—that is, as solitary individual divided from other human beings by deep walls and barriers. . . .[33]

In the West, identity is a way of organizing physical characteristics, beliefs, accumulated knowledge, experiences, abilities, and personality into attributes, the particular mix of which makes each individual unique and thus identifiable. Identity is that core part of the individual that provides continuity to the self as it moves through life. This core of identity is thought to form early in childhood and to be quite stable under normal circumstances. Changes to identity are events worthy of special notice and sometimes even ceremony (graduations, religious ceremonies, initiations, and other rites of passage). Global Politics has also adopted the term identity to talk about the "basic character" of states.[34] In this corporate sense, identity refers to a collectivity's culture, territory, resources, and relative power in a metaphor for an individual's personality, physical traits, and social roles. Although the idea of an individual having an identity is ultimately as arbitrary as that of a state having one, identity was originally coined as an attribute of an individual, and most scholars who have employed the metaphor have assumed rather than explained the appropriateness of the implied comparison.

Within the Western tradition, the formal study of identity has been the domain of psychology, which has tended to reify the Freudian individual, and to explain social dynamics through reference to individual characteristics, attitudes, or orientations.[35] It was not until Erik Erikson needed a way to talk about the social-psychological dimension of the person in 1950 that the term *identity* came into wide use.[36] To the degree that psychological theories of identity informed the study of politics, they did so mainly by positing country-specific personality types or by explaining terrorism as a cry for attention.[37] Others, such as Uri Bronfenbrenner and Sam Keen, worked to explain the dynamics of the Cold War through a psychological need for an "enemy image," a remarkably similar image of each other that Soviets and Americans tended to maintain even in the face of contradictions.[38]

Henri Tajfel's "Social Identification Theory" led the break with this North American style of social psychology.[39] The theory deals with what Tajfel calls "social identity," that part of a person's identity associated with group membership and the value attached to that membership, and thus adds a social component to the field. Another difference with past psychology is the proposition that society tends toward conflict rather than cohesion, thereby problematizing a neutral, rational image of society as context. By dealing with group membership generally, in the terminology of "in-groups" and "out-groups," rather than as some specific type of group identity (national, ethnic), the theory makes the concepts quite mobile. Lastly, social identification theory treats group membership as subjective and interpretive rather than objective, suggesting that people actively select information from the environment and interpret it in ways that simplify social distinctions. Tajfel and others translated these concepts into experimental data, including one study of the ways in which Afrikaners group people of different races.[40] Tajfel's theory broke through the logjam of individual-based psychology, but it still essentializes both biological and psychological drives. There also seems to be very little role for the individual as agent to alter any of these processes or meanings. In Tajfel's theory, individuals strive to change their identity in order to construct the best position relative to those around them. The process, however, only includes using the group labels to which they have access in the existing, essentialized social environment. There is no theory of social change or of agency.

Another often-cited book on identity in International Relations, William Bloom's addition to the prestigious Cambridge Studies in International Relations series, suffers from the same problem.[41] The book was published in 1990, and in the post-Cold War world, the "somewhat crude" question he asks ("With which entity do the mass of people identify—nation-state or class?") seems narrow and outdated.[42] In order to answer the question, he builds an "identification theory," an essentialized, individualized vision of identity, further circumscribed by the limitations of the nation. Using theories of identity to explain how a nation is "evoked into being" and "how that national public may then tend to behave" is a valuable goal, but the post-Cold War dynamics and politics of identity are so much more rich and interesting that Bloom's theory seems narrow and incomplete, even in a field whose disciplinary boundaries have been constituted from the beginning by such concepts. In general, such psychological theories of identity tend to essentialize biological and psychological drives and downplay or ignore social power, agency, and change.

Scholars who privilege power, agency, and change use the concept of identity to talk about the boundaries that separate people into groups and the politics of those boundaries. The set of boundaries available in the dominant traditions of Political Science, however, is very limited. Most modern thinking about global politics (and by implication most politics on a global scale) tends to focus on one of a very select set of reified manifestations of group identity—nations, classes, blocs, or levels of economic development (and perhaps a few others). Given its dominance of contemporary global politics, scholars traditionally have focused their theorizing on the idea of nation. Examples include Benedict Anderson's extremely influential contribution to theories of nation creation, R. B. J. Walker's more critical perspective on the role of nation in global politics, and Partha Chatterjee's postcolonial critique of how nationalism has been theorized in the West.[43] The end of the categorical dominance of the ideological and nation-state identities that defined the Cold War era caught most scholars unprepared to handle issues of diversity that resist the nation-state mold.[44] As group identities other than nation increasingly are asserted as strategies for the acquisition and maintenance of political power in the global arena, scholars of Global Politics have had to adapt to the growing importance of cleavages like ethnicity, gender, civilization, development, and religion, cleavages that are increasingly recognized by the mainstream as important sites of social and political power.

And yet this expansion into the broader realm of identity and difference has been somewhat haphazard. In the rush to deal with the expansion of types of politics in the post-Cold War environment, it seems that the field of Global Politics has forsaken a rigorous, holistic theory of identity in favor of theorizing a few of its splintered manifestations. Work that focuses on how global politics is influenced by cleavages of gender, for example, is separated from scholarship on ethnicity by barriers of jargon, methodology, and disciplinary politics. This pattern of abstracting and politicizing particular parts of what is a complex and fluid whole, while often very helpful and theoretically productive, perpetuates the reification of identities and agents, often restricting the ability of theory to deal with change. Scholars who narrow their analysis to a single factor of identity often ignore in-group differences and reify actors as undifferentiated, solid things—an Afrikaner or the Zulu people or the South African nation. In this understanding, identity becomes the essential core or personality of these reified, largely static entities. The complexity lost in abstracting and stereotyping agents at whatever level they are posited could be captured better in a wider discourse about the concept of identity.

In recent years, scholars have problematized how International Relations deals with identity, and the theoretical framework that follows is indebted to many of them.[45] William Connolly's 1991 book *Identity/Difference* argues that contemporary politics are dependent upon an antinomy between those within and those beyond the boundary of "us."[46] He argues that those who are cast as different are imbued with some form of "evil" in order to maintain the importance of the boundary between self and other and the cohesion of those within it. Connolly's main concern is not how this evil other is created (the "first problem of evil"), but rather the ways in which this evil justifies a static and defensive approach to maintaining the self in relation to that other by accentuating certain types of similarities and hiding or diminishing others (the "second problem of evil"). My goal in this book has been to translate these ideas into a basis for empirical research using identity.

Another valuable critique of identity in International Relations is David Campbell's post-structuralist examination of how statements of identity both enable and drive U.S. foreign policy.[47] In his second edition, Campbell adds an epilogue in which he critiques constructivism. He argues that the constructivist treatments available at the time either give agents volitional and supreme control (agents consciously construct reality) or construe language as reigning supreme over agency. I agree with much of what Campbell says, and in some measure this text was designed to answer some of the criticisms he has raised.[48] The most important distinction between Campbell's poststructural approach and the constructivist one I present below is that post-structuralism seems to settle for the sterility of perpetual critique. There is nothing wrong with restricting oneself to the project of unsettling everything, including new identities that rise to fill the voids created by previous critiques, but post-structuralists should not be too surprised when actors choose to pursue logocentrisms anyway. Abstract deconstruction inevitably turns into constructivism in practice.

Since the mid-1980s, constructivism and identity have experienced a kind of symbiotic growth in the field of Global Politics. Several edited volumes are indicative of the increasing prominence of identity as a conceptual centerpiece.[49] Some scholars of identity have appropriated constructivist terminology to depict the conscious, tactical nature of the political mobilization of, for example, national or ethnic identities. The result is often a dilution of the constructivist ontology. Most constructivist literature to date has lumped identity together with interests, often in order to critique Neorealism and Neoliberalism for assuming these factors to be given and constant or to focus on norms or rules or some other variable. The process of identity construction, as many scholars have pointed out, has remained undertheorized.[50] It has served mostly as a placeholder between norms and interests, and for many constructivists that chain itself is assumed rather than explained.

> Far from being created and instantiated through the process of social interaction, identity follows from the combination of exogenous interest and circumstances [in most constructivist literature] and so remains a component of the social construction of institutional preferences. Thus the same (neo-)functionalist perspective on identity transformation is replicated. While identity may indeed serve as an initial barrier to the recognition of more efficacious institutions, the causal prioritization of interests means that the transference of identities and loyalties to those alternative institutions is (despite protestations to the contrary in the literature) theoretically overdetermined.[51]

While most constructivists may indeed treat identities as a function of interests, a theory rooted in a strong constructivist ontology allows agents to create and change identities, making identity the focus of the process of social construction rather than merely an offshoot of interests. Alexander Wendt has begun to correct this problem. He argues that identity (who a person *is*) exists in a complex relationship with interests (what a person *wants*) and that they play complimentary explanatory roles.

Much in Wendt's theory of identity is powerful, well argued, and helpful to constructivism generally. His description of how identities as roles work to regulate interactions is very well developed and, I believe, right on target.[52] However, I believe significant difficulties flow from his choice to root his constructivism in a scientific realist ontology. This choice demands an analytical unit of action that tends to overemphasize structural stability, both in general and with respect to identities. Wendt also locates identity as a property of agents, rather than a meaning that exists only within a social context.[53] Wendt distinguishes four kinds of identity—personal or corporate, type, role, and collective.[54] From a thicker constructivist point of view in which reality is based on importance rather than existence, these four types of identity are easily condensed into a single type—role.[55] Ted Hopf's distinction between conventional and critical constructivists based on assumptions about change and identity is helpful in clarifying where Wendt would disagree with the theory of political identity presented below. While critical constructivists are most interested in the naturalizing power of identity, conventional constructivism is focused on the relationship between identity and action.

> In other words, critical theory aims at exploding the myths associated with identity formation, whereas conventional constructivists wish to treat those identities as possible causes of action. Critical theory thus claims an interest in change, and a capacity to foster change, that no conventional constructivist could make.[56]

Critical constructivism gives more power (and encouragement) to actors as agents of change, and is, in my opinion, more true to the two-way process of social construction than conventional constructivist understandings of identity. It is especially useful when examining the relationship between identity and social change. While major structural change is very difficult because of the tendency for actors to frame their activities as reproducing their identities and thus the existing social structures, actors are sometimes able to bring about major social change by evoking identities outside of or opposed to those structures (and dealing with the incumbent risks).

This kind of shift in the social foundations of identity is modeled in the fall of South African apartheid, where a hegemonic order based on colonial, modern, European discourses lost its power to define otherness, and conflict did indeed follow. In this way, South Africa is a strong analogy for this global explosion of cultural and ethnic identities in the post-Cold War world. The next section distills from the discourse on identity a theory of political identity developed with the South African experience as a backdrop. Before moving on to the empirical specifics of the transition that makes up the heart of this study, this chapter concludes with an attempt to tie that theory back into the constructivist understanding of social dynamics more generally.

A Constructivist Definition

The reconceptualization of identity advanced in this chapter requires a change to what might be called the "unit" of identity, and a distinction between identity and identity labels. In this understanding, *identity* is a repertoire of descriptive *identity labels,* arranged in a continuously shifting hierarchy of importance.[57] This hierarchy of labels is constantly changing as interlocutors and environmental circumstances vary. Even though an individual or corporate person may be said to possess an identity as the aggregate list of descriptions that can meaningfully be applied to the "self," either by the self or by others, the meaning of each of those constituent labels is determined in a complex, social process. Who a person is at any particular time is defined by the socially meaningful codes asserted in the interactions between self and others. An actor's hierarchy of labels is continuously rearranged as interlocutors and environmental circumstances change. Because identity is an aggregate of these intersubjectively defined codes, individuals are dependent upon the ideas and acquiescence of others for the meaning and power of their identities. When contrasted to the western psychological understanding currently dominant in Political Science, this framework presents identity as more fragmented, power-laden, fluid, and contextual.

Each descriptive label in an identity is itself a social construction and is only meaningful in the context of the power of social arrangements. The labels are empowered from early childhood and ingrained through language. Social arrangements specify which labels have garnered attention in the social past and thereby imply which ones deserve the current attention of society's members. Language is a good indicator of social values of importance; important/real things have labels while it takes strings of words to describe those things that are less important. A description like "person who gets seasick" does not have a handy everyday label because it is generally not important enough to merit its own category in our language. Specialized jargon (those who run charter fishing services may indeed find it important enough to have such a label) is one of the primary markers of expertise. The purpose of language is to share meaning, but in the process prejudices are smuggled in because the structures inherent in the capabilities and limitations of words and grammar filter the experience of the material world.

The effect on identity is demonstrated by the differences between Japanese and English. In Japanese, identity is significantly more problematic than the Western self inherent in English.[58] The Japanese concept of the individual is diluted by the use of the word *I*. The *I* that takes orders from a boss is an entirely different word from the *I* that disciplines a child.⁵⁹ The verbs for the same activity even vary depending upon the person to whom the *I* is speaking. In English, the same linguistic *I* confronts all situations. These kinds of language structures constrain thought processes. The idea of the self in English is unitary, self-contained, and predominantly static, while in Japanese the self is fragmented, contingent upon social relations, and always changing with respect to context.⁶⁰

Because constructivism asserts that reality is based in social assessments of importance rather than some nature inherent in the material world, the kinds of descriptive labels that Political Science currently considers political—citizenship, class, ethnicity, gender, development, civilization, and a few others—are not naturally so. Every description carries an implicit cleavage—those who are cub scouts and those who are not—and, in the context of modern dualities, differences carry judgments and implications for power. As William Connolly argues, "Identity requires difference in order to be, and it converts difference into otherness in order to secure its own self-certainty."⁶¹

Each self/other antinomy carries implications for power whenever it is invoked, and if its invocation is systematized into social rules, it becomes political. A decision to begin discriminating against people with green eyes would suddenly make people conscious of eye color and could very well result in the mobilization of that identity label for political activity.⁶² If someone with enough power decreed that all people under six feet tall were henceforth to be slaves of all those over six feet tall, it seems fair to suggest that height would become more important to members of that society than, say, race. Such hypotheticals may seem ridiculous and arbitrary, but it would not take many generations before such cleavages would begin to seem appropriate, even natural ways to divide humanity. How many generations did it take before people who lived on the border between Zimbabwe and Zambia began to believe that there was some important difference about those who lived only a few miles away? At a broad enough level of abstraction, all schemes of categorizing humans are equally valid. What separates the eye color cleavage from the Zimbabwean-Zambian cleavage is a history of political decisions in which people attributed importance to abstract national boundaries. As R. B. J. Walker describes, we inherited a world in which people believe national differences exist and in which people make decisions based on that existence.⁶³ People live *as if* imaginary lines represented on maps are true, and therefore they become so.

By beginning with the broad concept of identity rather than one or another of its manifestations (like gender or ethnicity or class), political importance is diffused throughout the spectrum of potentially descriptive labels. As Ian Burkitt argues, identity becomes political because the labels that make it up are social constructions whose meanings are susceptible to the actions and assertions of all who use them.⁶⁴ The meaning and importance of labels is constituted by their use in the everyday negotiations of power that make up social interaction and, by constructivist implication, that produce rules and society and reality. While changes in the meaning of labels may take place in dramatic social convulsions, it is wrong to treat either identity or identity labels as static in the long stretches between such upheavals. It also seems wrong to limit political analysis to a few categories of identity.

Identity changes more often in this constructivist vision in part because the hierarchical arrangement of the repertoire is based on those descriptions that are immediately important to the person and to those with whom she, he, or it is interacting. The possibility of adopting this more focused frame of reference is one of the key contributions of a more fragmented vision of identity. The top position in a person's hierarchy will be occupied by many different labels during the course of any normal day, with important implications for social power. For example, in the course of the half hour that it takes me to leave my house and arrive at school to teach a class, my hierarchical arrangement goes through many shifts. At home I might be interacting as "daddy" to my daughter or "boss" to my baby-sitter, positions of relative power (at least theoretically). On my way, I am one "driver" among many and in a position of equality with respect to the traffic laws and of mutual dependence with respect to our collective and individual safety. As I arrive in class, the driver label fades out of my top ten labels, replaced by "professor" and "expert" and "grader," labels that meant almost nothing in the context of driving. Unless someone brings it up, "golfer" would probably not even crack the top thousand. In other contexts, such as a free afternoon in late spring, "golfer" may be my most important description. Even labels like "speaker" and "listener" which circulate among interlocutors add and subtract a relative and momentary dosage of power in the course of a conversation. In most egalitarian circumstances this dosage is usually insignificant in relation to the power of other labels, but in some circumstances the ability to contribute to public conversation or even to speak to others is a closely guarded privilege, which is, I would argue, organized and distributed through social categories of identity. Other labels, such as "American," "male" or "White," are more politicized and hence more likely to be invoked in situations where power is an explicit part of the interaction.

At any point in time, each aspect of a person's identity can usefully be seen as a temporary assertion. These assertions can be made explicitly or implicitly through behavior that conforms to the expectations attached to one so described. Who someone is in an interaction depends upon the mutual acceptance of these identity assertions, and such acceptance is at least partially dependent on prevailing social rules and the relative social power of the person doing the asserting. According to the theory of symbolic interactionism, what might be called the rules of identity—the patterns of acceptable or reasonable assertions of descriptions and the processes for asserting them—are also learned through these interactions with significant others.[65] The process of interaction closely parallels the negotiations with respect to rules that Onuf described above. The weight of social expectations attached to labels is not a "pregiven collective interest," but the system of rewards and penalties erected and perpetuated by social elites does channel society's members toward actions that reproduce those structures.[66] Society is at least partly dependent upon actors asserting intersubjective, socially meaningful identities in their interactions with others. This social momentum makes structural change difficult. As Wendt argues,

> identities are always in process, always contested, always an accomplishment of practice. Sometimes their reproduction is relatively unproblematic because contestation is low, in which case taking them as a given may be analytically useful. But in doing so we should not forget that what we take to be given is in fact a *process* that has simply been sufficiently stabilized by international and external structures that it *appears* given. A methodology should not become a tacit ontology.[67]

For heuristic purposes, assertions may be best organized into personas, the three or four labels that are most important to that interaction—courteous, law-abiding driver or a democratic, capitalist superpower. While a persona is presented as if it is self-contained and consistent, it is only a convenient transitory fiction. These personas are cobbled together from the broader list of labels and shift as labels intersect in new and interesting ways as situations evolve. Each persona is political because it advances a vision of reality, rules, and privilege distribution and asserts that future action should conform to that vision. By investing agency in labels and temporary personas rather than in an individual or a state as a static whole, the framework of political identity can, for all practical purposes, bypass the so-called level of analysis problem and be applied to societies made up of any kind of units.

Levels of analysis are the analytical distinctions between the international arena in which actors are states, the domestic arena in which actors are bureaucratic and civic institutions, and the individual level in which particular people are the primary focus of analysis. Political scientists often have trouble spanning these heuristic chasms, a problem which justifies the disciplinary boundary between International Relations, Comparative Politics, and the study of domestic politics. The tendency in the field of International Relations to restrict agency to the corporate level often simplifies complex processes in useful ways (especially given the field's dominant meta-theoretical foundations), but it also constrains scholars' ability to confront that complexity more broadly.[68] While analytical distinctions between types of actors are often useful, the constructivist perspective on political identity refuses to presume the particular identity labels each society uses to distinguish between its members. Analysis becomes focused on how the society under consideration distributes power, privilege, agency, or whatever else. By seating the quality under consideration (for example, agency) in labels, the *unit* of analysis becomes the interaction between actors rather than the actors themselves. This perspective allows the analyst to make conclusions about the conditions under which assertions of a particular (in this example, agency-laden) label have been successful. This removes qualities from the actors and instills them in the relationship. Rather than understanding actors as largely static entities confronting a variety of situations, political identity allows us to look at interactions within which actors are defined. It thus provides a way to grab hold of the Foucauldian idea of power.

The perspective also allows the disaggregation of actors (corporate or individual) that were previously considered whole. These internally consistent wholes oversimplify the complexity of agency. Even those persons who are sometimes agents are not agents all of the time. Actions are still carried out in the material and social worlds through human or corporate bodies as the material component of agents, and this process is important because for constructivists, action is how reality is constructed. However, in this interpretation, both physical and institutional bodies are merely sites, screens upon which various labels and the roles they represent are consistently actualized with respect to others.[69] This relationship between identity and action in the material world seems crucial to understanding complex political phenomena. Avoiding the reification of the actor and adopting a small, contextual unit of analysis—interactions—in which power and identity often shift make it possible to study consistencies across interactions as indications of importance. When this concept of identity is woven back into the abstract theory of social constructivism, each identity label becomes a nexus where the mutual constitution of agent and society takes place, and identity becomes a useful concept to anchor the study of politics generally.

IDENTITY LABELS AS UNITS OF A CONSTRUCTIVIST METHOD

Placing the concept of identity at the center of a constructivist understanding of social reality enables the analysis of the overwhelmingly complex and fluid process by which agents and structures interact to construct each other in society. While analysis of this recursive process could take place at any point, selecting identity as the object of analytical intervention is no more (or less) violently logocentric than any other. Identity need not replace other methodological choices for studying this process, but it does constitute another point of entry through which constructivism can be translated into empirical research. Wendt agrees, at least in part, with this choice.

> [S]ocial identities have both individual and social structural properties, being at once cognitive schemas that enable an actor to determine "who I am/we are" in a situation and positions in a social role structure of shared understandings and expectations. In this respect, they are the key link in the mutual constitution of agent and structure, embodying the terms of individuality through which agents relate to each other. These terms lead actors to see situations as calling for taking certain actions and thus defining their interests in certain ways.[70]

Identities and identity labels are socially constructed, but they are also located within the process by which reality more broadly is constructed. This process of construction is continuous and recursive, but the theory of constructivist political identity developed here holds that each movement passes through identity.

In order for this theory to work, identity must be implicated in both directions of the two-way process of co-constitution.[71] First, how identity mediates the process by which society constructs individuals will be presented, followed by the reverse process.

Identity and the Social Construction of Agents

A society's intricate and shifting systems of identity labels are the principal means by which agents know which social rules to translate into action, and how to do so in such a way that their behavior not only makes sense, but is coordinated with the behavior of others. Identity labels are codes, statements that give cues for how individuals should behave and how others should behave toward them. They are not Weberian ideal types or Platonic forms, but containers of social meaning that are renegotiated continuously through the actions of society's members. Action is authorized and legitimated through reference to standards that actors feel the pressure of social expectations to actualize, and thereby re-affirm, in their everyday interactions. People behave as a scientist, as a mother, as a thief, and generally try to be a "good" one, even if they do so unreflexively unless pressed for justification. Wendt points out that, as collective representations, labels help explain aggregate continuities even if actors have no intention of behaving as "good Canadians," for example.[72] It is also the case that actors may perceive the meanings of or rules associated with the labels incorrectly. When confronted, however, actors will seek to justify their activities by calling upon models and tropes that match the descriptions they accept for themselves. These descriptions, encased in labels, are useful because they carry the power of social expectations.

All social arrangements include definitions of freedom and responsibility that empower some actors and restrict others with respect to particular contexts. The arrangements also spell out social or even physical penalties for those who behave in unexpected ways. While some societies are more restrictive than others and some labels bestow more social power than others, all identity labels are susceptible to the social pressures of the expectations attached to them. When actors evoke these labels, or are saddled with them by prevailing visions of reality, those shared expectations become part of the context in which actions are weighed, carried out, and evaluated. How an actor is identified is critical to understanding her act and judging whether it is normal or not, justified or not, innovative or not.

There is a utilitarian reason for this. To the degree that their meanings are shared, labels make the enormous complexity of interacting with others more predictable by helping interlocutors select from the bank of social behavioral patterns. Labels are generalizations, assertions that the identified person is the same in important respects as all others so labeled. These generalizations allow agents to draw parallels with other previously experienced situations or at least to tap into conventional wisdom about interactions.[73] "Don't take candy from strangers." "[Good little girls] Always say please and thank you." "This joker in the red car is going to cut me off." "Democracies do not go to war with each other." The social arrangements of rules and values in which labels are embedded provide actors not only with guidelines for themselves, but also for others, and simplify the highly complex set of possible interactions in society. These social arrangements are negotiated through the medium of identities, albeit as codes for rules, norms, and arrangements. Participants negotiate rules by asserting identity labels for their interaction, thereby determining each party's position and relative social power. Mere acquaintance with a society's rules is not enough; each socially competent actor must know which rules to activate when. This information is encoded in the identity labels applied to both self and other.

The meanings behind the labels are embedded in (largely implicit) hierarchies that supply the predictability for dealing with a highly complex set of possible interactions with others. Because a general consciousness of the functioning of such a system would reduce its efficiency, the invented and arbitrary nature of identities as codes for sets of rules is forgotten or ignored.[74] Societies function more smoothly if their categories of identity and the accompanying rules are accepted as natural. In normal times, these structures confront actors as what Wendt has called "obdurate social facts."[75] Constructing identity "is a continual and never-completed project, but it cannot appear as such. In other words, the people must simultaneously be presumed as a given and at the same time be continually reproduced."[76] In the rhetoric of social arrangements, momentum is presented as stability.

Through labels and personas, the structural power of social arrangements is most obvious. No one is an agent all of the time. At those times when the actor's persona has no labels that signify agency, or in those cases when interlocutors reject the actor's (most often implicit) assertion of such labels, the actor cannot be considered a social agent, and actions that do not abide by existing social rules are likely to be punished. If an actor successfully asserts agency-laden labels in a particular context, actions in that context may come to be perceived by others as legitimate, authoritative, and structural, or perhaps as acceptable anomalies with no repercussions outside of that highly circumscribed context. The momentum of existing relationships bestows power on people relative to how they have been defined up to that point. So auto mechanics have structural power with respect to transmission repairs, and in that realm they may indeed have power over corporate executives or senators or popes. It is not that subordinates normally have no power in society; they just have power (which is always relative) in far fewer situations than social elites. This power is organized for daily use by the identity labels that participants assert within the course of a relationship. It is important to note that this is not a causal theory of action, but a suggestion for how to tap into the process of social co-constitution. Because these labels are normally on the surface of the interaction or just below it, the mutual characterizations of participants in social activities provide an excellent opportunity to study the hierarchies of value and role that govern social and political life in a society.

Negotiation is also an appropriate metaphor for the cycle of these assertions in each interaction. Because the power of these labels to define the interactional context is dependent upon the mutual acceptance of assertions, each party in the relationship has power. Any party could simply refuse to accept another's assertion, even though disproportionate social power may make this strategy very dangerous. This refusal happens in many subtle ways in everyday life and is part of the process of defining a relationship. But a refusal to accept another's assertion is also a challenge to the set of social arrangements for which it is a code, and there are instances when the enactment of such a refusal becomes important for the shape of social structures. In times of explicit social change, changing conceptions of structures make rebellious assertions more acceptable, and more actors can become agents who think of themselves and are thought of by others as capable of formulating new behaviors and negotiating them as rules with others.[77] This is the power of agency.

IDENTITY AND THE CONSTRUCTION OF SOCIAL ORDER

While social arrangements organize and control agency through identity labels, identity labels are also the medium through which agents affect the social system. Social arrangements, "although difficult to challenge, are not impregnable. Alternative actors with alternative identities, practices, and sufficient material resources are theoretically capable of effecting change."[78] As agents interact, they assert identities, in some cases explicitly, but most often simply by obeying the rules characteristic of an identity in the particular context. The circularity of the co-constitution process is perhaps best grasped by privileging acts over cold materiality or interpretive meanings. In the beginning was the deed.[79]

> Even though agents and social structures are mutually constitutive and co-determined, the mechanism through which this occurs, the first cause of social life, is what actors *do*. "We are—or become—what we do." Actors can do things even if they do not already have the identities which those practices will eventually create.[80]

Because each situation and context is unique (if only because of the flow of events since the previous similar situation), each time an agent actualizes a behavioral rule, a rule is applied to a new situation. If change is privileged over stability in thinking about society, then to the degree that particular labels can be thought of as having metaphorical weight with agents, the corresponding identities have momentum in society. To the extent that observers accept that an agent embodies a particular label, that person's actions come to constitute (that is, either reinforce or change) the social momentum of that label. Depending on whether their actions fit expectations, agents either add to or, in effect, challenge the existing meaning of the label.

Through this process of assertions and negotiations, identity constitutes not only the conduit of social expectations, but also the point of entry through which current social patterns of privilege distribution can be challenged. The power of a hierarchy depends upon the general acceptance of its assertions. The ability of agents to reject characterizations of relationships that place them at a disadvantage seems, from this perspective, the basis for all effective resistance to power, and thus the greatest threat to those who enjoy positions of privilege within a social order. Resistance to the behavioral patterns of society comes from questioning the assertions about identity that make certain behaviors seem natural. But this resistance depends upon the ability to formulate and activate alternative identities. "Constructivism conceives of the politics of identity as a continual contest for control over the power necessary to produce meaning in a social group. So long as there is difference, there is potential for change."[81]

From this perspective, the transformation of the South African social order was accomplished by people who stepped out of the identities and personas that apartheid sanctioned and adopted new ones that empowered them to become agents of social change. To some students, being a protester suddenly became more important. Members of ethnic groups, Asians, and Coloureds became Black, a term that was appropriated as a symbol of common oppression rather than race. Miners and factory workers became union members. Clergy and other leaders adapted into activists. Apartheid used identities to restrict the perception of competency to change the social order. As actors supplanted officially sanctioned descriptive labels with others that demonstrated opposition to the legitimacy of the governing order, they activated identity labels that allowed political resistance and empowered them to fundamentally alter hierarchies of privilege. These new labels coalesced into personas, sometimes through the actions of White elites originally intended to condemn and delegitimize the resistors. What follows is a study of the transformation of the South African social order as seen through the labels and personas that people assert as descriptions and explanations of major social events.

From this constructivist perspective on political identity, agency exists in rhetorically asserted personas rather than in individuals or groups. Agency is organized by attributing it to labels that agents then assert in particular contexts. In this perspective, individuals are only agents when their interlocutors accept that agency-laden descriptive labels apply to them. Such labels and their distribution are governed by social rules that are themselves susceptible to change. If one adopts this perspective, South Africa's social transformation is usefully framed as the process of enacting a change in the conceptual boundary between political agents and political objects.

CONCLUSION

This chapter has presented a constructivist framework of political identity. In it, identity labels are a nexus between social structures and the actions of agents. Socially competent actors read labels as signals for what kind of behavior to expect from others and for how to behave toward them. In this way, identity labels tie interaction into the system of intersubjective assumptions, expectations, and patterns of behavior and, at the same time, serve as the mechanism by which social agents organize the adaptations they continually make to those social structures. Such changes most often appear to be structural from the perspective of those not involved in the initial creative acts that produced them. Identities, in this perspective, are the key tools of politics, serving either stability or change depending on the context. Through the assertions of these labels in rhetoric intended to justify or limit social behavior, the process of mutual constitution is available for analysis.

In contrast to social science traditions that root agency in either the human/corporate body (individualism) or disembodied social forces (structuralism or holism), studying change through identity labels allows scholars to better represent some of its overwhelming complexity. Labels are social structures, but here they function only as a methodological tool for tracing such changes in society (what Roxanne Doty calls "nodal points"),[82] not as a universal causal source of change in a scientific sense. A constructivist ontology and a methodological focus on labels allow actors to specify through their actions which identities, interests, and aspects of the social and material environment are real and privileged in any particular context. From a deep constructivist perspective, the complexity of causality, the uniqueness of individual and cultural realities, and the randomness of human creativity will always elude efforts to articulate a single causal theory of agency and social change.

If change is represented as passing through identity, then actors become agents only when they are able to successfully assert particular labels as part of their contextualized identity. Rather than reifying agency into particular social entities that only sometimes act as agents, thinking of agency as residing in fluid and contextual identity labels allows much more specific theories of social change and politics. People that International Relations scholars categorize as Americans or Chinese or Zambians only sometimes act as Americans or Chinese or Zambians. At other times they may act more as mothers or drivers or golfers. This is even more true of states, whose character depends upon the coordination of a diverse and very complex set of internal factors. Whether South Africa was a democracy (and thus able to claim the benefits the modern world offered those so labeled) was dependent on which of its characteristics were emphasized. To refer to individuals as Americans or a state as a democracy is to stress only one aspect of a complex and evolving identity. Only in very limited contexts can an individual or state become an agent with respect to the definition of American-ness or democracy. In the post-Cold War world, the traditional categories of identity in Global Politics seem to capture a decreasing sector of the actions that have importance in the global arena. Using identity labels as the unit of agency helps scholars be more specific about the distribution of power when studying social phenomena, especially when they focus on large-scale, explicit social change.

The large-scale explicit social change with which this book is concerned is the transformation of the apartheid social order. I argue that this transition is aptly represented through three of the conflicts that constituted it. But before delving into the specifics of the last thirty years of South African discourse, some historical and logistical errands must be run. The next chapter introduces the reader to the South African historical context and explains in much greater detail how the conceptual, ontological, and epistemological framework outlined above was translated into a methodology.

Chapter Three

SOUTH AFRICA AND IDENTITY

The rise and fall of apartheid is one of the most compelling stories of twentieth century politics. The moral simplicity and practical complexity of the South African problem captured the imagination of individuals around the world, making apartheid a global issue. When social change came through largely peaceful negotiations rather than the cataclysmic violence that even the most optimistic analysts considered likely, the quest to understand South Africa's politics became even more earnest. The case studies that make up the heart of this analysis frame the process by which apartheid was dismantled and an alternative social order laid out as a series of conflicts. I argue that these conflicts, which represent different stages in the transition, provide an excellent opportunity to apply the theories of constructivist political identity to the process of social change. The project, therefore, examines how the ideas that South Africans have used to make sense of who they are in relation to each other can help us understand the transformation of their society. The purpose of this chapter is to provide the reader with some of the historical, analytical, and methodological context for the events and processes on which I have chosen to focus. It is organized into three sections that introduce the reader to South Africa and apartheid through a necessarily simplified historical overview, explore some of the ways that South African politics and identity have been analyzed in the past, and present my own approach to studying the transition.

APARTHEID AND ITS HISTORICAL CONTEXT

A Brief Political History of South Africa

The land that is now the Republic of South Africa has a long history of the same types of conflict that were indicative of the spread of capitalism elsewhere in the non-Western world. Colonialism, however, did not overpower all contexts uniformly. What has made the South African case interesting is the particular racial adaptations that capitalism made as it confronted the circumstances of the South African context, and the tenacity with which the ruling elites held on to their distinctive institutional inventions as the dominant tenor of global social and cultural norms turned against them. Understanding the process by which race became institutionalized as the governing divisions of society demands an examination of South Africa's political history.

What we might today call racial diversity was prevalent even before 1652 when Europeans, in the persons of Jan van Reibeeck and the Dutch East India Company, began a colonizing mission and inserted themselves into the South African mix on a permanent basis. Anthropologists identify the hunter-gatherer San, the herder Khoikhoi, and the farming Bantu as distinct groups occupying southern Africa during the Iron Age. Colonization by Europeans stands out as a watershed because it forced the area into a global political economy, making the relationships of similarity and difference that formed the basis for identity global in scope.[1] Clashes between European settlers and indigenous groups dominated the region's history as Europeans edged inland and continued after 1806, when the area known as the Cape became a colony of the British Empire. In the first half of the nineteenth century, a major disruption in the traditional governance patterns of the Bantu peoples, brought on by the imperial aspirations of Shaka Zulu and referred to as the *mfecane,* coincided with a precipitous invasion of the interior (the Great Trek) by Dutch and other settlers unhappy with British rule. Meanwhile, British imperial expansion to the north and east in search of both land and labor resulted in a series of wars against both the Xhosa in the eastern Cape and the Zulu in Natal.[2]

All of these events slowly solidified European dominance. As diamonds (1867) and gold (1886) were discovered in the interior, British colonialists moved to take control of the land, the mines, and the people. These expansive drives also sparked two "inter-European" wars between the British and the two Boer Republics, entities established after the Great Trek by Whites whose national identity was based mostly on animosity toward the British, a rejection of the Enlightenment's early liberalism, and a fiercely independent attitude often justified by a strict Calvinism.[3] The British conquest of the Transvaal and Orange Free State republics resulted in the 1910 Union of South Africa and the consolidation of discriminatory White rule.[4] Three years later, one of the most important foundations of institutionalized racism and the exploitation of Africans as laborers, the 1913 Land Act, was promulgated. After another thirty-five years of sometimes tense power sharing between predominantly British and a variety of Afrikaner nationalist parties, the narrow parliamentary victory by the Afrikaner-based National Party (NP) in 1948 shifted power to Afrikaners, who constituted three-fifths of White citizens, but just over ten percent of the population of South Africa. This victory resulted in the implementation of policies designed to benefit the party's Afrikaner constituency. These policies were known as apartheid.

From the late 1940s until the middle 1990s, apartheid was the dominant social order in South Africa. Sometimes translated into English as "separateness," the word has become a translingual representation of institutionalized racism. In the context of South Africa, however, the term must be used much more specifically. Apartheid was first and foremost a systematic legal structure that divided South Africans into racial groups, legitimated the uneven distribution of South African economic, social, and political goods according to those racial categories, and systematized White exploitation of those South Africans labeled African, Indian, or Coloured. Apartheid laws were attempts by powerful Whites to invent solutions to what they saw as the problems of racial coexistence. Implicit in each of apartheid's acts of social engineering was a metaphysics that posited the central importance of groups, specifically racial groups, for predicting the qualities, abilities, and behavior of individuals. The entrenchment of this metaphysics into the formal political system provided it with legitimacy and allowed it to leach into every aspect of social reality. Apartheid forced South Africans to live their lives as if racism were true.

The cornerstone of apartheid was the Population Registration Act of 1950, according to which each person was labeled either White (also called European), Coloured, Native (also African, Bantu), or Asian (also Indian). These categories served as the foundation for a system of laws that allocated social advantage according to racial difference. The Group Areas Act (1950) and the Natives Resettlement Act (1954) systematized the practice of racial segregation of residential areas and were the justification for the wholesale movement of African, Coloured, and Indian neighborhoods. The Reservation of Separate Amenities Act of 1953 enforced segregation of public facilities. The Suppression of Communism Act (1950) gave the government sweeping police and detention authority, and a series of laws in the early 1950s established "Bantu education," which emphasized racial and ethnic difference and purposefully trained African students for nothing more than manual labor. Mixed marriages were prohibited (1949), as was all sexual contact between Whites and other South Africans (Immorality Act of 1950).

Apartheid's legal structures explicitly promoted the material and ideational divisions of racism for the benefit of Whites as capitalists, guaranteeing the availability of cheap labor. The creation of African land reserves known as "Bantustans," or homelands, and a draconian system of registration documents called "passes" regulated urban migration and ensured a steady supply of unskilled African laborers while maintaining the spatial segregation so essential to the disproportionate distribution of privilege. The totalitarian system legalized almost any abuse by members of the privileged minority, and patterns of mistreatment were backed by the coercive forces of the state in the name of "security." Both entitlement and exploitation became almost entirely dependent on race.

APARTHEID AS ORDER

While apartheid was a particular set of racist laws, it was also a vision of reality that influenced what people noticed and understood about the world and how they behaved in it. The apartheid social order was built upon what Kathryn Manzo calls the "postulate of difference."⁵ In contrast to the postulate of identity, a basic tenet of liberalism that holds that *individuals* can aspire to the same standards of civilization because of the universal gift of rationality, the postulate of difference posits that *races* are fundamentally different. According to this view, each race has unique qualities that may develop over time, but such development simply moves the race further down a predetermined, natural, and discernable path. It does not change a group's relationship to other groups.

For people raised in cultures soaked through with the postulate of identity, it is often difficult to grasp how different reality can be when it is populated by groups, rather than individuals. Those responsible for justifying apartheid recognized that many in the global audience needed to be convinced of this distinction.

> The population of South Africa does not comprise a conglomerate of individuals, some of who merely happen to be White and others Black. History (British Imperialism) brought together within the confines of the same geopolitical entity various nations, each with its own culture, language, traditions, political and social systems, and area of hegemony.⁶

To this theory of racial divisions, South African Calvinism added a strong current of predestination that ruled out trying to change what God had established. Apartheid's architects believed that races were established by God as essential human categories and that social relations should reflect these fundamental biological and social cleavages. Within apartheid reality, every group had their responsibilities, based on the talents and foibles inherent in their God-given (later "genetic") nature. The inherently uncivilized Africans were destined to be followers, "bearers of water and hewers of wood."⁷ While individuals and even groups as a whole could develop, the overall system of human categorization and the basic characteristics of each group were static.

Whatever its political origins, over time this categorical scheme became a naturalized part of the South African reality. Because South Africans of all races used these generalizations in their daily lives, individual actors experienced the expectations of others as social pressure to behave according to the rules. As a result, the stereotypes and generalizations were true; that is, they accurately predicted how people would behave. The "grouped" nature of reality of groups was subtle and pervasive.

> South Africans were born into institutions in a sense. It wasn't a politics of choice. I think that's what the liberal mind still failed to understand: some people are not individuals and even when you become an individual, when you experience that paradigm shift in a value system, you are still caught up in structures of your old paradigm. You can't move out of it.⁸

Unless there is reason to believe otherwise, most people take for granted that those around them interpret reality in the same way they do. Apartheid institutionalized this tendency by putting people in high, strong racial boxes and making life much easier for those people who internalized group stereotypes. The system was designed to deny South Africans knowledge of the other. When South Africans of different racial groups interacted, it was usually within the context of what James Scott calls the public transcript—a set of unspoken rules that govern the open interaction between subordinates and those who dominate.[9] Apartheid's public transcript was racial; it was designed to make race-based behavior make sense in everyday life. In order to get along under apartheid, South Africans needed to assume that their actions would always be interpreted through the categories of race. People behaved as White mothers or Coloured drivers or African drivers. As long as the legitimacy and the logic of that social order were intact, there was no reason for people not to behave racially.

While it is impossible to measure the extent to which South Africans believed in apartheid's interpretation of reality and truth in these years, its rules and hierarchies did hold sway over the practicalities of everyday life, governing behavior and coordinating social interaction. During apartheid's heyday, conflicts between members of society were confined almost exclusively to socially acceptable arenas and processes. At its height, the apartheid order was hegemonic in the Gramscian sense.

> Rather than creating a police state, the makers of modern apartheid wanted to create a self-policing state in which blacks knew their boundaries. When the government boasted that New York City had more police per capita than Soweto, it was boasting about the success of the psychology of repression which had blacks so convinced of their impotence that actual repression became necessary only on occasion.[10]

Through control over education, employment, and mobility, apartheid successfully organized an ordered racist society.

This order was built upon the brutal oppression of Blacks as Blacks. For all the physical and economic violence that apartheid heaped on the lives of Black people, however, perhaps apartheid's greatest tragedy for the group as a whole was its psychologically debilitating image of Black agency. Steve Biko, founder of the Black Consciousness movement, eloquently depicted the self-image apartheid inflicted on Blacks (here in the androcentric language of the day).

> The type of black man we have today has lost his manhood. . . . He looks with awe at the white power structure and accepts what he regards as the 'inevitable position'. . . . In the privacy of his toilet his face twists in silent condemnation of white society but brightens up in sheepish obedience as he comes out hurrying in response to his master's impatient call. . . . Celebrated achievements by whites in the field of science—which he understands only hazily—serve to make him convinced of the futility of resistance and to throw away any hopes that change may ever come. All in all the black man has become a shell, a shadow of a man, completely defeated, drowning in his own misery, a slave, an ox bearing the yoke of oppression with sheepish timidity.[11]

Under apartheid, Blacks were treated as a unitary group whose only political importance was as a problem to be dealt with. "Politics was about whites deciding the destiny of both whites and blacks: Blacks were part of the audience—the objects of politics, not the participants."[12] Because those within each subordinate group were politically identical, a small group of leaders could speak for them, and extending political agency to cover regular Blacks was both unnecessary and unwise. The force and hegemony of the state was able to effectively impose this identity for years.

The spatial implication of this grouped reality was geographic divisions. Government authorities divided the "native" areas of South Africa up into ten distinct homelands and assigned them to officially sanctioned ethnic groups. In many ways these spatial entities produced rather than conformed to pre-existing human groupings, but the government presented its new states as merely the codification of the boundaries chosen by historical Black ethnicities to separate themselves from one another. The government cast this policy as "separate development," and framed it as an extension of the independence movements that swept Africa in the 1960s. As the South African ambassador to the United Kingdom explained it,

> South Africa was, therefore, faced with this agonizing dilemma: how to provide for the inevitable progress to self-determination of the Bantu nations, without infringing on the autonomy of the white nation. . . . [T]o this problem, posed in this way, history and the realities of Africa, dictated only one solution. And that solution was the separate, but full, development of South Africa's people. And that, briefly, is what we are attempting to do.[13]

Because the government cast Whites as an African nation deserving of its own self-determination, it was able to use the rhetoric of the decolonization movement to argue that the world should think of the homelands as Black states and South Africa as a White one.

> Perhaps the major consideration [in deciding to pursue separate development instead of an integrated system] was that in a population as mixed as South Africa's, a one man one vote dispensation would be an absolute negation of self-determination. It would inevitably mean the supremacy of the numerically strong Blacks over not only Whites, but also the Coloureds, Indians and, not least, the smaller Black communities. Imagine the potential for conflict in such a situation.[14]

The homelands constituted only thirteen percent of South Africa's land, but homeland citizenship was imposed on all Africans (more than 70 percent of the population) in 1970. Four of the ten homelands were declared independent between 1976 and 1981, but no government besides South Africa's recognized them.[15]

This attempt to manage space was only one of the policies that made apartheid among the most comprehensive projects of social engineering in human history. Apartheid claimed that all political interest, all social interaction, indeed all human activity was predictable on the basis of a single variable—race—and a state was erected to institutionalize this principle. Apartheid domination was carried out by reifying that single manifestation of identity and empowering it over all other possible identities. It was an attempt to impose order on society by forcing all activity to be understood as determined by or at least infected with the race of the actor. This intrusion into everyday life marks the hubris of institutional control of nature—in this case "human nature"—that was the hallmark of the Westphalian state in the twentieth century. The modern state is certainly one of humanity's most complex inventions, and the apartheid state could very well have been among our most ambitious projects. To the degree that all South Africans accepted a single criteria as the governing principle of their interactions, and to the degree that the government was then able to manipulate that criteria through education, force, and economic incentives, apartheid's system of identity created the illusion of human and institutional control over social interaction. However, many forces were working against the apartheid project, not least of which were the actions of individuals and groups who rejected apartheid's vision of the world. These actions can be grouped together under the term *resistance*.

Resistance to Apartheid

The four-stage model of resistance presented in the previous chapter defines resistance as any act whose effect is something less than the hegemonic reinforcement of the momentum of an existing social order. This very broad definition sets up an antinomy between resistance and order, which societies by definition are continuously striving to maximize. The South African order has been built through innumerable conflicts, countless assertions and counterassertions over what that order should be, and there is a long and distinguished history of resistance to racism as a component of those negotiations. This overview of that resistance to racism cannot pretend to be comprehensive, but is intended to give the reader some context for the arguments presented in the case studies.

Any first encounter between people is bound to provoke resistance, but to cast early struggles between Africans and Europeans as resistance to racism is to mischaracterize acts that took place in a very different reality than that which prevailed during the twentieth century. The Khoi and San who refused to work for the earliest Europeans in Cape Town and the Bantus who waged war against encroaching colonizers certainly had more proximate issues than race to explain their actions to themselves. Anthony Marx interprets events in 1879, 1898, and 1905 as important acts of resistance, but acknowledges that they were "generally neither described nor understood by participants as being based on racial identity," but rather as "various expressions of disparate ethnic assertiveness."[16] Marx's argument is that only after race was used as a vehicle for domination did it begin to make sense for Africans to use it as a means for rallying resistance.[17]

"The high-water mark of racial domination produced a correspondingly high point of unified racial identity, thereby inspiring mobilization."[18]

The founding, in 1909, of the organization that was to become the African National Congress was spurred by the consolidation of English and Afrikaaner politics following the Boer War. The organization reflected a realization among elites who were not White that ethnic divisions would serve only to assist Whites in gaining and maintaining control of South Africa. For the first four decades of its existence, the tactics of the ANC demonstrated its abiding faith in the promises and rhetoric of British liberalism. It was not until a new generation of African leaders formed the ANC Youth League in 1944 that the tactics of polite petitions began to give way to leaders with a more aggressive approach. Soon after the National Party began to implement apartheid policies in 1948, this new aggressiveness was actualized in what the Youth League called the Programme of Action. The Programme consisted primarily of acts of nonviolent civil disobedience—strikes, noncooperation, and boycotts.[19] Tactics became even more assertive with the Defiance Campaign of 1952, which spread the idea of resisting apartheid much more widely.

In June of 1955, more than three thousand delegates from a wide variety of institutions and all four racial groups attended a Congress of the People hosted by an alliance of racially based organizations including the ANC. At this meeting, delegates officially adopted the Freedom Charter, which had been drafted before the meeting. The document, which later became the basis for Charterist resistance movements, made claims based both on liberal individualism and the idea of group rights.[20] This apparent contradiction and other aspects of the Charter have been the focus of controversy since before the document was promulgated.[21] The Charter lays out a vision of a multiracial (some argue nonracial) society based primarily on an inclusive national identity. This idea, epitomized in the statement "South Africa belongs to all who live in it, black and white," eventually led to a schism in the resistance movement, with those committed to "Africa for the Africans" breaking away in 1959 to form a rival organization, the Pan-Africanist Congress (PAC).

The PAC, led by Robert Sobukwe, argued that the ANC was not radical enough in its approach to ridding South Africa of racial oppression and that its proposed solutions were based on Western rather than African ideals and structures. South Africa did not belong to all who lived there, but to Africans, and the PAC would make no concessions to Whites in their drive to return the country to African control. The PAC saw the struggle in South Africa as part of a larger struggle against colonialism in Africa as a whole and dreamt of the creation of a United States of Africa.[22] While, like the ANC, the PAC claimed to be working toward a nonracial state in which people would be treated as individuals, they rejected the involvement of anyone besides Africans in the establishment of that state. Presaging the widespread misunderstanding of Black Consciousness in the 1970s, much of the PAC's advocacy of a nonracial society was lost on its rank and file. The PAC was, however, able to mobilize masses into action. The Sharpeville

Massacre of 1960, in which sixty-nine people were killed by police, took place during a protest against the pass law organized by the PAC. A PAC protest march on the Parliament buildings in Cape Town by thirty thousand Blacks nine days later has been described as the day on which "the Bastille might have been stormed in South Africa and wasn't."[23] After the marchers dispersed peacefully, the government declared a state of emergency and outlawed the PAC, ANC, and all other major African political parties.

Both the ANC and the PAC moved into exile and, forsaking their previous commitment to nonviolence, declared guerilla war on South Africa. During the 1960s, the ANC's military wing, UmKhonto we Sizwe (MK, or Spear of the Nation), and the PAC's forces, Poqo (Pure, later renamed the Azanian People's Liberation Army or APLA), carried out dispersed acts of sabotage and terrorism, but their impact was minimal. From 1960 until 1976, the government successfully suppressed organized internal opposition to apartheid, and order was maintained with increasing efficiency. Although there certainly was resistance to apartheid law, as witnessed by the almost routine violation of the pass laws, resistance took place almost exclusively at a personal level. The most important ideas about resistance during this period came from Steve Biko and the Black Conscisousness (BC) movement, which was directed at changing psychological aspects of apartheid oppression.

When the philosophy of Black Conscisousness began to spread in the late 1960s, many in the government welcomed it as evidence that Blacks were embracing race and racial groups as important.[24] In addition, its advocacy of an inwardly directed struggle over self-image rather than an outward challenge to the physical circumstances of the apartheid system meant that the government initially considered it less threatening than the armed resistance of the exiled groups. But as the radical nature of BC philosophy became obvious, Biko and other BC leaders were increasingly subjected to the wrath of the apartheid police state. Biko believed the mind of the oppressed to be the biggest weapon in the arsenal of the oppressor, a weapon that apartheid wielded very well. BC challenged apartheid by reconstructing the self-image of inferiority that apartheid had imposed upon Blacks through a reconceptualization of identity. While it used many of the same labels as the apartheid government, it sought to claim the power over the labels by redefining "Black" as an indicator of oppression rather than of race. The subtleties of this distinction were lost on rank and file supporters who instead focused on rhetoric about Blacks' power and used BC to argue for a simple inversion of apartheid's racial hierarchy. But the psychological repositioning that BC promoted proved to be integral to how South Africans were able to challenge apartheid. "It was the dissemination of Black Consciousness thinking throughout schools, universities, and other community groups that in an important sense was a hidden transcript of resistance to domination that enabled the mass protests which shook South Africa within a very few years."[25] Biko's Black Consciousness was about ideas, but the philosophy was reinterpreted through the 1976 student uprisings in Soweto into a basis for action. It was only after Soweto, as the resistance of ideas evolved into an active rejection of apartheid's hierarchy of privilege, that South Africans began the process of undoing apartheid.[26]

Like members of any society, South Africans have experienced periods of both more and less order, but for the decade and a half immediately prior to 1976 and the events of the first case study, South African society functioned very smoothly. This high level of order permitted many South Africans the luxury of being certain about their institutions. For most people (even for most of those exploited by the order) it was very easy to believe that the rules of apartheid were the correct ones for South Africa's particular situation. Apartheid, it was argued, solved South Africa's problems, problems defined, of course, from the perspective of the existing social order. The events of June 16, 1976, proved to be a turning point for that success. The intensity of political protest throughout the ensuing decade and a half, both violent and nonviolent, and a variety of other trends (demographic, political, and economic) led the White leadership to reach the difficult decision that apartheid must end. It was resistance that ultimately altered the apartheid government's decision-making calculus and made the radical transformation of political structures seem not only possible, but necessary. The transformation of a social order is, of course, a much deeper, continuous project. However, it has been the success of South Africa's "negotiated revolution" that has attracted the attention of journalists, scholars, and others. Before I add my analysis to this group, it seems necessary to organize the existing studies in a way that makes room for one more.

ANALYSIS OF SOUTH AFRICAN POLITICS

Understandings of Social Change

The end of apartheid has not significantly altered the broad analytic boundaries that define Political Science's perspectives on South Africa. Scholars have traditionally adopted one of three primary focal points to study the country: race/ethnicity, political economy, or political institutions. While these issues are most certainly intertwined and most scholars deal with all of them, they almost always do so from a perspective that privileges one as a framework for dealing with the others. Valuable insights into South Africa can be gained from any of these perspectives, but the insights of one perspective are often the misreadings and lacunae used to justify more study from another.

From the first perspective, apartheid and the transition away from it were fundamentally about racial and ethnic groups. Because apartheid privileged race as an explanatory social principle, this perspective has been one of the most accessible and incisive ways to slice South African reality. This focus is epitomized in Adrian Guelke's insightful book *South Africa in Transition*.[27] This well-argued text rehearses a variety of perspectives, and Guelke emphasizes the complexity of factors that make up the continuing transition. However, Guelke always comes back to race, using the concept to explain electoral politics, the debates over economic transformation, and the operation of the Truth and Reconciliation Commission.[28] One of the primary tasks of this book is to debunk what he calls the "myth of nonracialism."[29] He acknowledges that society and social change are complex, but he organizes and explains that complexity against the backdrop of race. Other examples of this racially centered analysis include Anthony Marx's comparative analysis of race in South Africa, the United States, and Brazil, a chapter by Grant Farred, and a volume by Heribert Adam, Frederick van Zyl Slabbert, and Kogila Moodley.[30] Others, like Sheila Croucher and Alan Morris, take racism as a presumption in studying particular aspects of society.[31] Given the importance of race in apartheid reality, this perspective of race as social structure is often very valuable.

From the position of the second group of scholars, however, studies of race often obscure a more important topic—apartheid as a means of producing and distributing wealth. Race, in Karl Marx's metaphor, is superstructural. Not all or even most of the scholars whose work falls into this second category are Marxists, but all emphasize economic criteria as the primary means by which the changes to South African society should be sorted and analyzed. Hein Marais' 1998 book is an excellent example of this perspective, in which "structures," unless otherwise denoted, are economic structures.[32] Marais argues against "overpersonalizing history" and obscuring the "structural underpinnings of the transition."[33] He justifies a political economy perspective by invoking the "extent to which the South African struggle itself became defined by a political reductionism that collapsed the political economy of privilege and deprivation into the form of the apartheid state."[34] The state, he argues, is important because it has been cast as the site of economic resource distribution. Many other authors, including Alan Ward, Charles Simkins, and Jonathan Michie and Vishnu Padayachee, also approach post-apartheid society from economic perspectives, assessing macroeconomic forces, the Reconstruction and Development Programme (RDP), and the Growth, Employment, and Redistribution (GEAR) policy.[35] The economic structures of post-apartheid South Africa are thus well represented in contemporary literature, and are one of the principal means for arguing that very little change has taken place.

The third category of analysis, while certainly not ignoring the other two foci, is centered on institutions of the formal and informal political spheres and the boundary between the two. Here, "structures" are political and represented by constitutions, elite-negotiated pacts, voting behavior, and various definitions of civil society. For example, Wilmot James and Daria Caliguire assess the prospects for a vibrant civil society and a democratic culture in South Africa.[36] This category is dominated by authors who use their analyses of South African specifics to comment upon general themes and concepts in political science. Both Anthony Butler and Thomas Koelble focus on how the lessons of South Africa reflect and inform contemporary literature on democracy and democratization.[37] Vincent Maphai uses the South African experience to comment on and adapt Arend Lijphart's theory of democratic consociationalism.[38] Jeffrey Herbst studies South

Africa's practicalities to assess the literature on peaceful transitions through negotiated pacts.[39] Andrew Reynold's studies of South African elections, Susan Collin Marks' book on institutions of conflict resolution, and Kadar Asmal, Louise Asmal, and Ronald Suresh Roberts' book on the Truth and Reconciliation Commission are all solid entrants into this perspective.[40] South Africa's new constitution is recognized by many as the most liberal in the world, and the transition that established it involved a wide variety of groups and individuals making demands and compromises to reach an agreement. The South Africa transition is therefore rich ground for the study of these kinds of institutional structures.

These three categories cannot encompass all of the recent literature on South Africa, but they do represent main themes of the discourse on the transition. Their rehearsal here is intended only to sort the numerous studies of South Africa in a way that makes a quite different study valuable. As David Horwath and Aletta Norval argue, the transition has been such a complex and multifaceted phenomenon that providing a singular, unified characterization of it by ruling out other interpretations prematurely would close down hard-won opportunities for discussion.[41] As a result, it is not necessary to assess the relative merits of the themes or theories described above, except as they are related to processes of political identity. For many, a focus on structures of race or economics or institutions may very well yield more useful conclusions about the overall process of transitioning away from an authoritarian, racist, capitalist, and violently divided society. This study glosses over details that other perspectives would consider of central importance, but these silences should not be read as a judgment of nonimportance with respect to the South African context as a whole, only with respect to the analysis of political identity. Because apartheid became politicized around the axis of identity broadly conceived and many of the conflicts of its transformation were waged in those terms, it seems valuable also to examine the social discursive structures of South African identity for any insights into social change they may provide. While the theory of political identity laid out in the previous chapter is, I argue, somewhat unique in its perspective, this assertion needs to be evaluated in light of how others have dealt with South African political identity in their studies.

Understandings of Identity

The list of officially sanctioned identities under apartheid was short and explicit. These racial and ethnic identities solidified over time as capitalism and the state structure emerged.[42] Apartheid's labels were ever present in the daily lives of all South Africans, and the rhetorical strategy that accompanied them was designed to make the racial foundation of policy seem natural, apolitical, and beyond the scope of possible change. Apartheid as social order sought to remove racial and ethnic divisions from the realm of consciousness and turn them into an unquestioned assumption about reality, a kind of unchangeable backdrop against which daily life was to be lived. In most social interactions, the most important characteristic of a person was race/ethnicity.

> To many South Africans it is self-evident, a matter of common sense, that the society consists of different racial and ethnic groups, each of which forms a separate community with its own culture and traditions. It is believed that such groups actually exist objectively in the real world, and that there is nothing anybody can do to change this.[43]

The value of nonracial labels, even occupational, gender, and citizenship labels, was nearly always secondary to that of race. Women, for example, rarely interacted just as women, but rather as White or African or Coloured women, actualizing racial stereotypes even when dealing with others within their group.

Kathryn Manzo suggests that it is important to pay attention to the global context within which this political reality was constructed.[44] The capitalist and European world system expanded economic, political, and religious spheres into South Africa and brought with them several iterations of a "civilizing mission." These spheres established dichotomous identities that served as much to define Europeans as they did Africans. Apartheid was an adaptation of this legacy of colonialism. The Afrikaners inherited a classic colonial system from the British, one that they as Whites had benefited from in many ways. But the Afrikaners had also suffered under it. When they gained power in 1948, Afrikaners began to hammer together a social order that continued many of the previous colonial segregation policies, but which put them together in a different way. The classifications of identity in the Population Registration Act, for example, were justified through a strange grab bag of criteria. Identity categories could variably be reduced to skin color (White and Coloured), country of origin (Natives), or continent of origin (Asian). In addition to these racial categories, the government also accentuated distinctions between cultural practices in order to justify dividing the African majority into nine separate ethnicities.

> In an important sense, then, the National party could not provide systematic criteria by which to differentiate blacks from each other and from whites because whatever measure was chosen—Christianity, private property, religion, culture, language, even skin color—would result in an inability to differentiate many of the black others from the white self. In other words, the lack of a clearly defined self and the lack of an easily recognizable boundary between the self and other were precisely what made ambiguity a political imperative and not a mere oversight.[45]

The point, made explicitly by Deborah Posel, is that apartheid as social order was not erected from a carefully outlined blueprint, but evolved as a response to a variety of pressures on the distribution of privilege.[46]

As it did, the discourse surrounding identity evolved also. The edited volume *South African Keywords: The Uses and Abuses of Political Concepts* explores the development and malleability of apartheid's discourse of domination.[47] The book is built around three main themes of apartheid's differentiation schemes—race, ethnicity, and first versus third world—each of which represents an adaptation of both rhetoric and understanding to account for the chronological development of apartheid's governance strategies.

> This [variation in terminology] does not mean, of course, that all reference to 'race' disappeared, or that the period witnessed any real decline in racist thinking or practices on the part of the dominant stratum of society: it is perfectly possible to be racist without stressing, or indeed even using, the term 'race'.[48]

Aletta Norval points out that the transformation of official categories from homogenous "Native" to a number of "Bantu" units was done to indicate the importance of separate ethnic and language groups in the ordering of the social.[49] As the rhetoric evolved, the racially distinct population was sliced again into thirteen separate groups: White (notice no legal separation between English-speaking and Afrikaans-speaking Whites); Coloured, Indian, Ndebele, Northern Sotho, Southern Sotho, two types of Xhosa, Zulu, Venda, Tswana, Swazi, and Tsonga. Outnumbered nearly six to one in the racial categories, White South Africans sought to even the playing field by dividing the Black population into smaller "nations." The White minority feared a wider African nationalism, which Bantu Affairs Minister M. C. de Wet Nel described as "the monster which may still perhaps destroy all the best things in Africa."[50]

To some degree, therefore, every study of South Africa must confront the idea of identity, even though some do it more explicitly and purposefully than others. Most of the work that has dealt with it tangentially has tended to equate identity with either race or ethnicity, or sometimes class, and to present even these limited categories in a static, essentialist way. Unfortunately, the same problems confront many of the analyses that are intended to deal specifically with identity. These analyses of South African identity fall into three groups.

The first group of studies, while often empirically rich and theoretically sophisticated when it comes to issues of political mobilization, treat the categories of identity with which they deal as primordial givens. Any analysis from the apartheid government, including those artifacts examined in this study, could be expected to exhibit these characteristics. In addition, much of the South African academic community was, for a long time, operating within the apartheid mind-set and many of the resulting analyses exemplify this perspective. Articles by Leroy Vail, Patrick Harries, and Hermann Giliomee advance good historic exegeses of ethnicity in the 1989 volume edited by Vail, but they treat ethnicity as somehow more primal than class or region or other collective labels.[51] Another study by a prominent scholar of ethnic conflicts, Donald Horowitz, analyzes ethnicity in South Africa without ever problematizing the concept.[52]

The second grouping of identity studies includes those that do problematize a particular category of identity, be it race, ethnicity, class, nation, or some other collective boundary. The problem here, however, is that the studies deal only with a single category. In the late 1980s and the 1990s, that category has usually been ethnicity. Examples include Rupert Taylor's study of township conflict, Paul Forsyth's article on the mobilization of Zulu ethnicity, and a similar study by Daphna Golan.[53] The exploration of ethnicity has been a popular entry point for the analysis of apartheid, and rightly so, for apartheid reified ethnic differences within the context of a grouped reality. These studies each contribute significantly to the understanding of one aspect of South African politics, but by reducing identity to merely one of its manifestations, they fail to appreciate the full diversity, both structurally and temporally, that constitutes the complex of identity for South African actors. While each of the categories of identity they choose represents a powerful tool in the South African strategies of governance, studying a single category is not the same as studying identity.

Gerhard Mare and Morris Szeftel (who relies heavily on Mare's analysis) are examples of the best of this group.[54] Both problematize identity as a whole and present a sophisticated understanding of the politics of identity mobilization. Even though they proceed to focus on ethnicity as a single category of identity, they acknowledge that political identity is a much more complex phenomenon. However, even Mare's much longer analysis presents a liberal, evolving notion of identity that cannot fully explain fundamental changes in how South Africans think about themselves and their relationship to the social order. In order to account for the transformation of the apartheid social order, analysis must be extended to a much wider variety of labels and to the power of those labels.

The third category of analysis problematizes identity very broadly. One example is Ran Greenstein's comparative study of identity formation and political conflict in Palestine/Israel and South Africa, which covers a variety of identity dimensions and argues that a diversity of identity categories were used in the solidification of racial domination (even though he does heuristically separate class from identity).[55] Also, Kathryn Manzo presents a very sophisticated Foucauldian analysis of the power of apartheid's identities (she calls them "subjectivities").[56] The analysis is particularly helpful to this study because she uses discourse analysis and acknowledges changes to the power of a variety of labels over time. She compares the power of civilization, Christianity, and racial modes of dividing powerful self from disempowered other, casts these divisions as means of organizing disparities of power, and pulls out the policy implications of each. She ties these discourses into global patterns of power and, in the latest book, describes the conscious search for and construction of symbols of nation in post-apartheid South Africa.

Also exemplary of this category are two texts by Aletta J. Norval.[57] Norval uses apartheid and the transition to post-apartheid identity to argue that the internal logic of identity construction in modernity could be challenged by the negativity of nonracialism as a goal. She spins out a very complex understanding of the strategies that create the politicized divisions between self and other and claims that apartheid contains an "identitary logic" characteristic of modernity itself. She argues that the crisis of apartheid and the entrenchment of nonracialism as a governing ideology create a crisis for the identity logic of modernity precisely because it is indeterminate. Her description of the pattern of de-articulation and re-articulation of identities accounts for both power and change, and closely parallels my argument about the two overlapping processes of the transition presented below.

This study strives to combine the best parts of the theoretical problematization of identity as a whole with empirical data culled from a discourse analysis of three political conflicts. The goal, as stated, is to understand the transformation of the apartheid sociopolitical structures and the constitution of those of the "New South Africa" using the changes to identity as a focal point. This goal is approached through a methodology of ethnographic discourse analysis, set within a framework of a constructivist understanding of political identity.

THE PRACTICALITIES OF STUDYING SOUTH AFRICAN IDENTITY

Framing the Transition

The South African transition can be disaggregated into two overlapping processes—the dismantling of the apartheid social order and the construction of an alternative. Both processes were accompanied by an enormous amount of conflict. The first, the delegitimation of apartheid, was by definition a process of disorder. Apartheid, as a set of social patterns and rules, was designed to fix in the minds of South Africans an understanding of reality and provide them a set of ideal images to guide their behavior. People were to behave as members of one of four hierarchically arranged racial groups. Social conflicts were to be settled by reference to the power of that hierarchy, meaning that Whites (nineteen percent of the population in 1968 and about ten percent in 1997) had tremendous power over members of other racial groups. Within apartheid, violence was an appropriate way for those with power to respond to conflict.

As more and more South Africans rejected apartheid's understanding of the world, the justifications that made such racial violence acceptable began to melt away, and were often replaced by attitudes of resistance. As more people questioned the existing social arrangements, it became more common for them to demonstrate their contempt through action, most dramatically through riots, unrest, and other disturbances. But the progressive denaturalization of apartheid's reality also affected people's daily interactions. People began rejecting the social rules that had previously helped them avoid and resolve everyday types of conflicts because they considered those rules to be part of the oppressive system, which they undoubtedly were. This disorder increasingly negated the principal benefit of apartheid—order—and created incentives for people to find other ways to organize their ideas about their interactions and about the world in general.

The second process, the construction of an alternative, also contributed to the atmosphere of conflict. As the legitimacy of apartheid's order declined in fits and starts throughout the late 1970s, the 1980s, and early 1990s, no single alternative set of rules immediately rose to take its place. The result was a gap of social legitimacy. South Africans rejected apartheid for a variety of reasons, and so their visions of how society should be different also varied significantly. Each person adapted apartheid's rules and patterns, or created new ones, in order to align their behavior with their understanding of the world, both as it was and as it should be. This variety meant that there was no widespread, stable set of social rules that all South Africans could call upon as mutually accepted standards for behavior in their interactions. As the functional consensus behind apartheid's rules dissolved, people going about their daily activities confronted others asserting a variety of different behavioral standards, resulting in increased social conflict and violence. This conflict supplied the dynamics by which these individualized alternatives slowly solidified into an order opposed to apartheid. It is only to the degree that legitimacy has coalesced behind a new alternative that order has progressively returned to South Africa. As evidenced by the problems of unemployment, poverty, and crime, this process of solidifying order is continuing.

The dual and overlapping processes of dismantling and reconstruction form a mid-level theoretical context that binds together the case studies that follow. It provides the conceptual frame within which it makes sense to examine the ways South Africans have used identity labels to organize and understand the political events and conflicts of their transition. To get at the more empirical questions about the power of South African identity labels, the social activity organized through these labels, and the changes in both the labels and their power during the course of South Africa's transition, I have turned to a variety of South African texts and artifacts.

ETHNOGRAPHIC DISCOURSE ANALYSIS

A methodology is a way of selecting and organizing information and its techniques are tools that should be applied as they are most useful. Studying the social transformation that has defined South African society over the past three decades requires a methodology adaptable enough to account for large-scale and complex fluidity. The positivistic methodologies that dominate social scientific research have been designed for more specific purposes. Positivistic analysis is radical, it "breaks cases into parts—variables—that are difficult to reassemble into wholes."[58] These methodologies were designed to approximate the techniques (and the claim to certainty) of the physical sciences. In their search for causes, therefore, positivist researchers have invented ways to isolate specific changes by holding the surrounding environment constant or by finding ways to approximate a control group, thus orienting the entire research agenda toward an assumption of constancy in the ontological and epistemological categories of knowledge, power, and value. The transition out of apartheid was precisely about unsettling these kinds of social foundations. When South Africans rejected their social order, they eliminated the stability of the categories that would have made the methodologies of positivistic "normal science" useful for studying identity.[59]

Instead, this study required a methodology flexible enough to expand and contract with the process of establishing a new social reality and to confront the creativity contained in such a fundamental transformation. It had to allow openness not just to new data, but also to new concepts and unexpected categories of data. Case studies are particularly well suited to this kind of endeavor.

> Case-oriented studies, by their nature, are sensitive to complexity and historical specificity. Thus, they are well suited for addressing empirically defined historical outcomes, and they are often used to generate new conceptual schemes, as well. Researchers who are oriented toward specific cases (area specialists especially) do not find it difficult to maintain a meaningful connection to social and political issues because they are concerned with actual events, with human agency and process.[60]

Case studies are particularly well suited to confronting the diversity of human institutions and have been used in a variety of studies of identity, including Dorinne Kondo's ethnography of a Japanese workplace, Kathryn Manzo's comparative study of race in South Africa, Britain and Australia, and Ran Greenstein's comparison of the conflicts in Palestine/Israel and South Africa.[61]

In order to study South Africa's broad social changes over time, I chose three moments spaced throughout the transition and approached them through a broad theme rather than searching for specific pieces of information. Given these parameters, the methodology that fit best was a qualitative and interpretive mix of ethnography and discourse analysis. Ethnography was helpful because the events and the meanings were foreign to me. The goal was to understand labels, rules, and patterns from a social context other than my own and to translate their meanings so that they make sense in another reality. This is just the type of alternative universe that ethnography was invented to study. The goal of ethnography is not to fix what others' actions "really" mean, but to translate the meanings of behavior so that they are comprehensible to a particular set of others.[62] The standard by which its research is judged is how well it clarifies what is going on for its audience, how well it interprets the culture that prevails in one reality for those in another. Practically, this means that the process is to "begin with our own interpretations of what our informants are up to, or think they are up to, and then systematize those. . . ."[63] Beyond this general philosophy, the specialized field of ethnography of communication provides a more specific methodological context.

The ethnographic study of communication analyzes communicative acts to attempt to uncover the patterns that underlie them and tap into the shared rules and procedures of communicative competence (that practical knowledge that qualifies a speaker as an authoritative actor within a culture). Ethnographers who study communication, like Donal Carbaugh, Allen Grimshaw, Muriel Saville-Troike, and Mary Jane Collier, focus on implicit and generative agreements that guide coordinated communicative conduct within interactions.[64] This perspective has been used successfully to study social structures of identity. Carbaugh, for example, uses this method to study the "model persons" through whom issues and actors in a social context are evaluated.[65] Collier focuses on the interplay between the social competence to communicate and the identity of the speaker. This identity is very fluid and changes quite often, even within the context of a conversation.[66] During interactions, each interlocutor may be attempting to assert different communicative rules, each trying to validate the identity that they have adopted in the particular context. The ethnographic approach to the study of communication emphasizes that the level of communicative competence is dependent upon the appreciation of cultural rules that dictate appropriate responses to specific situations. This study uses similar processes to describe the structures of identity that have defined actors and their social power in South Africa, and to track changes to these structures over time.

To actualize this perspective, I turn to the methodology of textual or discourse analysis. Discourse analysis is designed to get at the meanings of social codes. In this case, the codes are identity labels. If culture is an intersubjective imaginative universe, behavior that activates that culture may be studied as if it is a text, a creative act produced in coherence with established patterns and therefore meaningful. A recent edited volume collects a variety of such analyses from the South African context.[67] The editors frame the project as following on the work of Michel Foucault. Their assessment suggests that the methodology works well not only in South Africa, but with identity discourses as well.

> Foucauldian discourse analysis, then, unravels notions of identity that we normally take for granted, and it opens texts up in three kinds of ways: first to analyse how they construct images of the self as if it were something coherent; second to explore how those images function to reproduce certain experiences consistent with a coherent self; and third to highlight how texts themselves are riven by variation.[68]

Speech acts (both oral and written) are important because they are explicitly designed to transfer meaning and are created through the rules and understandings of the culture. For this study, therefore, I examined a variety of texts, including interviews, newspaper archives, government publications, and academic monographs. This diversity is important. "The power of apartheid was relayed through millions of channels of communication, from the government-controlled media through to everyday conversation. Power is, rather, a function of a multiplicity of discursive practices that fabricates and positions subjects."[69] My data consist of these texts as representations of the general patterns of communication that frame South Africans' understanding of identity.

The South African discourse on identity is extraordinarily rich and complex, and to try to analyze the discourse of the whole transition would be foolhardy. In order to narrow this task, I have chosen three political conflicts as moments when negotiations over patterns of identity took place. These conflicts are not explicitly about identity, but South Africans have organized them through categories of identity, and these identity labels reveal the process of social change.

Social Conflict as a Research Opportunity

When a social order is functioning well, few interactions are defined as conflicts. Instead the social order's shared rules and understandings of power relations align interlocutors to the same goals and procedures before they have an opportunity to negotiate this consensus for themselves. If everyone shares a common set of assumptions about the world and about who has the power in each circumstance, agreement is maximized, and very few opportunities for conflict arise. To the degree that the social order is in a state of flux, however, there is greater chance that interlocutors will be uncertain about their roles and relative power, and conflicts will be more common.

Conflicts, situations in which parties perceive their ends and/or means to be mutually exclusive, are opportunities to negotiate new social meanings and to adapt the social order to changing patterns of ideas and action. Such changes often take place in, and produce more, social conflicts. Conflict can provide a visceral tool of connection between individual actors and particular group identities. In addition, specific conflicts are often the primary elements in histories of division between self and other that in turn form the basis for most political mobilization of identity. Myths of glorious victory or tragic loss in battles long over often become fodder for those who stir up present-day conflict. Experiencing conflict powerfully influences an agent's attachment to particular labels. Merely siding with one party in a public conflict can invest a person in a package of expectations that accompanies a label.

Because conflict reduces efficient cooperation, every society has its own set of rules and procedures by which conflict is recognized, regulated, and resolved. To the degree that these rules are widely accepted, interactions are governed by intersubjective cues that let interlocutors know how to behave. The way people behave and the rules and patterns that regulate and guide their behavior are, from this perspective, matters of strategy, although this term generally connotes far more conscious decision-making than I mean to evoke here. Each actor asserts definitions and sends cues to other participants, usually in attempts to define the situation favorably. The assertion that an interaction is "political," for example, is a stratagem that demands the application of a framework of governance rules and identities, to the exclusion of other possible frameworks, such as those that regulate conflicts classified as moral, economic, or private. If other participants define the situation differently, a conflict exists and a negotiation usually takes place. Interactions are continuously redefined through this (most often implicit) negotiation process.

In the years after 1976, apartheid's rules progressively lost the legitimacy that kept conflict under control, and people turned to disorder as a form of resistance. As South Africans defied apartheid's rules, producing riots and disturbances and states of emergency, they demonstrated their contempt for the governing social order. They made apartheid political, and so debatable, through an assault on the mechanisms of order and its most visible benefit, the efficient control of conflict among its members. The crumbling of order depreciated the benefits of apartheid as a set of rules and institutions. At the same time, people tried to assert new rules, rules that carried with them new identity labels and new meanings for old labels.

The chapters that follow present three political conflicts as specific sites for analysis: the violent conflict of 1976 that began in the townships of Soweto, the political conflict that surrounded the proposed constitutional changes in 1983–1984, and crime in post-apartheid society. These conflicts are prominent features of the transition and each has a wide variety of texts that serve as data. The first two conflicts are primarily fights over the dismantling of apartheid, but the debate concerning constitutional changes also helped begin the process of legitimating an alternative to apartheid. The third conflict is almost exclusively about the solidification of that alternative social order. It is, however, important to understand these conflicts not as snapshots, but as dynamic parts of an ever-changing reality.

> The constitution of identity is an elaborate and deadly serious game of mirrors. It is a complex temporal interaction of multiple practices of identification external and internal to a subject or population. In order to understand the constitutive process it is, thus, necessary to be able to situate the mirrors in space and their movement in time.[70]

This study does both. It provides the social and political context for a discussion of political identity and then picks up those dynamics in three different time periods throughout a tumultuous social transition.

Overall, this combination of ethnography and discourse analysis is an attempt to systematically understand changes to South Africa's political identities. It analyzes the identity and role hierarchies through which political leaders, the media, and the public at large have thought and acted by studying contemporary and historical South African perspectives on these three conflicts. As events in the material, lived reality of South Africans, the conflicts are catalysts around which ideas of identity coalesce and discourses within which the social power of identities is negotiated. Participants seek justification for their actions in the labels they apply to themselves and their opponents. Observers within the society also make assertions and judgments about who the participants are and the rules that should govern their actions. These assertions of identity carry important implications for how other participants act and how other nonparticipants assess the conflict. The labels that are accepted as valid tie actors into social structures that determine standards of normality and assumptions about rules that should guide their behavior.

The discourses that surround these conflicts therefore provide compact and relatively explicit opportunities to access some of the dynamics of social change. By analyzing the substantive issues that permeate and define the conflicts, it is possible to interpret the actions of the participants as meaningful events and to draw conclusions about the identities through which those actions are organized. Because conflicts are sites where identities are employed, renegotiated, and even created, in conflicts identities are closest to the surface and most easily observed by outsiders. The methodology of this study focuses on extracting from social texts the words and phrases that South Africans use to make sense of the conflicts; on gleaning the stereotypes and labels that people call on to describe and explain the behavior of participants; and on understanding how those ideas have changed with the transition. What groups are referred to? What labels are used to group people together? As people use categories of identity to describe these conflicts, they reveal which identities are powerful in their understanding of reality. The practicalities of translating these textual identities into the empirical data for this study require a little more explanation.

TEXTS

Applying an ethnographic and discursive methodology requires access to texts. In this case, those texts are South Africans' descriptions and opinions of the three political conflicts. Many of these texts are accessible from the United States through published academic works, the internet, or newspapers available in various libraries, but a much larger bank of statements exists in South Africa, including a variety of unpublished conference papers and theses, government publications, newspaper archives, and of course interviews with South Africans. During my research in South Africa, I cast a very wide net in search of textual artifacts. My research by no means completely reflects the range of South African opinion on these conflicts, but by focusing my search thematically rather than on a narrow set of sources, I obtained a more well-rounded picture of the discourses as wholes.

I spent several months in the winter of 1997 researching in the libraries of Cape Town. As the site of the South African Parliament, Cape Town houses the South African Library, which is the equivalent of the U.S. Library of Congress. The library archives are a repository for government publications, and also house the newspaper archives for, among others, the *Argus,* one of Cape Town's English-language newspapers. At the University of Cape Town, the main Jagger Library, the African Studies Library, the Manuscripts and Archives library, the library of the School of Education, and the Government Publications Library each yielded important and helpful information, as did the Mayibuye Centre at the University of the Western Cape, which houses the archives of the ANC while it was in exile. At these libraries and a variety of secondhand bookstores, I accumulated the books, articles, posters, postcards, and other artifacts discussed herein.

On the same trip, I also conducted over one hundred interviews all over the country. I carried out several types of interviews. Some of the interviews were with scholars, whom I interviewed as experts in a particular field and as fellow researchers, rather than as South Africans with personal opinions about the conflicts. These interviews influenced the study in evolutionary and theoretical ways rather than as data. To get data, I interviewed a wide variety of South Africans, including both people on the street and elites. These interviews were semi-structured, meaning that I had some questions that I asked in every interview, but the bulk of each conversation was unique and dependent upon the particular dynamics of the interaction for its specific direction. Interviewees from this last category are identified only by their first names or by pseudonyms to protect them from any social impact based on the opinions they shared.

The vast majority of the interviews were on the topic of crime, the most contemporary and, therefore, tangible of the three conflicts. In many of these interviews, the subject of crime served mostly as a distraction. Identity is so politicized in South Africa that asking questions about people's identities would have elicited mainly politically correct answers. Data about such explicit self-identifications are easy to come by.[71] These data, however, are not very useful as evidence of how South Africans categorize people after apartheid because people know what they should answer. One of my interviewees summarized the situation well, saying "There are many reasons why being an interviewee is a context where [ethnic] labels wouldn't rise to the fore, while there may very well be times when they would. Asking someone to self-identify is a political question, it places people in a context where they respond in a political way."[72] To compensate I asked respondents to talk about a common politicized topic and listened to the words they used to describe the participants. I was interested in the stories about crime, but mainly as texts that employed contemporary social structures of identity.

The nature of my research topic prevented me from trying to randomly distribute my interviews. In order to develop a random distribution, the categories across which the samples are to be distributed must be known and secure. Before I did my research, I had no way of knowing which categories would be currently powerful for sorting South Africans. As a result I tried to talk to the widest possible variety of people: people from all four of apartheid's racial groups, people from the far reaches of the wealth spectrum, a wide geographic distribution (including both urban and rural areas), women and men, educated and illiterate, employed and not, people who had traveled the world and those who had never been more than one hundred kilometers from where they were born. I talked to young, poor Coloured men at a train station and to middle-aged wealthy White women in their homes. I talked to a mixed-race couple at a bar and to poor unemployed Black men who had only just moved to Cape Town from the former Transkei. Basically, I talked to any unsuspecting soul who happened to make eye contact with me. I spent a large amount of time wandering around, handing out business cards, and asking people about crime. This was surprisingly easy to do. As soon as I opened my mouth, people knew that I was from the United States, and because I was usually in places where tourists were rare, people wanted to know what I was doing in South Africa. When I told them what I was researching, people were very forthcoming with opinions and the conversations usually flowed very easily. I attribute this partially to the fact that South Africans have had the opportunity to formulate opinions about crime in their own discussions, and so had confidence in them and were less hesitant to share them in public with a foreigner. This phenomenon seems to validate my strategy of using conflicts as a window into identity categories.

I interviewed South Africans in the Cape Town area, Port Elizabeth, Durban, Pietersburg, rural areas of the Northern Province and Mpumalanga, and Johannesburg, giving me a good regional distribution of interviewees. In general, I interviewed slightly more men than women and more city residents than rural, but otherwise got a fairly representative sample of a wide variety of potential social groupings—race, ethnicity, economic status, political party. The mean education level of my sample was probably higher than that of the general population, but I talked to people with doctoral degrees and to those who had never been to school. I talked to an ANC Member of Parliament, the highest levels of the Truth and Reconciliation Commission, and a former general in the South African Police. I talked to admitted criminals, people on the equivalent of welfare, and a homeless woman who seemed mentally ill. All of these people had opinions about politics, all of which I have treated as valid interpretations of South African political reality.

While I found people very approachable, I also learned how much effort it takes to interview in this manner. I usually began by asking a question about current conditions, saying that we heard news about South Africa in the United States and I had come to see for myself and to ask people who lived here what things were really like. As I listened to the substance of people's opinions and stories, I also had to listen for the words that they used to communicate those messages. I had to group those words into categories and, at the same time, think about how to direct the conversation once the current thread was played out. Often, I also had to be focused on remembering exact words and phrases because, for one reason or another, tape recording was impractical. In these cases I would sit down immediately after the interview and write or type out the important aspects of the interview while they were still fresh. Often I would also revisit these reports as I entered them into the laptop and add additional context to the report. The interviews varied in degree of formality. Some of the most formal interviews were scheduled with people ahead of time and therefore were easier to tape. Scheduled interviews tended to last at least an hour, while unscheduled ones varied greatly from as little as ten minutes to as much as two hours. I found people on the street, especially women, more hesitant in the initial stages of the interviews, but people generally warmed up to the topic as they became convinced that I really was just interested in their opinions of their country. Still, this initial hesitance often made me refrain from even asking if I could tape-record the conversation.

Each interview and each written item thus became a text, an artifact of the South African political discourse. My task has been to mine these texts for information on identity. I used the three political conflicts to limit the proportions of the analysis. Another limitation, the choice of 1976 as a starting point for the transition, should in no way be seen as dismissing the long and distinguished history of resistance to racism in South Africa. The conflicts, each with its own chapter, are some of the milestones in contemporary South African history, and each has redrawn social boundaries and changed the power of social labels in significant ways. The substance of each of these conflicts anchors an analysis of how identity labels have been used within the transition. In the conclusion, I offer some summarizing analysis and propose models of identity in social change that may prove useful in other contexts.

Chapter Four

SOWETO 1976

Following the election of Nelson Mandela as State President of the Republic of South Africa in 1994, the sixteenth of June was declared an official state holiday—National Youth Day. Over the previous eighteen years, June 16 had become an unofficial holiday for Blacks, a day dedicated to commemorating the sacrifices of the struggle against apartheid as symbolized in the 1976 police shootings of schoolchildren marching in protest through the streets of Soweto (Johannesburg's SOuth WEstern TOwnships). For most Whites the day had become little more than a predictable disruption of work, a day when the normally ubiquitous Black labor was largely absent. With the end of exclusively White rule, however, the new government sought to transform June 16 (and a whole host of other formerly Black or formerly White institutions) into a symbol for a single, unified nation. Celebrations of Youth Day were supposed to be symbols of the rhetorical themes of the Government of National Unity, an opportunity to reclaim stories of division and make them serve a diverse, but national, unity.

June 16 was again chosen as a site for this transformation project in 1999, when it was called into service for the inauguration of Thabo Mbeki as the second State President of the "New South Africa." As one newspaper editorial put it,

> This time round all South Africans, black and white, will be celebrating a new day; a day that liberated not just blacks but whites as well from the bondage of apartheid. When President Mbeki steps down from the podium on Wednesday, we must all help him to attain his greatest wish: to be president of One Nation, not two nations. 16 June will never be the same day again.[1]

This chapter examines June 16 as an icon of the transformation of the South African social order by looking into the discourse that has surrounded it and defined its meanings.[2] It analyzes how this symbol has been presented, interpreted, and commemorated in a variety of ways for a variety of purposes. The stories that came to define the events of June 16, 1976, empowered many South Africans, especially young Black South Africans, to change their relationship to the apartheid state. This alteration in the relationship is, I argue, accessible through the politics and the power of the identity labels South Africans have used to define those associated with the events of June 16. This chapter analyzes the competing discourses on Soweto by focusing on these descriptive labels. For most of its life as an icon, June 16 was intimately interwoven with and often synonymous with Soweto, not as a geographic space, but as an event. An examination of the power of Soweto should begin with the "facts" of the case—those elements upon which the various stories seem to agree.

SOWETO, JUNE 16, 1976—A STORY

The sixteenth of June 1976 began as another mundane late autumn Wednesday in Soweto. The morning air was thick with the smoke from tens of thousands of coal fires, and people trudged to the portals of the wealthy White city where they sold their labor. The only ones particularly anxious would have been the teenagers who had organized a march to protest a decision to enforce a long-standing rule governing the language in which their classes were taught. Since the 1950s, Black students had been studying Afrikaans as a required subject (and this continued until after the 1994 elections), but the policy of using Afrikaans to teach half of the nonlanguage subjects in Black postprimary education, the so-called 50–50 rule, lay dormant until a mid-1970s change in leadership at the Transvaal Department of Bantu Education. In Soweto, a small number of junior secondary students were being forced to take their mathematics and social studies tests in Afrikaans, a language in which most were barely conversant and that many considered repugnant. Students from other schools empathized and knew that they would soon face the same prospect. Frustrated in repeated attempts to stop the policy or even to express their grievances to the authorities, the children had coordinated a march.

The march had been planned by an Action Committee composed of two delegates from each junior and secondary school in Soweto.[3] In order to confuse the police, students were instructed to leave from a dozen assembly points, each with its own departure time, and move toward Orlando West, where they planned to meet and then proceed to a soccer stadium for a rally. As the streams converged and climbed up Vilakazi Street, students were singing and chanting. They carried signs with slogans such as "Afrikaans is an oppressor's language" and "If we must do Afrikaans, [Prime Minister John] Vorster must do Zulu." Shortly before nine in the morning, a senior pupil told the students that the police were approaching and reminded them to be calm and cool. "We are not fighting," he said. Police vehicles soon arrived carrying forty-eight policemen, eight of whom were White, and two police dogs. The police lined up across Vilakazi Street in an arc about one hundred paces from the students. Colonel Johannes Kleingeld was in charge, but had no effective way to address the crowd. The time was approximately nine-thirty in the morning.

What happened next is unclear. The events of the morning were quickly politicized and competing accounts of which side was responsible for the initial aggressive action became part of South Africa's political mythology. While the circumstances are a matter of debate, the police did open fire, even though Colonel Kleingeld apparently gave no order to do so. The first to die, at least as far as history is concerned, was thirteen-year-old Zolile Hector Pieterson, whose bloody, limp body is being carried in the famous photograph that made Soweto personal to millions around the world.[4] An autopsy found that he had been shot from behind by a bullet fired directly at him, contesting Colonel Kleingeld's theory that he must have been killed by the ricochet of a warning shot. At least one other marcher was killed and twelve more injured in this initial encounter.

While many students stood their ground and threw rocks at the retreating policemen, the bulk of the crowd dispersed down side streets where they began to spread the news, set up roadblocks, and exact revenge on any symbol of White authority they could find. They killed two White employees of the West Rand Administrative Board (WRAB), the body that governed Soweto and therefore presented the most proximate symbol of White authority besides the police. They destroyed government liquor outlets and beer halls, which they blamed for their parents' political passivity. Newspapers reported the attacks on these establishments as looting, but much of the alcohol was poured out in the streets by youths who eloquently condemned its anesthetizing effects in slogans painted on charred walls.

For several hours after the initial encounter the police merely waited in their stations for reinforcements. In the afternoon, however, they moved out into the streets and, according to some witnesses, began to shoot into crowds of people.[5] By the middle of the afternoon the destruction had intensified. The shootings expanded the constituency of the protests in two directions. On one hand, normally law-abiding citizens were driven by the shootings to vent frustrations built up over years of apartheid. On the other hand, the chaos gave *tsotsis,* the young criminals adapted to the peculiar reality of urban apartheid, expanded opportunities to exploit Soweto.[6] This produced two threads in the unrest, with some distributing bread from delivery trucks to "the people" before setting the trucks alight, and others seeking merely to get drunk or profit from the anarchy.

Over the next few days, the violence in Soweto intensified, and protests and violence spread to many places around the country. Alexandra, a township that abuts northern Johannesburg, exploded on June 17, causing even greater concern than Soweto, which had been cordoned off easily. Black students at the University of Zululand burned an administration building to the ground, and students at the University of the North tried to. As they protested the police action in downtown Johannesburg, White university students and Black office workers were attacked by a hundred White vigilantes wielding steel pipes, clubs, and chains. The government's violent reaction only added fuel to the fire, and even its decision to rescind the policy on Afrikaans had no discernible effect on the scale or scope of the protests. In August, Cape Town erupted and Coloured students demonstrated alongside African students for the first time. Three worker stayaways called by the students in August and September were increasingly successful. Sporadic unrest continued in townships throughout 1976 and the first three quarters of 1977, after which things calmed down. Calms after Soweto, however, were much less naive than those before it.

While these and many other "facts" about the events of that decidedly abnormal Wednesday have become part of the history of South Africa's transition, there has not always been such agreement on either the events or their meanings. "The truth about Soweto" became the subject of a competition for adherents, a contest among interpretations of what "really" happened. In a word, Soweto, June 16, 1976, became politicized. The next section analyzes the struggle over the authority to interpret Soweto by three categories of contestants.

COMPETING DISCOURSES ON SOWETO

Each story told about Soweto is politicized in subtle ways, through the choice of events to include, the labels given to those events, and the internal order that is constructed to present them as distinct and significant. These choices provide the audience with information about the teller's purpose and goals. Rather than assess the validity of these stories, this section divides the range of accounts into three broad categories and examines some of the differences among and within those categories.

Reporting the Events—The Riots

Some stories have a certain immediacy attached to them that allows them to qualify as news. The first category of accounts comes from the archives of South African newspapers and is an attempt to recreate the details that would have been available to most South Africans in the days immediately following the events. What the South African press found newsworthy about what happened on June 16 was the disturbance of the social order, most often referred to as rioting. This was synonymous with looting and burning, pillage, chaos, rampage, and anarchy. In newspaper accounts, the actors were rioters (rioting pupils), looters (*plunderaars* in Afrikaans), tsotsis, thugs, and spivs. They were drunk (drunken rioters, drunken youths, drunken tsotsis) and acted in mobs (angry mobs, rioting mobs, roaming gangs, an angry crowd).

Newspapers accentuated racial violence and destruction. In *Die Burger,* Cape Town's Afrikaans paper, the top of the front page on June 17 was dominated by a picture of the body of a White WRAB employee with a little sign left by his killers that said "beware." Inside, an editorial said, "Among other things [the present incident] can be attributed to the fact that it is fatally easy to whip up a Black mass into acts of unthinkable savagery and violence."[7] The *Star* led with "Mobs Take Over" with a picture of a burning building and stories like "Rioters storm hospital" and "Drunken tsotsis on prowl."[8] One headline the next day read "A white skin is a death warrant."[9] *Die Vaderland* described the riots by evoking *die Swart gevaar* (the Black menace), a phrase that represented White South Africa's collective bogeyman.[10] Photographs showed policemen firing at schoolchildren armed with trashcan lids and rocks, Black workers marching with White university students in downtown Johannesburg, blazing cars and shattered windshields. The White culture's patriarchal obsession with Black rape was evident in stories of White women who were "seriously assaulted" or even pulled from their cars and raped.[11]

The language issue was almost completely eclipsed by the violence. According to Denis Herbstein, the television news in Afrikaans did not even mention the language issue in its June 16 evening report on the riots.[12] While the issue slowly gained more prominence in some editorials and among opposition politicians, editors clearly rated effects of the disorder as more important than causes. Only a few side stories on the initial confrontation described participants as pupils, students, and schoolchildren.

Other stories stressed the relationship between Whites and "regular" Blacks. Common to all the papers were reports of Whites saved by "Blacks who didn't give in to hate."[13] The stories of J. Beeby, a pest control officer who was sheltered by a Black family overnight, and a South African Broadcast Corporation (SABC) reporter and cameraman saved from an angry crowd by a passing Black driver were told over and over.[14] By the weekend, papers were reporting a "Black Backlash" against "mobsters who have brought chaos" to Soweto.[15] Such stories seem designed to cater to a strange duality evident in much White South African discourse of the time, namely that Whites could know Blacks as one whole, and yet always seem to find exceptions to the rules of Blackness among the Blacks that they knew personally. The ability of Whites to find people in Soweto with whom they could feel comfortable contributed to the perception that the riots were the result of drunken criminals among an otherwise contented populace.

Despite a consensus among newspapers that the events were dangerous racial violence, significant discrepancies among stories emerged before the police gained a fairly secure hold over information. There were numerous estimates of the number of students who participated in the initial confrontation—ranging from hundreds of students to four to five thousand to ten thousand. Subsequent analyses place the number as high as twenty or thirty thousand. Some of this discrepancy can probably be attributed to the students' strategy of converging from a dozen gathering points. In any case, after Justice Minister Jimmy Kruger spoke to Parliament on Thursday, most newspapers tended to report his estimate of ten thousand.

Reports also varied as to which side took the first aggressive action. Some sources stated that the violence began when the police tried to take away the marchers' placards, which led to stones being thrown and shots fired.[16] Others said that a White policeman simply "lost his cool" in the face of the crowd and threw either a teargas grenade or a stone which resulted in retaliation and then shootings.[17] Others claimed that no stones were thrown until after the police started shooting.[18] Minister Kruger presented the official version, telling Parliament that police "were immediately stoned," that subsequent teargas canisters failed to have an effect, and only then were there "heavier attacks which forced them to use their firearms."[19] This rhetoric of defense had a thousand police officers "pinned down" in the Soweto darkness overnight.[20]

The facts also change over time. In the versions of events offered in morning editions of newspapers on Thursday, June 17, filed by reporters covering the story from Johannesburg, the police took the initial provocative action in the confrontation with the marching students, even if that action was simply trying to take away the student's protest signs.[21] In contrast, in later Thursday editions and subsequent reconstructions reporters on the parliamentary beat in Cape Town increasingly followed Minister Kruger's parliamentary speech in which police were stoned first and "[w]arning shots were fired only when it became clear that tear gas would not stop the rioters."[22] (Notice that in Kruger's account the students are already "rioters.") A police colonel speaking to the foreign press immediately after the shooting claimed much more than warning shots. "We fired into them. It's no use firing over their heads," he said.[23] Later, police claimed that the injured must have been hit by ricochets of warning shots fired into the ground.

The government was not entirely happy with initial reporting of the events. The Cillie Commission later argued that the papers were too critical of the police and, presaging the tighter government controls over the media in the 1980s, questioned whether "any publicity at all was desirable."[24] But as the government imposed severe restrictions on travel and as violence spread over a much larger area, the police increasingly gained control over information. Reporters became dependent upon police for both information and escorts through the townships. On Friday the 18th, police instituted "a total clamp down on the release of information regarding the number of people killed and injured in the riots."[25] Minister Kruger was reported to have answered questions about the number of dead by instructing reporters to "count the graves."[26] From this point on, much of the information about the events must be seen as having been filtered through official government sources. Alternative stories, primarily anecdotal, were occasionally filed by Black reporters who continued to have access to the riotous areas, but any overviews of the events were largely controlled by (or at least "infected with") the information that the government released and often by the tone with which they released it.[27] This spin quickly solidified into an explanation.

The Government's Story—The Conspiracy

In hindsight, it appears that the government simply did not know why Soweto was rioting. Officials seem to have been caught completely off guard. When asked in late May if there was any danger of "a blow-up in Soweto," Manie Mulder, the WRAB official in charge of Soweto, replied, "none whatever . . . the broad masses of Soweto are perfectly happy."[28] M. C. Botha, Minister of Bantu Administration and Education, had told Parliament on June 11 that he had "no knowledge of any unhappiness in Soweto."[29] When Minister of Justice Kruger addressed Parliament on June 17, he acknowledged that the government "did not expect something like this to happen."[30] Police officials seemed unable or unwilling to discern patterns or reason in the violence, seeing only "burning, looting, stoning and chaos"[31] in a situation that was "very confused and ugly."[32] Minster Botha claimed that the "alleged aversion" to Afrikaans as a medium of instruction could hardly be the only reason for the riots because almost all of the students taking part were not subject to the regulation, and because the 50–50 language rule "had been unaltered since 1955."[33] From within apartheid reality, African students would not, indeed could not, express opposition to government policy by planning a march, and normal Sowetans had no reason to attack the government violently. June 16 literally did not make sense, which made it all the more threatening.

Into this contextual vacuum the government inserted the framework through which it understood opposition to its policies in general—conspiracy. The government asserted that the Afrikaans issue and the march to protest it had been designed as a means to provoke the police and give a pretense for the rioting that followed. This theory took shape on Thursday. In a front-page story entitled "Behind the scenes planning?" the *Cape Times* quotes senior government officials as incredulous that ten thousand schoolchildren could have "mobilized themselves into riot action without some kind of behind the scenes backing."[34] Prime Minister John Vorster said he was convinced that the riots were not spontaneous, but a "deliberate attempt to create polarization between Blacks and Whites in South Africa."[35] According to Minister Botha, the conspirators were not Sowetans, but "professionals," and Whites were definitely "involved in inciting the people of Soweto to riot, loot and arson."[36] For his part, Minister Kruger directed blame toward "the nihilism of Marcuse," Black Power movements in the United States, and, of course, communists. Government officials focused on claims of responsibility made by both the African National Congress (ANC) in New York and the Pan-Africanist Congress (PAC) in Dakar.[37] They attributed the timing of the violence to Prime Minister Vorster's upcoming trip to Germany to meet with American Secretary of State Henry Kissinger and the impending independence of the Transkei homeland.[38] Vorster, Kruger, and Foreign Minister R. F. "Pik" Botha each argued in interviews that a substantial number of the deaths were the result of agitators trying to establish control over the townships, that Blacks were killing Blacks.[39] Another slightly different theory put forward by the government was that the riots were actually a tsotsi-coordinated effort at plunder.[40]

In these theories, the police were restrained defenders of the peace, reacting to an insidious plot to overthrow the state. Kruger said that the police had fired in self-defense and used the minimum of force possible. He said the police maintained the "greatest measure of self-control" throughout the rioting.[41] He even evoked a Battle of Britain invasion metaphor, claiming "Never had so much been owed by so many to so few," in this case by South Africans to the police.[42] Whether or not he meant to draw Nietzschian parallels, one Member of Parliament certainly opened the door when he praised the police for "superhuman self-control."[43] Kruger also justified the need for deadly force, claiming that rubber bullets would not work to control rioting because "[t]he moment people in a riotous situation know you have rubber bullets it means, in effect, that you also have rubber guns."[44]

Politicians, the police and, to a lesser degree, the press instinctively resorted to conspiracy theories in an attempt to divert responsibility from the government and from apartheid generally. As John Brewer has argued,

> The government still sees these incidents as the result of agitators urging participants to acts they would not otherwise commit—participants merely represent a suggestible mob. It sees the causes of these incidents as lying outside government policies and the society they create. Participants are not seen as making a case, for there is no case to be made; rather intimidators transform participants into a mob thinking they have a case. In this way the deciding factor in the occurrence of collective action is the existence and ability of agitators. Hence collective action is seen as transitory, *ad hoc*, and unpredictable.[45]

To present the government theories as part of some grand strategy, however, is to fall into the same sort of conspiracy trap. Theories emerged quickly in response to a muddled and confusing crisis. Facts were less important than understanding. (A month after the violence began, the Commissioner of Police, General Prinsloo, told the press, "Intensive police investigations have not brought any conspiracy to light," with no noticeable effect on the government's story.[46]) The government's agitator and tsotsi theories reflected a real inability to comprehend what was going on in Soweto coupled with a defensiveness bred by decades of standing up for apartheid. The conspiracy theories fit with reality as the government understood it and that fit made them valuable.

As more information became available, these theories coalesced into the story that the government told about Soweto. The more thoroughly constructed story that emerged in the weeks after the events is represented in several artifacts found in South African archives. Three of these government publications, a poster and two pamphlets, were produced in the weeks and months following the initial violence. The final artifact examined here, the report of the official Commission of Inquiry, represents the government's attempt to lay the whole issue to rest four years later.

The poster, entitled "John and Mary Boycott School," is a series of cartoons depicting "strangers in the townships" who were "richer and better dressed" than township residents handing out fliers and organizing meetings to boycott school. The children are portrayed as being convinced to shout *'n Maand lang,* Afrikaans for "a month long," so that the teachers would know how long they would be gone. (It is interesting that the poster depicts children actually using Afrikaans.) According to the poster the children were unaware of "another organization" whose slogan was *Amandla* (Zulu for "Power"). The poster says that John and Mary and others who wanted to continue studying were "threatened with violence by the tsotsis who waited outside the school." John and Mary are then depicted ten years later—poor, sad, and disheveled. They now see the strangers were using them, with a picture of a sinister-looking puppet master controlling the riots. The poster concludes by imploring the reader, "Stop being used! Stop being bullied into your own destruction! The power is in *your* hands! Your defence force is here to protect you and enable you to attend classes again!"[47]

The second publication is a pamphlet prepared by the Publications Division of the South African Department of Information entitled "A 'Ghetto' in South Africa."[48] The pamphlet is filled with photographs and descriptions that present Soweto as an organized and middle-class living space. After the virtual tour, the author confronts the issue of the riots head on.

> It is well known that since June 1976 there have been sporadic demonstrations and riotous incidents in Soweto instigated and carried out by a small minority. The majority of Sowetans are peace-loving people, and this was clearly underscored by the goodwill shown to Whites in danger and to the police during the unrest. Although the commission appointed to investigate the causes has not yet made its report, Mr. F. A. Tabeev, a member of the Presidium of the Supreme Council of the Soviet Union, said in Dar es Salaam in October 1976 that the riots "were the result of the work of organised national liberation movement officials of the African National Congress (banned in South Africa) operating on a broad front. . . ."[49]

The organizers' expectation that the demonstrations would escalate into a general uprising failed because there was a "lack of sympathy for their cause." The author celebrates the "great reservoir of goodwill between Blacks and Whites" that was proven during the "testing time" and says that such urban violence is common to many industrialized states.

A brochure put out by the Foreign Affairs Association entitled "The Challenge of Soweto" is a much more detailed argument.[50] The author, F. R. Metrowich, begins with a series of questions.

> The Soweto demonstration had been organized two days previously. It was announced as a peaceful demonstration. Why, then, did it get out of hand? And why did it take place in June shortly before the Prime Minister of South Africa, Mr. John Vorster, and the American Secretary of State, Dr. Henry Kissinger, were to meet in Germany to discuss peaceful settlement of Southern Africa's political problems, when Afrikaans was introduced as a medium of instruction in Black schools as far back as 1953—23 years ago?[51]

Metrowich's answer, under the heading "Enter the Agitators," is that "the so-called language issue was merely used by agitators as a pretext for rioting."[52] The pamphlet presents an argument comprised principally of exiled anti-apartheid organizations claiming credit for the riots and stating that the "Afrikaans medium is our weapon for revolution," of government officials' stated belief that the riots were not spontaneous, and of unattributed statements taken from newspapers. Police conduct is represented as defensive actions against largely adult rioters. Key to the argument is the assertion that the police were not responsible for all of the violence that took place. "Layabouts and Black gangsters known as 'tsotsis' moved in on the first day of the rioting to exploit the situation and terrorize, rob and beat up law-abiding Black citizens."[53] This "moving in" is presented as the cause of the rising death toll. Metrowich accentuates the "Good Samaritans" of the conflict—the White social workers who were killed, the Blacks who saved White lives, and the non-Whites who were "generous in providing comfort" to police in the form of coffee, food, coal, wood, and even a tent while they manned roadblocks in the autumn cold.

In his conclusion, Metrowich again asks a series of questions.

> Was the issue that ostensibly started the rioting a grievance or a pretext; was there incitement and exploitation; was it a racial clash involving Black and White; to what extent was there gangsterism rather than genuine democratic protest; were the Police brutal and repressive or were they fulfilling their role as law-keepers in the interest of the majority? . . . If it was a Black-White racial confrontation, why did Blacks select other non-White groups (Indians, Coloureds, Chinese) as targets; and why was there so much apparent good will between the Black and White majorities?[54]

This string of questions goes unanswered, but Metrowich does comment on them generally.

> What is abundantly clear and requires no judicial investigation is the absurdity and callous irresponsibility of the consortium of politicians, churchmen, newspapers and government representatives who declared the riots to be (a) a threat to world peace (b) monstrous in its [sic] extent (c) evidence of a deliberate oppressive action by the Government of South Africa to teach Black people a lesson (d) a spontaneous peaceful demonstration by schoolchildren against an inferior and oppressive educational system and (e) a classic race riot.[55]

The pamphlet emphasizes the relatively low death toll (reported as 176) and claims that the unfavorable world attention is part of the conspiracy. "This intellectual dishonesty might help the consortium of critics of South Africa to manipulate the facts as it suits them but it will not help anyone, Black or White, in South Africa one iota. This is the lesson of Soweto."[56]

As part of its response to the riots, the government immediately set up a one-man Commission of Inquiry to investigate. Such commissions are the primary method by which South African governments have traditionally dealt with major policy questions and events like Soweto. The Judge-President of the Transvaal, Pieter Cillie, was appointed to the task. He began his investigation in late July 1976 and finally submitted his 760-page report on March 1, 1980.[57]

The report presents a fairly in-depth analysis of the events. It is more critical of the police than any previous government report, but still finds that there were no "deliberate and impermissible assaults by members of the police force."[58] The commission also found that "it was never the policy of the police force to shoot rioters indiscriminately, nor did this happen."[59] Its reported death toll—575 for the period from June 16, 1976, to February 28, 1977—was significantly lower than several independent analyses.[60] It acknowledges that problems with the educational system were the reasons for the initial march and that the frustrations of apartheid life often contributed to the violence, but it still claims that intimidation and agitators were a necessary component of both the violence in Soweto and its spread.[61] As Brewer has said, the report presented the incidents as "a purely transitory, unpredictable, essentially non-rational, and apolitical occurrence unconnected with the activities of the state."[62] When the report was released, newspapers reported the conclusion that the police force had to "collectively bear responsibility" for the outbreak of violence because of poor investigative skills, but that the actions of specific officers were not excessive or wrong and did not cause riots or worsen them.[63]

This report constitutes the apartheid government's final position on Soweto and represents its attempt to extend its authority to cover the interpretation of the events. According to this story, the riots were an unfortunate chapter in South African history, an attempt by anti-South African forces to sow racial conflict that would best be forgotten. In contrast, the anti-apartheid story of Soweto became part of a living mythology that was continually reinterpreted over time. Those working against apartheid appropriated and sloganized "Soweto 1976" and "June 16" and used the story in a host of ways in their efforts.

THE ANTI-APARTHEID STORY—THE UPRISING

A significant portion of those who paid attention to the events in Soweto were predisposed to believe the worst about the South African government and its agents, the police. Within South Africa, millions lived the frustrations and indignities of everyday apartheid, inflicted by the same entities the people of Soweto were fighting. Outside, a decidedly antiracial liberal individualism had become the dominant standard of justice and equity in the West. To many, both in South Africa and abroad, the White government was a repressive regime and the institutions of apartheid governance were inherently and actively unjust. There was a receptive audience, therefore, for an account of the events that began with an assumption of government illegitimacy and the desirability of change, rather than the government's assumption of the need to protect law and order. In this anti-apartheid story, the main participants, their motives, and the implications of their actions are quite different from those the government described. While the explanation of the Soweto *riots* coalesced rather quickly after the initial violence, the story of the Soweto *uprising* became a living part of the rhetoric of struggle, and as such has continued to evolve.

At the time of the events, only a few opposition organizations had enough legitimacy to get their views into South African newspapers. Even though the word later came to dominate thinking about Soweto, at the time newspapers only used the word *uprising* derisively, in a report on how the Radio Moscow Africa Service framed the events.[64] The South African Council of Churches "expressed support for the students' protest against the offending regulations and deplored what it called totally unwarranted actions against them."[65] The Young South African movement of the White, liberal United Party condemned the police for "turning a peaceful protest into a bloodbath."[66] The Federation of Black Women of South Africa and the South African Black Social Workers' Association expressed sympathy with the protesters and deplored the action of the police. A meeting of Soweto school principals blamed the Bantu Education Department, which "refused to listen to pleas to stop teaching in Afrikaans." The riots, they said, were sparked by children who hated the imposition of a language they resented.[67] Other elites, including Reverend Desmond Tutu, Reverend Sam Buti, and Winnie Mandela, berated the government for ignoring weeks of protest on the language issue. Dr. C. F. Beyers Naude, a dissident Afrikaner whom the government (in its search for all possible conspirators) had ordered to "disassociate himself" from the events in Soweto, called the crisis the "most serious the country has ever been involved in."[68]

World attention snapped to South Africa and those opposed to apartheid used the opportunity to spread their message. People demonstrated in London, Paris, New York, Bonn, Geneva, and many other sites around the world. The matter was debated by the Security Council of the United Nations, which passed a resolution condemning South Africa, and by the Council of Ministers of the Organization of African Unity, which declared June 16 "the day of the Soweto Martyrs."[69] Before the government could perfect its restrictions on the media, both domestic and foreign, television pictures broadcast around the world made apartheid important to Western middle classes, and apartheid became a policy that everyone could hate. That basic unity insured that South Africa held a reserved spot in global public consciousness. The apartheid government treated these condemnations as attacks on the sovereignty of the state, and in many ways the coalition that came together around the anti-apartheid story of Soweto represented one of the first truly global political movements.

While the story of the uprising began with a belief that Afrikaans was an issue of enough significance to provoke a march, language quickly became tangential as the story evolved. From this perspective, what caused the violence of the uprising was the apartheid system generally. Focusing blame on the spark rather than the powder keg into which it fell would only have diverted attention from the issues that those opposed to apartheid wanted to accentuate—racialism, oppression, injustice. The actions of the police were presented as typically extreme and brutal, an overt manifestation of the violence experienced by the majority of South Africans on a daily basis. In contrast to the government and press stories which focused solely or primarily on violent destruction carried out by Blacks, the anti-apartheid perspective saw schoolchildren shot by White police and "the people" retaliating. The following short summaries are illustrative.

> On Monday 17 May the 1,600 students at Soweto's Orlando West Junior Secondary School marched out of the school gates on strike. They would not return, they said, until the South African Government removed Afrikaans as a medium of instruction in the schools. The protests rapidly spread to other Soweto schools until, by mid-June, the movement became too powerful for the apartheid regime to tolerate. The racist rulers in Pretoria resorted to their time-tested methods of bloody repression. On the morning of 16 June, para-military police opened fire on peaceful crowds of student demonstrators, killing a 13-year-old and setting of a train of events which brought the most massive uprising in recent South African history.[70]

> On the morning of Wednesday, June 16, 1976, Soweto unexpectedly rose up against white rule and became the focal point of a countrywide revolt. It was on that day that thousands of Sowetan schoolchildren marched to protest the use of Afrikaans as the language of instruction in their segregated schools. The police fired on the unarmed demonstrators, killing several and wounding many more. Soweto exploded. Stores were looted, government buildings were burned, and people were killed. South African history reached one of its decisive turning points, and Soweto became an international symbol of black protest and white oppression.[71]

Opposition rhetoric clearly was meant to inspire action by describing events as constructive rather than destructive. In contrast to the government's use of the terms *riots, rampage, chaos,* and *pillaging,* opponents of apartheid used *uprising, protest, revolt,* and *rebellion.* The events were described as "the uprising of an entire people, the bugle-call to revolt, the herald of a new dawn after the long and seemingly endless night of the terrible torture of apartheid, oppression and servitude."[72] Where the government focused on material ruin and crime by calling participants "rioters," "tsotsis," and "criminals," critics of apartheid saw "innocent children," "peaceful marchers," "heroic dead," and even "revolutionary martyrs." The ANC, which was invested in the events being seen as part of a larger anti-apartheid and communist movement, even called them "comrades."[73] While the government emphasized the protective, defensive posture of the police, opponents called them "Nazi-like," "fascist," "para-military," "trigger-happy," and "cold-blooded" and their actions "murder," "war," "massacre," and "genocide."

Anti-apartheid stories treated all of the resulting violence as part of a "struggle," imputing political rationales to all participants and ignoring the criminal elements involved.[74] Some later sympathetic academic analysis suggested that the students had significant success in curbing the tsotsis, but most stories just completely ignored them.[75] This created an image of unity among Sowetans that belied significant initial chaos. Anti-apartheid interpretations definitely discounted the trouble students experienced getting parents and workers, especially hostel dwellers, to support their cause.[76] From some accounts, the rioters spoke and acted for "the people,"[77] but the vast majority of Black South Africans neither participated in nor supported the uprising.[78] They may have sympathized with the students' frustrations and decried the injustice of the shootings, but active resistance was almost exclusively the province of young students, and most others found it unwise, if not suicidal. The constituency claimed by the anti-apartheid rhetoric did not exist, even if it did slowly solidify over the next twenty years, in part because of Soweto.

As time went by, an interesting tension developed among some of the anti-apartheid stories with respect to the spontaneity of the violence. Everyone agreed that the *march* had been organized. The government's story was that the *riots* were also planned and spread by design. The exiled African National Congress and Pan-Africanist Congress both provided fodder for this interpretation by trying to take credit for the uprising in an attempt to aggrandize their organizations.[79] Other apartheid opponents seem adamant about stressing the lack of organization.

> The most important point of all, however, is that the student revolt was a spontaneous furious reaction to the shooting on 16 June 1976, not a planned insurrection with a country-wide organization network, funds, and a series of strategies and fall-back positions worked out in advance. Bravery, militancy, and even the resourcefulness which the SSRC [Soweto Students' Representative Council] revealed in the campaigns which it did quickly organize, were no match for the considerable resources of violence which the State was able to deploy.[80]

Later analysts found that "[t]he speed of the chain reaction in other townships virtually rules out the possibility of organization on any significant scale."[81] Overall, the ANC's participation in the events of 1976 seems to have all taken place after the fact.[82] "Although ANC pamphlets were distributed in Soweto and elsewhere, and the exiled organization later claimed that it had played a major part in organizing the revolt, there is every sign that is was taken by surprise by the events of 1976–7."[83]

As the anti-apartheid movement gained momentum, the Soweto uprisings were often constructed as a turning point in South African history, a watershed that began the serious decline of apartheid as a social order. The processes of resistance, the processes of repression, the social fabric of Soweto, even the Sowetans themselves, especially the youth, were all seen as fundamentally changed by the events of June 1976. The outburst of action on June 16, 1976, was represented as breaking a kind of seal on opposition politics, producing a qualitative change in both the methods required to police the apartheid order and the ways South Africans thought about resistance, and therefore it was seen as beginning a new phase of active resistance to apartheid. This theme of active resistance was developed over time around the mythology of Soweto and the anniversaries of the events.

The first several anniversaries of June 16 were tense and anxious. Police aggressively dispersed gatherings, but the commemorations and ceremonies were focused almost exclusively on specific individuals who had been killed and feelings of personal loss. In 1980, there was a change. That year, the day corresponded with an existing student boycott that had been going for two months in the Coloured communities around Cape Town. June 16 was evoked for a two-day work stayaway in defiance of sweeping government measures trying to prevent disruptions.[84] This mobilization of the anniversary for contemporary political purposes changed the meaning of Soweto. From 1980 on, Black South Africans were called on to commemorate the uprising and the violence more than to remember the specific people who had been killed. All of the dead got rolled into one name, Hector Pieterson, and a statistic, usually a number between 575 and 1,000. Most newspaper stories about the anniversary condensed what happened in 1976 into a sentence or two to serve as a reference point for either contemporary political activity or an assessment of how the country had changed since. The Soweto uprisings became about the present rather than the past. June 16 became an excuse for political gatherings (especially in Soweto),[85] for police to use force to disperse those gatherings, and for Black youths to vent frustrations. From 1980 on, June 16 became a backdrop for political activity.

Each year, the legitimacy of commemoration spread further into civil society. Throughout the early 1980s, the day was usually marked with partial worker stayaways, closed shops, and scattered police/demonstrator violence. In 1983, the annual memorial service in Soweto drew its largest numbers since 1977.[86] The Black Sash, a liberal White women's group, began sending letters to school principals encouraging them to recognize the day as a holiday. In 1983, the Coca-Cola bottling plant in Soweto reinstated three workers that it had fired for missing work on June 16 and said subsequently June 16 would become a paid holiday for its Soweto workers.[87] Other companies began to follow Coke's lead.

On June 16, 1986, the tenth anniversary, the situation was particularly tense. On June 12, in anticipation of the anniversary, the government issued a State of Emergency covering the entire country, and the Minister of Law and Order banned all commemorations. Significant violence occurred anyway, and the annual stayaway was largely successful. Newspapers interviewed former student leaders, people photographed in 1976, even the police brigadier in charge of the riot squad ten years earlier.[88] It was a natural milestone and many papers printed both summaries of the events ten years earlier and detailed accounts of resistance highlights during the years since. Both kinds of stories solidified June 16, 1976, as a date of tremendous historical significance.

Another shift in thinking about June 16 took place in 1987, and for several years the anniversary was significantly calmer. In 1987, opposition movements called for June 16 to be commemorated with respect and restraint as a day of dignity. "Although the symbolism has not waned, this momentous event has over the years turned from the confrontational to the ceremonial."[89] They had solidified June 16 as a "*de facto* public holiday for most South Africans," and the annual call for a worker stayaway was unnecessary, as most employers had arranged some kind of agreement with their workers. This change took place against a general shift in opposition strategies, as the state successfully adapted to resistance tactics of mass mobilization. This larger context of shrinking participation in resistance was evident on anniversaries, which shifted from "the politics of anger to the politics of introspection."[90] In this period, June 16 was used less as a stage for resistance activity, but it continued to be solidified as part of the mythology of resistance. Even the staid *Business Day* editorialized that "[June 16] has become a commemoration not so much of resistance to the Soweto education system but of another milestone in the black struggle for freedom from oppression."[91] One professor of education said that in the process of trying to prepare his students to teach history, he found his classes in the mid-1980s largely ignorant. "White students knew nothing about 1976. Black students were aware, but they weren't aware of the details of what happened."[92] The events of 1976 became less important than the symbolism that engulfed them, mostly because "the events that followed year after year since that day have been even more remarkable."[93] During the late 1980s, June 16 was a day of solemnity.

When politics were once again unleashed after the 1990 unbanning of opposition parties, the symbolism of June 16 became a battleground for opposition politics. Once the struggle for the future of post-apartheid South Africa was overt, June 16 became a day for opposition groups to hold competing rallies, each calling for unity with the others. Each party used their rally to parade their opposition lineage and claim responsibility for the Soweto uprising.[94] In 1991, the Inkatha Freedom Party (IFP) held its own rally for the first time.[95] This proliferation of remembrance rallies is indicative of the intense political and violent struggle between parties at this point in the transition. By 1992, one editorialist complained that the day had become so trivialized by party politics that "even the Nats [the National Party] might hold a June 16 rally."[96] He lamented that solemnity had been replaced with a "grotesque parade of party political flags" and "platforms to vilify opponents."[97] In a spot survey, one out of four students interviewed professed not knowing what the holiday was for.[98] This divisiveness was accentuated in 1992, when the ANC chose June 16 to begin a "rolling mass action," a strategy to force government movement in constitutional negotiations. Other parties objected to this call, and the next day in an attack by hostel dwellers in Boiphatong, a township near Johannesburg, over 70 residents of the township were killed. This massacre and the subsequent hostility toward the government and its "moderate" Black allies finally forced constitutional discussions out of their stalemate.

Upbeat, an educational magazine for Black students, is indicative of how June 16 was important to resistance in South Africa. Not until 1985 did the magazine acknowledge the anniversary, and then only with the words *June 16* on a black background and a picture of a Black child holding a handkerchief to his face.[99] In 1986, a bolder one-page story appeared with a vague description of students protesting about education and hundreds of children killed.[100] In 1987, a two-page story with pictures said, "the police opened fire" and "more than 1000 people died in the uprising," and described the material conditions that led to the protests.[101] After 1987, however, there were only two small reminders of the day. In 1989, eight sentences conclude with "People all over South Africa remember this day. It is a symbol of student resistance to apartheid education."[102] The story in 1995 does not even mention Soweto, but discusses Youth Day in the context of the United Nations Convention on the Rights of the Child.[103]

Through such rhetoric, June 16 became an indicator of South African resistance politics. Opponents of apartheid successfully sloganized *June 16* and *Soweto*. These terms became shorthand for

> not only the June 16 uprising but also a whole series of subsequent events: School boycotts and strikes; marches of tens of thousands; demonstrations extending into downtown Johannesburg; the burning or sabotage of symbols of white oppression, including government offices, beer halls, and liquor stores in African townships; clashes with police; police attacks on gatherings at funerals, where the slogan often heard was "Don't mourn—mobilize."[104]

After the 1994 elections, June 16 became an official holiday commemorating youth and a nation-building exercise, with youthfulness and responsibility emphasized over divisiveness and injustice. For years, opponents of apartheid used June 16 as a vehicle to legitimate, glorify, and mobilize resistance. In post-apartheid South Africa, it has become an opportunity to promote South African rainbow nationalism. The events in Soweto changed the framework within which South African politics were understood. The spontaneous actions of the students demonstrated that active resistance was a possibility for Black South Africans, especially for youth. The breadth of frustration in the society provided a ready-made constituency that, over time, found the students' attack on the authority of the state legitimate, desirable, even praiseworthy and exemplary. The gradual expansion of this constituency is what eventually brought down apartheid. These dynamics of resistance and social change took place in an atmosphere charged with the politics of identity.

THE POLITICAL IDENTITY OF SOWETO

June 16, 1976, was a site where important changes to South African political identities were negotiated. This is evident in the competing discourses about the events of the day. Each story attempts to describe and explain the events so that they fit into a broad understanding of South African reality as a whole, and in so doing asserts a system of political identities. A story is believable and events are described and explained to the degree that they fit into the preconceived world of each observer/listener, even if hearing the story subsequently alters that world irreparably. What makes the stories political is the influence they have on audience attitudes toward the existing order and its implicit hierarchies of privilege. The stories can be analyzed for the assumptions that the storytellers make about what their audience already knows or believes, and for the ways they try to steer images of reality into the future. The differences between and within the competing discourses become clearer by examining the images of identity they assert.

Protagonists and Social Power

One of the ways that the three types of accounts—news stories, government stories, and anti-apartheid stories—differ from each other is in the interpretation of the actors involved. In news accounts of the events, actors were grouped by their relation to order. Apartheid reality forced newspapers (and society generally) to present Soweto participants according to group characteristics rather than as individuals. On one side was a violent mass—an angry horde, the youth, or, as the violence spread, the prospect of a whole race acting as one. Headlines and pictures focused on the violence and destruction and evoked the specter of Africans out of control. These images were a trope for White South Africans and played upon the ever-present threat of the White minority being overwhelmed by a savage majority bent on revenge for apartheid. On the other side were the agents of law and order. Police were praised because they were seen as preserving order, although some also criticized the police for contributing to the violence. Other labels were based on action, either violent—marchers, rioters, looters, tsotsis—or orderly—police, the folks who brought sandwiches and coffee to the police, "regular" Sowetans. These labels complicated apartheid's strict racial hierarchies. White university students protested through downtown Johannesburg and many Blacks continued to act lawfully. So while much of the racialism was subtle, the defense of order, and thus apartheid, was explicit.

The government, however, was responsible for more than just suppressing disorder; it also had to explain it in such a way that the core of apartheid reality remained intact. Apartheid's rules for attributing agency made this difficult. For a person living the fundamentals of apartheid, Africans, and especially young African schoolchildren, were incapable of even imagining a demonstration like the march through Soweto. Blacks could not spontaneously overwhelm a police state constructed by Whites for the sole purpose of preventing such an uprising. And average Africans, content with their lot, would be repulsed, not inspired, by such illogical, lawless conduct. Such actions were beyond the scope of their role as Africans in apartheid society.[105] The government's social architects believed that the institutions of apartheid were the solution to "the racial problem" and that they had negated *die Swaart gevaar,* even if its continued containment required constant vigilance. From within apartheid reality, therefore, Soweto was unpredicted and unpredictable. For this reason, it was a primal threat to White security and the social order on which Afrikaner hegemony depended.

The disturbances of 1976 were traumatic for South African whites, not because the objectively shook apartheid (which they did not), but, more intangibly, because they indicated reserves of black political energy where none were supposed to exist and where any were seen to be dangerous. In this sense 1976 called forth the need for new responses on the part of white South Africa, not because it had actually lost control, but because the paranoia of total control bred the belief that any loss of control is tantamount to surrender.[106]

The government had to prevent the events from appearing anomalous to the core of social reality, for if apartheid could not explain Soweto (as it clearly did not predict it), people would be forced to question the entire social system.

Plausible explanations were therefore a necessary part of the defense of the order. For those within apartheid, the safest possible explanation for Soweto and its aftermath was that the violence was a foreign plot, an attack on the integrity of the South African state coordinated by foreign (i.e. White) communists.[107] The default explanation for anti-apartheid feelings, developed over years of defending apartheid in the international arena, was that communists wanted control of South Africa. The conspiracy theories were widespread and solid. The police colonel in charge of the riot police, a purported expert on communist guerrillas known as "the Red Russian," claimed that he confronted crowds using "a well-known communist tactic."[108] In his speech to Parliament, Minister Kruger, commenting on young people walking around with upraised fists, said, "Surely this is a sign of the Communist Party."[109] Even opposition Members of Parliament were dubbed "communists" and "traveling ambassadors of Moscow" for suggesting that the real agitator was apartheid.[110] From inside the worldview of apartheid, Africans were too simple minded to outwit the police, but this same quality made them easy to manipulate. These theories manifested the public roles of Africans under apartheid—stable and content, simple followers dependent on others for creative ideas. The causes were therefore not specific policies or even general discontent with the system, but outside instigators and agitators. The Cillie Commission condemned the South African Police, not for its violent repression of the unrest, but for the failure of its intelligence services to uncover the plot.

The identities through which the government understood and explained Soweto were deeply implicated in the apartheid social order. Within apartheid's four racial groups, the government did make distinctions for students and criminals, youths and adults, agitators and lawful residents, but racial identities were always primary. The social order had clear rules for the types of people who could be an agent in the political arena and for the kinds of actions that were available to those who were agents and those who were not. Africans were unimaginative laborers who could be trained but not educated. Afrikaners possessed South African sovereignty and had a duty to defend their right to self-determination and governance. Criminals sought personal gain at the expense of those who followed the rules. Communists were intent on taking over the country for its resources. By portraying the impetus for the riots as coming from outside normal society, either from foreign agitators or domestic tsotsis, the government's story preserved the inertial force and direction of the existing social order. Through its descriptions and explanations government officials sought to divest the violence of any romance and rather connect it to broadly shared social negatives, which in their minds were criminals and communists. At the same time it attempted to maintain the integrity of "African scholar" and related labels to encourage people to abide by the established rules of those roles. It was this defense of the government's image of normality that produced statements about the police being in the townships to protect residents and allow them to go to school and work.

In contrast, the anti-apartheid stories undermined the normality of apartheid's existing system of political identity in two ways. First, these stories claimed political agency for identities that apartheid interpreted as mere objects in the political arena—those for whom decisions needed to be made. In the years prior to 1976, throwing rocks and burning down liquor stores were not readily available as political statements, and they were certainly beyond any interpretation of the standards of normality attached to the label "student." Afterwards, this was no longer so. "Youth" also became re-empowered as a category of action. In the 1940s, the ANC Youth League led the reformation of resistance strategies from polite petitions to mass action, and secondary school students were very important to national politics in the 1950s, but youth opposition had withered with the rest of resistance in the early 1960s.[111] The students in Soweto and around the country reawakened this constituency, creating significant intergenerational tensions, but ultimately pulling their parents into action through a combination of guilt and inspiration. Perhaps most important, the anti-apartheid Soweto stories doomed the government's efforts to keep Africans (at least those not part of the limited and pliant homeland hierarchies) strictly apolitical. The story of the uprising accentuated the political power that Africans had—the power not to abide by the rules of order, the power to disrupt, if not yet replace, apartheid.

Second, anti-apartheid stories of Soweto redefined the meanings of many labels that were already part of the political lexicon. People claimed legitimacy for labels that the government sought to apply negatively—"protester," "rioter," even "terrorist" and "comrade." Within the opposition stories, these labels were valued precisely because they signified action against the existing order. The stories presented these identities as accessible to average Black South Africans. When "unarmed schoolchildren" and "peaceful student demonstrators" became "revolutionary martyrs" and "heroic dead" by marching and attacking the "racist rulers" who "declared war on our kids," then "protesters" and "rioters" were transformed from trouble makers, people whom all those who benefited from an orderly society could agree to condemn, into legitimate spokespersons for "the people" who had no other voice. The stories justified, legitimated, and even glorified acts of violence done in resistance to apartheid. The identity labels associated with these acts already existed in the political arena, but in the anti-apartheid stories of Soweto their meaning and their value were changed.

These then are the variety of protagonists that populate the stories of Soweto. Each story makes an implicit claim to be the truth about what happened. But the events that took place in Soweto in June 1976 were, as most societal occurrences are, quite complex. They *were* part riot, part uprising, and even part conspiracy, loosely and broadly defined. All of these strands coexisted, waiting to be noticed and accentuated by participants and observers. Rather than trying to discover which of these stories about Soweto, June 16, 1976, is factually true, it seems more interesting to study how the stories were told and how they have been used politically in the years since. If the differences between these stories represent a competition, a contest for adherents who believe one explanation over another, then the anti-apartheid version has surely won. Opponents of apartheid kept the day important, adapting the mythology of Soweto and using it in their struggle. In contrast, the government's story of crime and lawlessness has shriveled and died.

THE WINNER

The anti-apartheid story won the competition for public opinion because enough South Africans knew the same frustrations, indignities, and dehumanization and could believe that apartheid alone was enough to engender the kind of violence Soweto produced. Apartheid, after all, was designed to subject all Africans to the same political experiences. People could believe that students would want to protest being taught in Afrikaans and that violence was how Sowetans would express their anger at the death of children. Ultimately, many simply believed that normal means of dealing with such feelings could be easily overwhelmed by the deluge of anger that the crisis between the students and police precipitated. Enough people also believed that the apartheid government was responsible. Even the government's Cillie Commission could not ignore the powerful impact that Soweto had on Black unity around the country.

> At first, the sense of involvement manifested itself as sympathy; the demonstrators made it clear that they sympathized with Soweto and its people. But the feeling of sympathy soon developed into a sense of oneness and of solidarity with Soweto. This solidarity was really an identification with everything that Soweto symbolised. This was Black Solidarity.[112]

All over South Africa, people expressed their outrage at the shootings and their empathy with the frustrations of apartheid life. Sowetan students traveled around the country, telling others what was happening in Soweto, teaching them slogans and songs, and helping to spread unrest.[113] Student leaders in other parts of the country considered the actions of their colleagues in Soweto an example and sought to organize similar actions in their own areas.[114] In spite of claims to the contrary by the government and a few anti-apartheid organizations, the reactive protests and violence were not centered around any alternative ideology. The dispersion of violence was based more on a widespread visceral empathy with the action of standing up to the police than any specific grievance. As word spread, the story of riots and criminal disorder that came from the press and the government was clearly reinterpreted and transformed. The Cillie Commission found that inciters had used newspaper reports and photographs of riots to twist the disorder into the popular story of the uprising.[115]

> Furthermore, there was a glorification of violence and of people who took violent action; because violence and acts of violence were often written and talked about without noticeable disapprobation, the misdeeds of the violent sometimes became feats worthy of emulation in the eyes of young people.[116]

The government's story accentuated violence as much as or more than the anti-apartheid version, but this similarity was obscured by definitions of the perpetrators. Violence by agents of the government was excused because it was against rioters and in the service of law and order. Even if some believed this story, however, the government eventually lost the battle for believability.

Indeed, the government's story had trouble right from the beginning. In a survey of five hundred racially diverse people living around Durban taken about a month after the violence began, respondents rejected key aspects of the government's explanation, even though it did play better with White respondents than it did with Blacks.[117] Across the racial groups, most respondents believed that the fundamental issue was the enforcement of Afrikaans on Soweto schoolchildren, that the police and schoolchildren were the prime participants, and that the violence was not rooted in agitators or the criminal element. No Africans, and only one percent of Indians, four percent of Coloureds, and two percent of Whites, saw the events as a conflict "between police and hooligans."[118] Substantial majorities of Blacks saw the events as a "rebellion, revolt and mass protest."[119] Those Whites who did believe the government were mostly Afrikaners. A 1977 survey found that English-speaking Whites were inclined to blame racial unrest on objective problems, while Afrikaners attributed it largely to "agitators" and "communists."[120]

Over the years, the government's story became essentially irrelevant to what Soweto came to represent, both to the South African community generally and to the global coalition aligned against apartheid. To be fair, this story was intended principally for constituencies predisposed to believe it—sympathetic foreign governments, foreign investors, and South Africans who lived by the principles of apartheid. While it is impossible to know what the government storytellers were thinking at the time, it seems fair to assume that they believed that the vast majority of South Africans were in this latter category, that their fellow South Africans interpreted political reality, and therefore the riots, through apartheid lenses. People generally tend to assume that those around them share their own understanding of reality. By design, apartheid prevented members of the four racial groups from having enough real contact with each other to know whether their perceptions of each other were valid. The ordered experience of the previous fifteen years provided a solid basis for believing that explanations grounded in apartheid reality would be the ones that South Africans would choose to help them make sense of Soweto. Apartheid had provided South Africa with a highly efficient social order and most South Africans had lived their lives according to its rules.

Soweto ended this efficiency. It disabused South Africans of all races of the assumption that Blacks were content with apartheid arrangements, provoking resistance to the momentum of the apartheid social order. By shattering expectations, Soweto forced people to notice and even question apartheid's political reality. As the soon-to-be-banned editor of the Black newspaper *World* put it, "White South Africa gasped at the intensity of the violence. They were shocked that it could happen on their doorstep. Perhaps they thought Blacks LIKED living in Soweto."[121] It seems that Blacks also gasped. The popular story of the uprising changed how many Black South Africans thought about their relationship to the state. Through that story, the lesson of Soweto came to be that Blacks had the power to disrupt apartheid society. By breaking through the placid, orderly surface of everyday apartheid life, Sowetans called attention to both their oppression and their latent power. As resistance movements found strength and empathy in the story of Soweto, and returned to it again and again as a rallying point and as a symbol of oppression and sacrifice, Soweto was mythologized. The students of Soweto had achieved the third level of resistance—their actions caused others to notice and question the social order. And because Soweto was represented as the beginning of the end of apartheid, that is what it became. Because South Africans believed the story of Soweto as uprising, it became a turning point in South African history, and post-Soweto politics became considerably different from what had come before.

Soweto as Political Resistance

Acts can be considered resistance to the degree that they oppose the existing social order, which, in this model, is assumed to be continuously in motion. In chapter 2, I proposed a definition that disaggregated the idea of resistance into four separate levels—noticing, questioning, causing trouble by acting in ways opposed to the dominant social order, and working for a specific alternative to that order. While these levels say nothing about the quality of resistance, in a sense the aggregate number of levels achieved by all the people in society would be indicative of the amount of resistance in a society at any one time. The primary impact of Soweto as resistance was at the first and second levels, and so the aggregate amount of resistance in society, while a sudden and startling explosion compared to the preceding decade and a half of high momentum, was quite low compared to the widespread and targeted resistance of the 1980s. So while Soweto did not undo the apartheid social order, it did slow its forward progress.

Soweto produced resistance primarily at the first two levels, but its impact varied by the individual. It would have been very hard for any South African to avoid noticing the events of Soweto, and apartheid as a system figured prominently in the stories that remained after the first day or two. Even those comfortably ensconced in apartheid's momentum had to remember that apartheid existed. Rather than simply the forgotten and ignorable backdrop against which politics occurred, the stories treated apartheid as a human invention with a name and a politicized history. For many South Africans, noticing apartheid was threatening enough to daily routine to drive them into full support of the state and any response it deemed appropriate.

For those who noticed and then questioned, the government was ready with an answer that made sense of Soweto in a way that those predisposed to an apartheid worldview found strangely reassuring—an anti-South African conspiracy. For these people, and especially Whites whose access to privilege was dependent upon that reality, it would have taken a significant effort to challenge the conspiracy explanation. This would have been especially so for those officials who wove the explanation together. For those less invested in the apartheid understanding of reality (including many foreign observers), the conspiracy story explained less of the case. Many of these people were pushed by the events of Soweto into a state of active skepticism about apartheid. Even if Soweto itself did not inspire them to activity, they were ready and willing to subject future events to a scrutiny they would not have in the years preceding Soweto.

There were also those who were inspired by the actions of the students to act in ways that caused trouble for the apartheid order. Many in this category were South Africans. As a student from the time told me, "People around the country copied what they saw in the newspapers about the uprisings in Soweto. For example in Moutse—we read about Soweto and then went around looking for things to be against. We boycotted, chased the principal, et cetera."[122] Soweto also inspired people around the world to protest in front of South Africa's embassies and to donate money, time, or just attention to the anti-apartheid struggle. In addition, while the number of people who caused trouble by acting out resistance against the available manifestations of the apartheid social order was, by any reasonable standard, quite small, many more attained a weak version of this type of resistance simply by incorporating elements of Soweto as uprising into the explanations of the events that they passed along to others.

While each individual involved in anti-apartheid activities would certainly have been able to justify their behavior by referring to some kind alternative social order, such alternatives were too varied, ill defined, and personal to qualify as the fourth level of resistance—working for a specific alternative. The legacy of Soweto was not the creation of an alternative social order, but the transformation of anti-apartheid sentiment into action and the sudden sense that future action was possible. It was not until the 1980s that the accumulation of forces pushing against apartheid would slow its momentum enough to allow others to try to steer the South African social order in a different direction. What made this dispersion and expansion of resistance possible was a discourse that cast Soweto as the beginning of the end of apartheid.

The success of this discourse is reflected in how Soweto is referred to in the words and actions of later resistance. Resistors adopted Soweto as justification for their own activities and the justifications slowly solidified into new standards of acceptable behavior.

> The '76 experience was, for us, a kind of physiotherapy. You know how a physiotherapist trains patients to be independent and to do everything for himself [sic] and that he shouldn't rely on the next person. So I say the June '76 uprising was just like a physiotherapist who trained the blacks to use their own initiative and not to depend on other people. It motivated us, especially the youth, to become more powerful.[123]

Another leader from the 1970s said, "after 1976, students came out openly to identify themselves with Nelson Mandela and the politics of the progressive movement for the first time since the repression of the 1960s."[124] Thousands of students fled the country to escape government crackdowns, most of them in October 1976. Many joined exiled resistance movements, and terrorist attacks by guerrilla forces increased markedly following a steady decline from the mid-1960s. One of the students involved said that, while there were plenty of student protests before 1976 about food and other conditions, they were not political. Afterwards, he said, students became politicized and whatever the issue was became related to apartheid.[125] This increasing politicization is one of the defining characteristics of resistance in the 1980s. The state's overwhelming superiority in the instruments of physical force had been a strong deterrent to disorder, but the legitimation of physical resistance changed that. The Cillie Commission found a general "loss of fear of violent action" which, it said, resulted from participation in violence, something it called "a baptism of fire."[126] Soweto produced a community that encouraged and held in esteem resistance activities, whether violent or not. This is the change that ultimately doomed the apartheid social order.

While there is a long and distinguished history of active resistance to apartheid (especially the Mass Actions of the 1950s), the dominant strain of resistance in South Africa immediately prior to June 1976 was Black Consciousness, which was targeted at psychological changes, not material ones. The uprisings changed the focus of resistance. The shootings gave people a reason to vent their anger in destructive ways, and for many it felt good. The story the resistance movement told about Soweto justified and legitimated action against apartheid. In the process, it also created new categories of social and political actors, actors directly opposed to how politics were understood in apartheid reality.

Changes in Identity Labels

While events created new political *actors* in Soweto, the stories of the uprising created new *categories* of actors in the political system. The Soweto uprisings added new labels to the descriptive identity repertoires of young Black South Africans. These new "selves," encapsulated into personas that were easily transportable and transferable to others around the country, legitimated activities opposed to the order the state sought to maintain. The students claimed violent action against apartheid in all its manifestations to be characteristic of Blackness, of youth, of resistance. Anti-apartheid stories turned the identities the government applied to the disorderly into implicit arguments for disorder. The same people who had been living their daily lives as Africans (presumably trying to be "good" Africans by fulfilling the expectations society attached to the label) suddenly began to act as protesters, as Black youth, as rioters. Through these actions, new identities were inserted into the political arena, bestowing on those who asserted them the power to disrupt order, and eventually the power to impose an alternative.

It is important to remember that Soweto seems to have been led by action rather than ideology. Anger and frustration spontaneously erupted into violence against the police and other symbols of authority, and this spontaneity left the average participant casting about for a rationale that could put the events into a larger context and justify such an explosion. What was most available was Black Consciousness (BC) and the positive images of Blackness that it offered. The student organization that planned the march was loosely affiliated with BC, but it represented only a very small part of the students that marched. So while its rhetoric proved to be extremely useful and powerful, the subtleties of BC philosophy were lost or reinterpreted in Soweto.

> The ideology of BC was boiled down by these angry youngsters to an emotional core identified by the students as Black Consciousness, even though it only vaguely resembled the set of complex ideas that had been elaborated by the movement's leaders. The leaders' subtle description of whites as historical oppressors who could be included in a postliberation South Africa was largely drowned out by the denunciations of whites as ascriptively distinct enemies who would remain "dogs until they died."[127]

Students grasped hold of the emotionally appealing idea that Blacks were powerful, but did not, or could not, grasp the much more complex idea that identity categories were constructed and mutable. They appropriated BC's slogans and images of powerful Black agents as a means to convey to themselves and others that they were fighting to be on top. The newspapers often referred to this as Black Power. Whether they understood the subtleties of the distinction between Black Consciousness and Black Power is unclear, but it is a good one. Black Power, which Molefe identifies as the ideology of the Pan-Africanist Congress, accepted race as a valid category of identity.[128] The students were thinking less about ending racial oppression than flipping the existing racial hierarchy and literally giving Blacks power over Whites. BC founder Steven Biko claimed Soweto as evidence of its success, but the story of the violence seems less an endorsement of redefining social categories than claiming positive, and more importantly powerful, images of Blackness.[129] Expressing themselves through the rhetoric of Black Consciousness and Black Power, Black South Africans endorsed the themes attributed to the uprising, even if the subtleties of these philosophies were lost on all but a few. "Ideological differences were not all that important. All we wanted was to push the Boers [Afrikaners] to the sea."[130]

South Africa's political and social transformation was also facilitated by the ability of actors to tap into, gain legitimacy from, and effect global patterns of thought. The ideas of Marcus Garvey and the United States Black Power movement were imported and adapted to the South African situation. The influence of recent Mozambican decolonization, in which Africans defeated Europeans, and the defeat of the South African Defense Forces who had intervened in Angola are repeatedly cited as contributing factors to the uprising. A multitude of voices around the world condemned the actions of the police and the entire system in which they operated. Global opinion coalesced around an interpretation that sided with the justice of the rioters against the sovereignty arguments of the apartheid state. These voices supplied rhetoric and arguments that the internal movement could use to understand and justify acts of resistance.

The government tried to present the riots as an unacceptable and dangerous breech of the social order and to keep those activities within the realm of the tsotsi, the criminal, the communist, and the agitator. They failed. Instead of criminals and communists on one side and policemen defending law and order on the other, the resistance movement succeeded in convincing people that the conflict was between peaceful schoolchildren and trigger-happy racists who did not value African life and were sent to impose White exploitation on Blacks. A significant portion of the Black population found the destruction that followed to be a legitimate response to the provocation, and such behavior became routine for Black youths. Both Black youths and the social standards by which their behavior were judged were changed by the experience.

When it was functioning smoothly, apartheid's system of political identity governed behavior by supplying the standards and expectations that actors were supposed to follow. Apartheid had the power of normality. The students' violent rejection of those standards created a whole new system of rules and expectations. The events in Soweto solidified and spread the interpretation of the state as actively oppressive, a portrayal which legitimated resistance for an increasing number of people. To the degree that people believed the stories that interpreted Soweto as resistance, it made sense for them to act against the system. The labels that defined the uprising produced a fundamental shift in how the students thought about themselves. The stories added labels like "youth," "protester," and "rioter" to their repertoire of identity labels and legitimated them. In this way, resisters who reached the third level of resistance were able to step out of their identities dictated by apartheid and embrace new activities opposed to the state and its social order.

CONCLUSION: THE BEGINNING OF THE END

Soweto is a useful marker in the transformation of apartheid, a site of dramatic political change, and therefore a very interesting opportunity to examine how identity and politics interact. That relationship is complex and multidirectional. When accounts of events legitimate identity labels as indicative of political actors, of agency, they can facilitate kinds of political activity previously unseen in people who claim those labels. On the other hand, spontaneous acts sometimes have obvious political implications, but no obvious explanations. When such explanations come to light, they often empower categories of identity that previously had not been recognized as bestowing political agency.

The Soweto students' spontaneous retribution for police shootings released emotional floodgates for a portion of the South African population. Anger came pouring out of people—anger at the shootings and accumulated anger at the everyday frustrations of apartheid life. Apartheid had established systems that effectively channeled the flow of everyday emotion, keeping it in acceptable limits and allowing apartheid society to function smoothly. The emotion that flowed out of the shootings, however, completely overwhelmed those normal channels, mixing with the rising tide of everyday frustrations and flooding out into the public arena. The upsurge was expressed in actions that existing categories of identity could not justify or explain. In the search for explanations, words took on new social and political meaning. For an increasing number of South Africans in the years since, these meanings validated active resistance to apartheid and the National Party government.

Soweto symbolizes a change in attitude, a change in action, and a change in the ways South Africans defined themselves in relation to one another. As Colin Bundy has said, 1976 is "the year the government finally lost its legitimacy in the eyes of the people, the year when the mantle of moral authority began to fall increasingly on the shoulders of the ANC."[131] The Soweto uprising and succeeding waves of unrest presaged the failure of apartheid's social engineers to regulate politics by squeezing it into the constraints of race. By attacking the prime benefit of constructing a social order—efficiency—the resistance movement eventually forced apartheid's social engineers to give up. The riots, though spontaneous, proved to be the perfect weapon to attack apartheid governance. Despite the armed forces' proven capacity to handle any military threat, disorder became increasingly legitimated among average Black South Africans. With no real prospects for a return to smooth cooperative social interaction within the confines of apartheid racism, there was no reason to continue it. Soweto demonstrated in a visceral way that Black South Africans could disrupt the system by exercising their power to withdraw their acceptance of their lot.

As the social legitimacy of apartheid's rules and codes of behavior came under increasing attack after the Soweto students' march, South Africans began to search for an alternative way to structure their interactions. The next chapter examines the discourse around a conflict that defined the middle stage of the transformation process—Prime Minister P.W. Botha's constitutional reforms of 1983–1984. This conflict produced resistance that not only continued to cause trouble for apartheid, but also began to solidify the alternative order that would eventually take its place.

Chapter Five

CONSTITUTIONAL REFORM, 1983–1984

If the South African social order is understood as a body in motion, rolling through time, then the Soweto uprising altered its momentum, changing both its bearing and its inertial force. While the revolt posed no real danger to the continuance of the state, which maintained both control over the apparatus of material production and a virtual monopoly on the use of force, Soweto did create new social frictions, altering many of the conditions that had allowed apartheid to prosper. Chief among these were changes to Black South Africans' implicit acceptance of their status as political objects. Soweto and its aftermath demonstrated that, while Black South Africans still lacked the power to create a new social order, they did have the power to disrupt the existing one and to render it inefficient. In order to deal with this newly realized power and try to regain the economic efficiency and social coherence of the previous decade, White elites decided to adapt apartheid. They called this process reform.

The idea of reform suggests orderly change, and it was employed by the South African government to frame its proposals as necessary, both to deal with an altered political environment and to prevent a much more dangerous, chaotic, revolutionary future. The mainstream political acknowledgment of a wide variety of pressures on the apartheid system, including global pressures for economic and social sanctions, unleashed a spectrum of political discourse previously unknown in South Africa. There was turmoil in White politics as the National Party shifted away from its roots in Afrikaner nationalism to a more class-based constituency, a move which alienated many of the more conservative Afrikaners but won it new adherents among the more business- and internationally-minded English-speaking Whites. The apparently genetic political incompetence that apartheid attributed to Indians and Coloureds was somehow undone and members of these communities were offered means to become responsible citizens of the republic. While Africans were still excluded from these official channels, they slowly found extra-parliamentary political power that they increasingly exercised in these years. As a result, the number of political agents inside South Africa increased dramatically.

Reform was not an attempt to end racism or White privilege, but rather to make these core principles more practicable by altering apartheid at the margins. It was designed to do this by investing more South Africans in the existing system, thereby releasing much of the mounting pressure for more radical changes. There was, however, no consensus on what the balance should be, and by raising the possibility of change, the government significantly widened a discourse that previously had existed only among a very insulated elite. The discourse surrounding this official politicization of apartheid and the official and unofficial expansion of political agency therefore provide a remarkable opportunity to study the political identity of South Africa's transition.

REFORM, RESISTANCE, REPRESSION

Reform

The end of the 1970s was a time of crisis for many White South Africans. The violence of Soweto had ended one of apartheid's primary benefits, the opportunity to live a rationalized life of privilege without being confronted with its more negative effects. A number of less dramatic, but just as far-reaching changes in the economy and in South Africa's international reputation led to an increasing sense of isolation and unease. For some, these changes elicited the kind of fiercely defensive responses reminiscent of the founding myths of the Afrikaner nation. For others, however, there was a growing belief that some changes needed to be made. These reactions accentuated existing divisions within the governing National Party. Beginning in the 1960s, the Afrikaner elite had split into left, right, and centrist groups. To distinguish themselves, the main left faction adopted the label *verligte,* usually translated as "enlightened," and the right called themselves *verkrampte,* a term related to the Afrikaans word for "narrow."

The verkrampte wing saw itself as the guardian of pure apartheid and worked to resist any change to its policy of radical separation. They preached hard-line racism, the chosen status of the Afrikaner volk, and apartheid as a moral vision. Yielding ground on any aspect of the policy, they argued, put the society on a slippery slope toward fundamental change. Verkrampte political rhetoric usually combined arguments for defending White interests and those about the divine and natural foundations of racial difference. For many verkrampte, apartheid was the social manifestation of fundamental truths and the institutional arrangement best suited to governing a racially diverse polity. This message seemed to play best with poorer Whites who stood to lose the most from increasing opportunities for Blacks.

The verligte, on the other hand, seemed less interested in the maintenance of apartheid as a coherent justification for White privilege than in the maintenance of that privilege itself. From their perspective, a variety of economic and social changes had taken place as South Africa developed into a regional industrial power, and the events of 1976 were only the most graphic indication that the apartheid system should be changed as well. White rule was not a moral imperative for them, but rather a mechanism to White privilege. In a purely pragmatic assessment of the factors that would contribute to the maintenance of that way of life, the verligte suggested a change in strategy to update apartheid policies, to make them more palatable to a variety of audiences. The verligte tended to come from the bourgeoisie, the English-speaking community, and the new wealth of the Afrikaners, and they had a deep interest in protecting their gains from the economic and social threats posed by internal disorder and South Africa's developing status as an international pariah.

Neither side in this elite debate was suggesting an end to Afrikaner hegemony, although the verkramptes certainly tried to frame the reformers as doing just that. In response, reformers sloganized a line from a speech Prime Minister P. W. Botha gave to the party congress in Durban in August 1979 in which he claimed that the government had to "adapt or die."[1] Because neither camp had control of all governmental decisions, policy remained somewhat schizophrenic. Reform produced many changes in laws that benefited Black South Africans.[2] At the same time, however, the government continued to push homelands into "independence," trying to fulfill the apartheid vision of making all Blacks foreigners in the Republic.

The reform that did take place was possible in part because reformers were able to portray South Africa's situation as a crisis. In a series of policy reports written while he was Minister of Defense, P. W. Botha framed the forces aligned against South Africa as requiring more than just military responses. Botha even gave that crisis a name—the "Total Onslaught." "This 'onslaught' was seen as an orchestrated attempt by the Soviet Union, naively assisted by western liberals, to destroy white political and economic power in South Africa."[3] In response, Botha proposed a "Total Strategy." After Botha took over as Prime Minister in 1978, the plan was implemented even more vigorously, combining concessions designed to broaden popular support for the White minority regime and an aggressive military posture aimed at neutralizing opposition both at home and abroad. Robert Price divides Botha's total strategy into three analytical aspects— reform, repression, and regional hegemony.[4] The strategy was to find the right mix of these policy ingredients to maintain the most important aspects of White privilege, even if it meant jettisoning other aspects that in the past had been presented as integral to privilege overall. Price says there were four principal objectives of reform: to free the economy of apartheid's inefficiencies; to create a Black middle class whose interests would be threatened by radical change; to co-opt a significant portion of the Black population by creating opportunities for economic advancement and by ameliorating living conditions in urban townships;

and to normalize South Africa's international status by bringing its sociopolitical arrangements into line with globally dominant standards.[5] The need to placate the international community provided a check on the amount of repression that the government could use to meet its other goals.

The widespread belief that South Africa was in crisis, albeit one created by others, gave the government freedom to investigate new solutions to societal problems. In the late 1970s, Commissions of Inquiry were assigned to investigate several pillars of apartheid policy that had come to be considered problems—political, debatable, and essentially solvable problems. But almost all of the commissions' specific recommendations were rejected by the government. However, these commission findings do represent a model for what the verligte meant by reform. The commission reports never questioned the fundamental division of society into racial groups or the proposition that race determined potential development paths or levels of civilization. Indeed, Adam Ashforth argues that for the first time in official discourse the authors of these reports were able to omit definitions and descriptions of apartheid's racial categorization framework, treating it as a simple, apolitical description of reality.[6] Race became subtly stronger because it became an assumed, natural part of the social backdrop against which decisions had to be made. From this perspective, change needed to take place only at the level of bureaucracy and implementation. Reform was about how to build a state that conformed sufficiently to anti-apartheid demands to allow South Africa to shed its status as an international pariah without upsetting White privilege.

Integral to the process of reform was the election of P. W. Botha to the office of Prime Minister in 1978. Botha quickly consolidated his power and reorganized the structure of the highest levels of government. These institutional changes provided him with the power to oversee a transformation in the basic structure of National Party rule. Afrikaner economic advancement had diluted "the glue of ethnic unity," and the new elites were more interested in protecting their capital investments than the ideological coherence of apartheid racism.

> In 1978, the appointment of P. W. Botha as Prime Minister not only confirmed the ascendancy of the Afrikaner bourgeoisie in the National Party but also marked the consolidation of a new political alliance between monopoly capital and the upper echelons of the military establishment. The Total Strategy doctrine represented a comprehensive political programme that aimed not only to restructure the dominant bloc of class forces but also to forge new forms of legitimation that relied more upon market forces than on formalized racial discrimination to secure bourgeois rule.[7]

Reform, however, was not instantaneous. Botha was very careful to hammer together this constituency and maintain it through what amounted to a questioning of many of apartheid's fundamental truths. The hand of the anti-reformists was strengthened by the good economic years of the early 1980s, when gold prices floated around $850 an ounce and even the smallest pieces of the economic pie were getting a little larger. The National Party compensated for the desertion of many hard-core Afrikaner nationalists and apartheid true believers by adding the support of English-speaking big business supporters. In 1982, the verkramptes left the NP and formed the Conservative Party (KP), which took over the mantle of Afrikaner nationalism and apartheid. While the schism was traumatic, this break freed Botha up from the politics of maintaining NP unity and allowed more reforms to be implemented.

The crowning achievement of the reform effort was the new constitution that Botha shepherded through Parliament and a White referendum in 1983. Its cornerstone was the creation of two new houses of Parliament—one for Coloureds and one for Indians. Even though Africans were still excluded from participation in Republic politics (ostensibly because they were able to participate in their homeland structures), these reforms shook the very foundations of apartheid. The constitution granted "other" races a say (albeit one neutered by a *de facto* White veto) in the governance of "White South Africa."

THE CONSTITUTION

In 1976, coincidentally a mere two days after the explosion of violence in Soweto, an official Commission of Inquiry released a report recommending improvements to the political status of Coloureds. The government immediately rejected most of the commission's recommendations, but in the aftermath of Soweto, the mere existence of even this limited constitutional debate made constitutional reform seem plausible. Unexpectedly, there seemed to be the political will to change the constitution, and in 1977, a committee made up of cabinet members produced a plan that came to be known as the government's 1977 constitution. The NP associated itself with these proposals during the 1977 White parliamentary elections and interpreted its ensuing victory as the electorate's endorsement of constitutional change. However, other political developments soon diverted the initiative's momentum, and the issue was moved into South Africa's political backwaters, consigned to a select committee chaired by Alwyn L. Schlebusch. Over the next five years, this governmental mechanism for studying the constitution went through several iterations. The Schlebusch Committee was turned into an official commission of inquiry, which in 1981 mutated into the President's Council, which included Coloured and Indian elites.[8] In the campaign to sell the 1980s constitutional changes to the South African public, the Council was presented as the "first multi-ethnic institution of its type on the South African political scene" and as a "living laboratory," for how a multiracial institution could share power in a framework of consensus-based politics.[9] In practice, however, the Council had no real influence on the final shape of the constitution, which was the result of backroom wrangling among National Party elite.

Botha unveiled the constitutional plan at a National Party caucus in 1982 and characterized it as "healthy power-sharing," a phrase that caused some turmoil and that was later replaced by "joint responsibility." After drafts and refinements, Parliament adopted the new constitution on September 9, 1983, and it immediately became law.[10] On November 2, 1983, Whites went to the polls to register whether or not they were in favor of the implementation of the new law. The Constitution was approved by a two-thirds majority of White voters. The government refused to sanction proposed referenda on the constitution in the Coloured and Indian communities because of the serious risk to the plan if the constitution were to be rejected. There is evidence that this was a wise decision. A boycott of the elections for the Coloured and Indian houses that were held in August 1984 produced a turnout of only 19.6 percent of eligible Coloured voters and 16.3 percent of eligible Indian voters.[11]

The political structure that the new constitution set up was a departure from the Westminster-style Parliament that had governed South Africa since 1910. It established a three-chamber, or tri-cameral, Parliament, with one house each for the White, Coloured, and Indian population groups and the proportion of representatives approximating that of the population—four Whites for every two Coloureds and for every one Indian.[12] Voters in each population group elected most but not all of the members for their house, with the remainder appointed by the president. Parliament was supposed to work by consensus, but if a stalemate arose between the houses, the issue was referred to the executive branch for resolution. The division of powers was handled through a conceptual distinction between "general" and "own" affairs. General affairs were those deemed to concern the society at large, while each house of Parliament would have responsibility for issues that, according to the logic of apartheid, needed group-specific policies and solutions.[13]

The executive branch consisted of the new office of State President and a body called the President's Council. Both were indirectly elected by a body of legislators drawn proportionately from Parliament, although the president also had the authority to appoint one-quarter of the Council's sixty members. The proportions and the labyrinthine rules of procedure guaranteed that the dominant White party would be able to implement any policy it wanted. This guarantee was the result of an enormous shift in power from Parliament to the executive branch, and to the State President in particular. One commentator compared the new system to "an executive autocracy."[14] Presidential power was basically unhindered; there was no bill of rights or provision for judicial review, and almost all of the constitution was alterable with a simple majority in Parliament.[15] Indeed, all the National Party needed to maintain control of the state was one-third plus one of the votes in the White body.

The exclusion of Africans was one of the major stumbling blocks for the government's attempt to sell the new constitution as a significant reform overseas. This aspect of the constitution came to overshadow all the other reforms in the minds of many, and rather than spawning the acceptance for which Botha had hoped, the reform era ended up bringing more concentrated international approbation. Anti-apartheid activists were able to portray Botha's reforms as entrenching rather than alleviating apartheid. The widespread, grassroots reaction against the South African government and their policies was translated into both domestic and international pressure for foreign governments to impose sanctions on South Africa. In 1983 and 1984, however, most Blacks still were largely uninterested in politics. "The struggle" was more likely to have meaning in relation to their constant efforts to keep their menial jobs and eke out a living on the margins of wealthy White society. Only 48.8 percent of African respondents to a survey conducted in the Vaal Triangle area around Johannesburg in June and July 1984 admitted to having heard of the new Parliament. Of those, 23.8 percent said it was a good thing and 60.5 percent said it was a bad thing while 15.7 percent did not know.[16] The accuracy of responses to such politically charged questions may be suspect, but the numbers certainly would have been much different six months later, after a wave of violent protests centered on the constitution had swept South Africa.

In the end, reform failed to staunch the flow of anger and resentment that apartheid engendered in Black South Africans. Instead, the new constitution provided a unifying focus for dissent and the national consciousness that fit local issues into a conceptual framework, politicized them, and linked them to a national and international resistance against apartheid. The primary characteristic of South Africa's new political era was defined not by Botha's reformed governmental structure, but by a surprisingly virulent strain of opposition that used the discursive opportunities of the new system to allow opposition activists to challenge the whole social order. The government's constitutional reform proposals became the catalyst that changed fragmented and distinct local resistance activities into parts of a nationwide struggle against apartheid and imbued those activities with the energy and confidence of a global movement against racism.

Resistance

In the years 1980 through 1984, Black political activity was decentralized. While widespread social order had been reestablished by the late 1970s, new strategies of resistance were created that organized and empowered Black South Africans in consciously political ways. These changes made resistance a real possibility for many more South Africans, further problematized the apartheid understanding of Black abilities, and fundamentally changed the relationship of Blacks to the government.

The resistance of the early 1980s began as empowerment of Black people at the community level. The state's successful restoration of control over the townships and the relative strength of the South African economy produced a political economy in which the most practical expenditure of energy seemed to be toward the improvement of living conditions. A proliferation of smaller community-based opposition groups focused on translating into political action the anger and frustration that had come to the surface and been justified through the Soweto uprisings. Neighbors came together to form organizations designed to solve community problems. These organizations came to be called "civic associations," or just "civics." Originally these township organizations were formed around local, practical, mundane issues. The first association was formed in

Diepkloof, Soweto, to help victims of a car accident. Because these localized movements were focused on the practicalities of everyday life, the government initially embraced them as evidence that Blacks were becoming invested in their situation. Civics, however, quickly became standing committees that sought redress for concrete community-based grievances against private businesses and local governments. Civics came into their own in the African townships around Port Elizabeth and the Coloured townships around Cape Town to deal with specific issues like street repair and bus shelter construction.

For the average urban Black in South Africa, participating in an organization that made and implemented decisions about community or social life was something novel. Apartheid reality was designed around the premise that Blacks were genetically less capable of making the kinds of decisions necessary to manage themselves in a modern society. Apartheid cast Whites as political decision-makers for Blacks who were incapable of understanding modern governance. The government and media interpretations of the events of Soweto as reactive mob violence did little to change White impressions of Blacks as easily excitable but uncivilized and unsophisticated with respect to politics. The resistance that bubbled up during the early 1980s embodied a political and organizational sophistication that demonstrated to all, not least Blacks themselves, that Black South Africans were indeed capable of political thought, organization, and activity.

This kind of resistance was in part a conscious decision. Anthony Marx argues that the economic recovery of 1979–1981 allowed opposition an interlude from mass militancy and state repression to begin to implement a change in strategy that had been discussed in group prison cells and encouraged by older veterans, like Nelson Mandela, who remained in jail.

> They set out to form local organizations of civil society to press for material gains and later for further political reforms. By 1983, mass participation, rekindled in the 1970s, had been channeled away from outbursts of anger and into more structured forms of mass organization following a national agenda consistent with that originally set forth in the ANC's Freedom Charter.[17]

This mobilization at the grassroots level was starkly different from, and perhaps represents a lesson of, the aftermath of the Sharpeville massacre in 1960, when the government efficiently decapitated resistance energy and imposed a stranglehold on social order for the next decade and a half, broken only by the schoolchildren of Soweto. The decision to diversify mobilization efforts was intended to prevent the uprisings of 1976 from becoming just another missed opportunity.

Government restrictions also helped to localize the political focus in the early 1980s. "[T]he pass laws restricting freedom of movement, the danger of detention, and inconvenient transportation links made it difficult for Black activists to travel from township to township."[18] The result was a decentralized and regionally diverse movement. This strategy produced a rich environment for grassroots, civil society mobilization that was completely different from anything urban

Black South Africans had ever experienced. When the government introduced its plans for constitutional reform, many of the informal organizations that "honeycombed the social fabric of all but the smallest and most remote of the townships" coalesced into a loose federation that formalized their opposition to apartheid into a national movement called the United Democratic Front (UDF).[19]

The idea of organizing these diverse activities around an anti-apartheid theme was first proposed by Allan Boesak in a speech in January 1983. In arguing against the government's constitutional proposals, Boesak exemplified resistance of the third level—causing trouble.

> This is the politics of refusal, and it is the only dignified response black people can give in this situation. In order to do this we need a united front. . . . There is no reason why churches, civic associations, trade unions, student organizations, and sports bodies should not unite on this issue, pool our resources, inform the people of the fraud which is about to be perpetrated in their name, and on the day of the election expose the plans for what they are.[20]

Although Tom Lodge has suggested that some form of nationwide movement probably would have arisen even without the government's constitutional proposals, it is clear that the constitutional reform plans "supplied the galvanizing impetus" for the UDF and provided its diverse form and initial strength.[21] Using the constitutional proposals as foil meant that the focus of UDF organizing was the apartheid system rather than Whites or specific groups. The special role of the constitutional proposals was attested to by one of its organizers, Patrick "Terror" Lekota. "If anybody is to be blamed for the formation of the UDF, it must be the government. If the government did not introduce that [constitutional] dispensation which was not satisfactory, we would not have had the ground to form the UDF."[22] In order to sell the process as democratic both at home and abroad, the government encouraged open debate on the constitutional proposals, creating opportunities that were deftly exploited by anti-apartheid groups. The most lasting effect of the reform strategy designed to divide Blacks against each other was that Blacks became united in resistance.

The UDF was officially launched August 20, 1983, at the Rocklands Community Center in Mitchell's Plain, a Coloured township of Cape Town. Estimates of the size of the crowd jamming the building to the rafters vary from 6,000 to 15,000 people, of whom 1,500 were official delegates from over 500 organizations. The UDF was a federation, organized through a hierarchy of committees that brought together representatives of existing organizations of all sorts. By November 25, the organization claimed an affiliated membership of approximately two million people.[23] In most localities, the UDF drew members from three types of groups: a civic association, a women's group, and a youth congress. These affiliates retained their own identities and purposes, making the UDF very diverse. For many of the groups, the only common ground was opposition to some aspect of the government's reforms.

This polyclass political approach was matched by an eclectic, barnstorming style. A host of tactics were used—free-wheeling petition drives contesting electricity billing procedures, mass meetings challenging rental or transport fare increases. These crusading mass campaigns, aimed at the redress of immediate grievances, were reminiscent in tone of the tactical approach of the ANC and its allies during its "over-ground" heyday in the 1950s.[24]

In order to keep this diverse group solidified, the UDF resisted all positively defined ideology and only defined itself negatively, in opposition to apartheid.[25] From the very beginning, however, the UDF relied heavily on "Charterism," a movement that grew up around the ANC's 1955 Freedom Charter, for a panoply of symbols, freedom songs, heroes, and legends. "By tying current acts to a historical tradition, it ennobled them, infusing the daily efforts of local activists and their sympathizers with moral and emotional weightiness."[26] Evoking Charterism's mythology to give power to a diverse group of organizations made sense both logistically and as a potential platform for reconciliation.[27]

The rhetoric of the UDF also politicized people's personal everyday struggles by conceptually linking them to apartheid as racism. As people fought to rectify their own troubles, they were able to claim that they were fighting not only a national fight against apartheid, but also contributing to a global movement against racism.[28] All sorts of ordinary South Africans were able to see themselves as local, national, and global *agents,* and to see each local committee's experiments in organizational structure as manifestations of "people's power," as "a new structure of government, first for the townships that they believed were being liberated from Pretoria's control, and eventually for all of South Africa."[29]

The people's power movement began in 1985 in the sleepy little town of Inkwenkwezi, a township attached to the Indian Ocean town of Port Alfred. In June 1985, the township's civic association initiated a boycott of Port Alfred's White businesses to try to bring attention and improvements to the living conditions in their township. The boycott met with stunning success, in part because the demands were local and within the power of merchants to affect. White businessmen worked hard to meet the residents' demands and the boycott ended after three weeks. This success marked a significant shift in opposition politics.

> Port Alfred's black township had seized the initiative and set the agenda, forcing whites to respond. For the first time, a black community had wielded power, not just resisted it. Within weeks, black consumer boycotts spread through the Eastern Cape, hammering white retailers in fifteen other towns.[30]

The boycotts not only won important concessions from local businesses, but they also lent a sense of unity to the civic associations who employed them. The boycotts began the process of linking individuals and grassroots groups together in resistance.

Such local organizations were becoming firmly entrenched all over the country and resistance leaders began to claim living spaces in the name of "the people" and to take over many of the services that are normally reserved for the modern state. In effect, civics weakened the concept of the South African state by implementing governance alternatives around which opposition could continue to solidify. "UDF activists were not so naive as to believe that the state would cede local power to such popular structures, but they did believe that state power could be offset, if not replaced, in the 'liberated zones' of townships that the local authorities had not been able to control."[31] This transition from the third to the fourth level of resistance is the most lasting legacy of the government's constitutional reforms.

Just as each person experiences the social order through individual filters and experiences, resistance is also personal. As some South Africans found civics and other more organizational forms of activism, others turned to violence. On September 3, 1984, the new constitutional structures were initiated with great ceremony in the parliamentary capital of Cape Town. The day was celebrated in a radically different fashion in South Africa's industrial center, the Vaal Triangle area near Johannesburg. A work and school stayaway called by the Vaal Civic Association was enforced by young people who stopped busses and burned shops and public buildings. The resulting police crackdown inspired students in Soweto and other nearby townships to join the stayaway. By mid-October, all the townships in the industrial heartland were involved. At the end of October, the government sent seven thousand soldiers of the South African Defense Forces (SADF) into the Vaal townships, but the repression only spread the resistance. Over the next two months, the violence in the Vaal Triangle intensified and became the catalyst for a countywide insurrection.[32]

> Six months after the Vaal uprising, news of violence became as routine as the weather report. A typical police bulletin carried news of a dozen incidents of unrest, ranging from stones throwings to shootouts. Thousands of Blacks took part in weekly rituals of angry confrontation, which often climaxed in deaths—which led to political funerals—which led to new confrontations. The violence took many forms—pitting police against blacks, black rebels against black collaborators, black rivals against each other. Some incidents were planned, others were spontaneous.[33]

The scope and intensity of this violence vastly outweighed the violence that followed Soweto. Official casualty figures for the sixteen months of violence in 1976–1977 were surpassed in the first five months of 1985 alone.[34]

In early 1985, the ANC leadership in Lusaka issued a call for Black South Africans to "make the townships ungovernable." The call became a slogan, and it was answered in unprecedented scope. "By mid-year Pretoria indirectly acknowledged that this goal had been achieved, at least in some areas, when it began to refer to the townships of the Eastern Cape as 'no-go areas'—places that were too dangerous for the South African police to enter except in convoys of armoured personnel carriers."[35] While in 1976, the violence was contained to about two hundred mainly urban Black communities,

> [t]he insurrection of 1984–86 gripped virtually the entire black population outside of remote rural areas. While the young comrades were its militant vanguard, the insurrection drew support and participation from virtually the entire social spectrum of black South Africa, save the tiny commercial petit bourgeoisie. The rich associational life that had characterized the townships during the early 1980s and the existence of the UDF which linked together geographically and functionally diverse associational elements and gave them a national political orientation, laid the organizational foundation for this aspect of insurrection.[36]

The violence and the death toll continued to grow throughout the first six months of 1985. In June 1985, one of the UDF's most successful and magnetic organizers, Matthew Goniwe was killed along with three other activists on a lonely stretch of road. As the organization converged on the town of Craddock in the Great Karoo desert on July 21 for the funeral, the government declared the first official State of Emergency since 1960. The timing was designed to help the government round up the UDF leadership and thus decapitate the movement. The declaration signaled a ratcheting up in the intensity of the conflict and the beginning of even more violence.

REPRESSION

The State of Emergency affected only thirty-six of the country's 266 magisterial districts. By limiting the geographical scope of the emergency, the government portrayed the unrest as limited and suggested that a few surgical strikes would restore order. The strategy of decapitation had worked twenty-five years earlier, when the arrest of Robert Sobukwe on the first day of the Pan-Africanist Congress (PAC) anti-pass campaign effectively set the PAC adrift.[37] Trapped in apartheid's grouped mind-set and misled by the assessments of right-wing security policemen on the ground, Botha and the government believed that without the leadership the organized resistance to apartheid would collapse in the same way. "Common perceptions of the township rebellions amongst whites are of mob violence, irrational boycott-tactics, fiery incomprehensible leaders and communist agitators. Very few understand the logic of township violence and where it is leading to."[38] In the 1980s, however, the resistance movement was very different. The UDF was not a centralized organization as the PAC had been. The diffusion of grassroots organizations in the early 1980s had dispersed political responsibility, and there were simply too many people who considered themselves political agents for the government's tactics to be effective.

Rather than disheartening the populace, the emergency inflamed it. Government arrests initiated a cycle of unrest, killings, funerals, and more unrest, and new leaders moved up to take the place of those detained, leaders who for a variety of reasons had fewer incentives to restrain the emotions and actions of the people. As Bishop Tutu had warned, by detaining Black leaders the government had created a "leaderless mob."[39] As student leader Mpho Mashinini told Steven Mufson,

> [t]he emergency caught people unaware. The leadership was picked up and no one was outside to direct things. There was no UDF to tell people what action to take. It was left in people's own hands. As a result it changed the pattern of daily struggle. More people were mobilized and conscientized than ever before.[40]

This was the power of the grassroots framework; the townships were full of people who believed they could be political actors and even political leaders. In some cases the emergency deflected UDF strategy toward consumer boycotts and action at the level of the street committee, but rebellion and political organizing also increased.

In addition, even though the State of Emergency was limited to thirty-six areas, those areas were widely dispersed and the violence was clearly a national issue. As a national organization, the UDF was able to frame the government's response as a reason for unity in resisting apartheid.

> Whereas activism in the early 1980s had been directed at local demands, repression made it clear that material concessions were no longer available and that grievances could only and finally be resolved by challenging national state structures. Although the protests remained locally organized, by 1986 the demand associated with such protests no longer were confined to local issues but now called for the unbanning of the ANC, the release of Nelson Mandela, and an end to all apartheid legislation.[41]

In the same way that the constitutional changes provided an impetus to unity, the State of Emergency helped to tie people's own experiences into national and global conceptual frameworks that justified resistance activities against the state.

The first partial State of Emergency was rescinded on March 7, 1986, after eight months and immediately before a seven-member delegation from the Commonwealth of former British colonies called the Eminent Persons Group (EPG) arrived to explore the situation and report back on whether sanctions should be implemented. After some initial conciliatory moves, President Botha unexpectedly sabotaged the negotiations, and the EPG returned to recommend comprehensive and mandatory sanctions against South Africa. The imposition of comprehensive sanctions and the accompanying damage to South Africa's claims to being a member of the Western, civilized, anticommunist club of nations severed many of the restraints that had been holding Botha back from more aggressive action. "Once it was prepared to absorb the domestic and international costs of massive repression, Pretoria, its security forces loyal and intact, was in a position to throttle the township insurrection."[42] With the tenth anniversary of the Soweto uprisings approaching, Botha declared a nationwide emergency on June 12, 1986. The era of reform ended, replaced by military repression and weak attempts to improve material living conditions in a few townships. The State of Emergency was renewed annually until 1990.

This nationwide emergency was more debilitating for resistance than the partial emergency of eleven months before. It included severe restrictions on the media, which often allowed the police to use extreme force with impunity. The state also intensified police and army activity, including deploying two new types of Black police officers, which increased the size of the national police force by one-third.[43] This time the government confronted the decentralized nature of opposition with a policy of police sweeps and massive detentions that broke the back of the local structures, except in Soweto, which was large enough to hide some organizers. At the same time the government set out to lure adherents away from the UDF through a program known as Winning Hearts and Minds, or WHAM. In an effort to dilute the resistance movement and create a sense that lives would improve more through the status quo, the government spent an estimated 3.2 billion rand in 1987–1988 on improvements to thirty-four locations.[44] This combination of increased police activity, the loss of leadership, and material improvements slowed the momentum of the UDF and quickly ended widespread popular hopes for apartheid's imminent demise. The government was largely successful because of the movement's ideological incoherence, which had been its initial strength. When government strategy targeted this weakness, the movement foundered and was unable to resist when it was banned in 1988.

Anthony Marx has argued that the UDF represented a necessary stage in the development of opposition—a consolidation of energy behind the dismantling of apartheid. Even though the government was eventually able to reimpose order through force and even to maintain it through the quasi-military occupation of the townships, it was clear that apartheid would never again be able to provide the same basis for efficient cooperation and order. This fundamental delegitimization created a kind of functional anomie among the bulk of the Black population. Into this space stepped the ideological coherence and focused resistance of the Black labor movement, whose small but coherent membership was able to combine the philosophical cohesion of the unorganized Black Consciousness movement with the diffuse praxis of the UDF.[45] This combination carried the torch of opposition in the phase immediately before F. W. de Klerk's dramatic move toward negotiation in 1990.

This is the story of the era of reform, roughly a decade of debate that altered the momentum of the South African social order in important ways. Insights into how these changes took place can be found in the rhetoric employed in the negotiations. As a practical matter, it is necessary to limit the discourse by focusing on the discussion of its culminating debate over the constitutional reforms of 1983–1984. Much of this discourse is preserved in artifacts of the campaigns surrounding the White referendum on the constitution in 1983.

COMPETING DISCOURSES ON THE CONSTITUTION

On November 2, 1983, White South Africans went to the polls to vote yes or no on a single question—"Are you in favor of the implementation of the Constitution Act, 1983, as approved by Parliament?" The question had been strategically worded to force together in the same "no" camp those who wanted more reform and those who wanted none at all. In this way Botha and the verligte movement were able to present the reforms as solidly centrist, and the constitution as the only real option for change. The middle of the road balancing act was successful in producing a resounding victory in favor of the new constitution. Two thirds of those who went to the polls voted "yes," including a majority of the traditional National Party base and an estimated twenty-five to thirty percent of voters who traditionally voted for the liberal Progressive Federal Party, the party of parliamentary opposition.[46] The strategy, however, proved ineffective in the political universe beyond the Whites-only referendum. The victorious Botha did not take into account the explosion of new resistance from people who were only then finding an effective political voice. For these South Africans, the referendum represented not an end, but the beginning of a discourse that both sealed apartheid's fate and determined the core elements of the social order that would succeed it. The discourse evolved from the opportunities presented by the referendum campaign

THE MEDIA'S STORY—REFLECTING SOCIAL DIVISIONS

The South African media played a large role in facilitating the debate over the constitution and the yes/no choice provided by the referendum, but by itself did not create a particular interpretation of the debate or even much of a vocabulary through which to speak about it. Unlike the sudden explosion of the Soweto conflict, an event that lent itself to an independent perspective as news, the constitutional discourse was initiated and largely contained within the formal political realm. The explicitly political nature of the debate meant that the primary components of the discourse originated with politicians. Mainstream newspapers, in what was probably thought of as a demonstration of journalistic integrity, framed the stories that they told primarily through the comments, speeches, and letters of others. These views came from a range of political parties, well-known non-politicians whose opinions became the stuff of full page advertisements, and regular citizens who wrote letters to the editor. These texts carried on a kind of dialogue with each other. While newspapers certainly benefited from the government's need to portray the discourse over the constitution as a truly democratic, free exchange of ideas, most of the English language newspapers waited until a week or so before the vote to formally advocate a yes or a no vote.

Given that the parameters of the choices were so narrow, with the referendum focused on a single question, newspapers really reflected the arguments put forth by the society at large. Even the state-owned radio and television outlets presented both sides of the debate, although the SABC was roundly criticized in the English-language press for the biased nature of its coverage. The main role of the newspapers therefore seemed to be to sift the various positions and to organize the information for their readers. The arguments were simplified under the titles "Yes" and "No." The Yeses were those in favor of the constitution, and their arguments were variations on the theme that while they were far from perfect, the reforms represented the best available way to deal with South Africa's changing political environment. The No arguments had several contradictory themes. The conservative right, represented by the Conservative Party and its leader Andries Treurnicht, argued that the changes went too far and were dangerous to the stability of South Africa. The liberal left, represented by the Progressive Federal Party and its leader Frederick van Zyl Slabbert, argued that the reforms were not an incremental change for the better but an entrenchment of racial politics and National Party rule. Much of the debate in the English-language press concerned the dilemma for liberals that all no votes could be claimed by the far right as a rejection of any reform.

In the week leading up to the Wednesday vote, newspapers tried to condense the diverse arguments into easy-to-handle lists. The editors of the *Star* found four principal reasons for each position. Those voting no argued that 1. Coloureds and Indians were not consulted about the changes; 2. Africans would see a yes vote as hostility; 3. the reforms would "constitutionalise" apartheid for the first time by institutionalizing racial groups; and 4. the constitution entrenched white party rule. The arguments for a yes vote were that 1. the reforms would bring a mixed race cabinet to power for the first time; 2. Blacks would be no worse off than they were before the new constitution; 3. a yes vote would humiliate and sideline the far right; and 4. reforms could set the stage all kinds of changes that are currently unforeseeable. These lists demonstrate that the editors presumed they were speaking to a liberal audience.[47] Political columnist Peter Sullivan came up with a slightly longer list involving arguments he had heard for each of four options: yes, no, abstention, and purposefully spoiling the ballot paper.[48] Many of the arguments repeat those in the *Star's* list, but Sullivan added several key phrases. In favor of a yes vote, he argued that the constitution was a step in the right direction, that the outside world wanted it affirmed, and that there was a "hidden agenda" that would bring Africans into the mix soon after the constitution took effect. For the no vote, he said the new constitution was a horrible legal document that was fatally flawed and unworkable, that the bureaucracy would be tripled and taxes raised, and that the NP should not be trusted with even greater powers. Spoiling the ballot, he said, would send a message that both choices were wrong. Abstention would demonstrate an unwillingness to participate in what was essentially an internal National Party squabble and would be a vote with the majority who had no vote.

When the editorial boards of these newspapers advocated particular positions in the final week or so before the vote, the divisions among the White population were evident in their respectful tone, almost always acknowledging the difficult of the decision. The major Afrikaans papers all came out in favor of a yes vote. The English-language press, however, split on the question. Of the major English dailies and weeklies, six advised their readers to vote yes and ten advocated voting no.[49] The *Daily Dispatch* editors voted yes, arguing that rejection of these reforms would probably stop any progress that had already been made. The *Citizen* argued that a yes would not end change, while a no probably would. The *Argus* voted no, calling the proposal half baked and ill-conceived. Kimberley's

Diamond Fields Advertiser argued that voting no would force the government to go back to the drawing board and come up with a better proposal. The *Pretoria News* said the constitution was at best wholly inadequate. One paper, the *Star*, advocated abstaining from the vote, arguing that there was no acceptable choice, that a large abstention would send the correct message to foreigners while keeping options open, and that it would show solidarity with the vast majority who had no vote. Spoiling the ballot by marking both boxes or neither was not advocated by any of the papers, but it was affirmed by Anglican bishop of Johannesburg and received considerable discussion in letters to the editor.

Reading the newspapers from this critical juncture in the transformation of apartheid conveys a sense of the passion stirred up by altering the apartheid social order. What is striking, however, is that even given the relative freedom afforded the press by the government at this point in history, very few opinions were unique to the press. With the exception of the *Star's* promotion of abstention, the newspapers simply reflected the arguments of the political parties to a greater or lesser degree. The papers would probably have argued that this should not be surprising, that the job of a free press is to reflect social views rather than to create them. In this case, it appears that they largely succeeded. The labels used in the newspapers, by reporters, editors, and writers of letters, were nearly indistinguishable from those that appeared in the quotations of politicians from the White mainstream. As was evident from the resulting victory, the government succeeded in setting the agenda and controlling the parameters of the debate in White society. This successful strategy is reflected in texts that represented the government's argument.

THE GOVERNMENT'S STORY—REFORMING APARTHEID

In the discourse over the constitution, because the government was not the defender of the status quo but rather an advocate of change, it is necessary to explore briefly the arguments for the continuation of apartheid. A sizable percentage of the White population still believed in the vision of reality in which apartheid made sense. The debate over reform was the government's attempt to pry these Whites loose from this metaphysics. Those who refused to budge found their perspectives were now represented by the Herstigte Nasionale Party (HNP), which had broken away from the National Party in 1969 over the integration of sports facilities, and the Conservative Party, which had splintered off in 1982 over the constitution. There was also an ominous fringe of unreconstituted racists for whom parliamentary opposition was not violent enough. From the right, the reforms were anathema not only to the Afrikaner "volk" (nation), but to reality itself, and the rhetoric focused on threats of a slippery slope leading to the ultimate consequence of Blacks coming to power. A leading Afrikaner columnist argued that "the continuing ethos of white South Africans is such that they would have recourse to arms rather than submit to 'power-sharing' with blacks—which they perceive as nothing more than a euphemism for black dominance, and a threat to their existence."[50] While this is the perspective that most concerned Botha as he began to push for reforms, in the end the position was effectively neutralized, and the resounding referendum victory marked the transfer of mainstream White political thought away from the philosophical defense of "grand apartheid" to a more practical defense of White privilege.

The victory in the referendum reflected the success of Botha's strategy of cobbling together a centrist majority by luring those demanding change while holding on to as many of those committed to continued White dominance as possible. The rhetoric that accomplished this is preserved in several artifacts. The first is the final report of the President's Council, the "multiethnic" body set up to study and advise the government on the new constitution, hereafter referred to as the Final Report.[51] The second is a pamphlet entitled "Constitutional Guidelines: A New Dispensation for Whites, Coloureds and Indians," issued by the Department of Foreign Affairs and Information in December 1982.[52] These artifacts and others present a discourse organized around three separate but interrelated themes—that change was necessary, that the proposed changes would solve the problems, and that the reforms did not go so far that they threatened White privilege.

The first theme justifying any change was directed at the core of the government's constituency, traditionally conservative Afrikaners who had benefited enormously from apartheid. This was a ticklish proposition—the government needed to condemn the current constitutional structure without blaming the architects. Additionally, many Afrikaners believed the rhetorical justifications (religious, scientific, or both) of apartheid's racism. The government solved this problem by evoking evolutionary change. The constitution was framed as the next logical step in the country's political development. The new proposals were said to "represent a stage in the sustained search for justice, orderly renewal and reform."[53] The constitution was an orderly, voluntary change that would prevent future imposed and disorderly changes. This strategy allowed the government to argue the need for change without condemning past frameworks.

To back up this claim, the government presented a new history of South African political development. Through a subtle shift in emphasis, the history of apartheid became one in which Whites were constantly searching for ways to bring Western-style democracy into a very difficult context. The President's Council used almost one-quarter of its Final Report to place the proposals into a historical context of "Political Decision-Taking" beginning in 1652. (It should not be surprising that Whites seemed to have made all the political decisions in South Africa's history.) It concludes that "It is clear from this brief historical survey that a totalitarian tradition of dictatorship has never gained a foothold here. In fact, the progress of constitutional development has gradually worked towards the establishment of a democratic polity, in line with Western democratic models. . . ."[54] While seeking to entrench its state identity as Western and democratic, the government also presented racial diversity as a problem that required skillful adaptations of the West's models. Past arguments grounding apartheid in the very nature of God's universe were replaced with apartheid as an exercise in institutional problem solving.

This rewriting of apartheid as solution dovetailed nicely into the image of the constitution as an evolutionary response to changing conditions and an opportunity to further adapt Western governance paradigms to South Africa's unique situation. The government's history stressed intergroup conflict but claimed that forces of urbanization, modernization, and economic development were creating shared interests.[55] According to the report, the politics of White domination were rooted in Parliament's "Westminster style" in which the "winner takes all" and "governs at the executive level to the exclusion of parliamentary minorities."[56] "In a multinational society such a conflict style must of necessity give rise to serious clashes and strife."[57] Clearly, proceeded the argument, such a system, though grounded in generally accepted Western standards, was incompatible with South Africa's evolving political landscape. The system was at fault and needed to be changed.

At other times, the reforms were portrayed as a necessary compromise. The government set out to convince Whites that they would be safer with the constitutional changes than without them. The fact that the African National Congress was urging people to vote against the constitution became campaign rhetoric. In a speech to a National Party meeting in September 1983, Botha drew the choice as dichotomous and crucial to survival. "We in the N.P. say: either we drive the Coloureds into the arms of the country's enemies or we try to make an arrangement so that there can be peace behind the backs of South African soldiers and police and we can look the enemy in the face."[58] In other contexts the threat of the White right became evidence of the need for change. A "Johannesburg banker" told a *Wall Street Journal* reporter, "We may be creating a dictator, but it's a risk we have to take. It's the only way to get around the right wing of the Afrikaners, who have enough power under the present system to prevent any change."[59]

This argument about the necessity of compromise interlocked with the second theme of the government's argument—that even if they were not perfect, the changes would alleviate the crisis. During the campaign for the White referendum, many supporters found themselves on the defensive, arguing that some change was better than none.

> Unlovely as it is, the new constitution is seen as an exercise in the art of the possible, it holds the promise of an Afrikaner-English consensus, of introducing recalcitrant whites—in the gentlest possible way—to the habit of sharing power with people of a different shade of pale and of the even more elusive promise that, with the first step out of the way, South Africa can achieve a consensus on the looming imperative of black reform.[60]

One supporter even suggested that the reforms could represent a "valuable psychological breakthrough and precedent—an opportunity to convince whites that they are not the only South Africans."[61] The government's sales pitch to potential Coloured and Indian voters used the same themes of a step in the right direction that would provide access to some power and improvements in material conditions.[62]

In the campaign, the government emphasized the constitution's ability to provide order and stability, buzz words that Whites equated with security and the continuation of privilege. According to the Final Report, the constitutional changes were intended to "ensure the highest possible degree of stability in the State so as to promote the security and the social and economic welfare of all its inhabitants."[63]

> At this stage, when the end of its task is in sight, there is a strong feeling in the Committee that it is necessary for a certain realisation to penetrate to all groups and levels of the South African community, namely that the success of processes of adaptation at the constitutional level will in the first few years be decisive for the survival of a civilised social order in which the prosperity, peace, and progress of all population groups can be promoted. This includes the Black man in Southern Africa.[64]

The goal of stability meant that changes should not be radical. "No step may be taken that will endanger *order and stability*. Political and constitutional adjustments must be embarked upon in a well-considered and evolutionary way and with a view to promote a stable society."[65] The President's Council encouraged a step by step approach that would eliminate the possibility of "greater instability than what it sets out to eliminate."[66]

While trying to convince the electorate, and the world at large, that the reforms were both necessary and effective, the intricacies of the political situation demanded that the government also focus on a third theme, that the reforms were not taking things too far. From the government's perspective, this meant guarantees to their White constituency that there would be no majority rule, meaning Africans would be excluded from the politics of the Republic. On the other hand, an attentive international community had to be convinced that the reforms were a step in that direction. The government used several different strategies to walk this line. One was to blame the African leaders for refusing to participate in the consultative commission the Schlebusch Commission of Inquiry recommended in 1977 and for their general unwillingness to compromise. "[B]y their insistence that 'majority,' i.e., predominantly black, rule is for them nonnegotiable, black leaders are, of necessity, excluding themselves rather than being brutally excluded against their will."[67] At other times, representatives of the government blamed African exclusion on the potential for conflict. Ambassador to the United States Brand Fourie said, "The notion that the diverse cultures of South Africa can be forced into a unitary society on the basis of a one man, one vote formula is ruled out because, like single-group supremacy, it promises only conflict."[68] Gerrit Viljoen, then National Education Minister, was even more blunt. "White South Africans, therefore, simply are not prepared to submit to universal suffrage in a unitary state under conditions in which they would be swamped by a vast black majority and be reduced to political impotence."[69]

Whatever the rationale used, the government presented its new plan as an evolution of the basic philosophy of separate development. It was evolutionary in that it redefined the groupings requiring separation from four groups to two. On one side were Whites, Coloureds, and Indians, who suddenly became "groups whose cultural values and value systems were relatively close to one another."[70] On the other side, Africans still required a different system, both because the government continued to treat African ethnic groups as separate entities rather than as parts of a single race and because of the conflict that would "inevitably follow" if these groups were included in the same political system.[71]

> The political rights of all South Africa's peoples must be recognized and guaranteed. However, the situation is too complex for all groups to exercise their political rights in the same way. The fact that Blacks [Africans] exercise their political rights in different ways and that methods are still being examined to ensure the political rights of some other Blacks, need not preclude Coloureds and Indians from enjoying their political rights.[72]

The Final Report unapologetically compared the exclusion of Africans to the practice, entrenched in "every democratic society," of excluding children from the franchise until they reach a minimum age.[73] From within the apartheid worldview, the comparison made perfect sense. In addition, the evolution argument left open the possibility that Africans would one day "develop" enough to join a unified system.

> A peaceful and successful performance of a highly divided and heterogeneous society will never be achieved by imposing an artificial uniformity from above, but only by allowing it to develop, through a greater variety of structures and truly pluralistic choices for all the different groups concerned. While this may occur it does not seem in any way contradictory that the political organization of South Africa as a whole remains segregated.[74]

Of course, the Whites would judge when the standards for such an organic development had been achieved.

The rhetoric that the government used to argue three themes—the necessity of change, the value of the particular proposals, and the guarantees against going too far—was constrained by the necessity of fostering the image of South Africa as a Western, civilized democracy. Because this was how the vast majority of White South Africans (including presumably all the top government officials) thought of themselves, the discourse was as important for domestic as for international consumption. South Africa's democratic and anticommunist identities allowed the conservative administrations in the United States and Britain to provide support for the apartheid regime (albeit tempered by their own political constraints). The government claimed that a vote against the constitution would be perceived in the West as a victory for right-wing racists, further damaging South Africa's image, foreign investment, and the battle against sanctions. The South

African government also looked to the West to justify the new constitution by tapping into rhetorical frameworks that had been successfully employed by other countries with diverse, group-conscious populations (Belgium and Switzerland, for example). The claim that the cultural differences between South Africa's groups were unique allowed the government to continue to stretch the definition of "democracy."

> In a democracy, minorities will accept the rule of the majority if they perceive a fair chance of becoming part of a future majority. This principle also limits the scope of an existing majority, which is fearful of having to submit to rule of today's minorities, which may become tomorrow's majority. The operation of this rule, and thus of democracy itself, becomes difficult if a society includes groups whose members will refuse, for cultural, economic, religious or racial reasons, to form majorities across the cleavages separating them. Under such circumstances, the integrating function of democracy is frustrated, unless democracy is allowed to operate for each group separately.[75]

However, the politicization of race and apartheid made selling these institutional and political parallels to an international audience difficult. In a search for other helpful rhetoric, some South Africans returned to a set of tropes centered around the idea of civilization. Kate Manzo argues that civilization has been the most consistent justification for White privilege in South Africa since 1652.[76] The manifestation of the civilization discourse that was most powerful at the time involved a series of concepts and theories centered around the concept of development. The international acceptance of development as a way of organizing and making sense of the observable differences in lifestyle provided a very useful set of justifications, and people began to argue that South Africa had both the first world and the third world in a single country.[77] The idea that South Africa's problems were caused by trying to build institutions to deal with this divide helped the government explain the continued exclusion of Africans in terms that they thought would sell abroad and make those at home feel better about social disparities.

Another aspect of the democratic persona that the government had to adjust was the concept of equality. The government's discourse was both built by and primarily directed at people whose fundamental assumptions about the nature of the universe included the idea that racial groups, rather than individual characteristics, were valid predictors of abilities and behavior. The reforms were based on, and further entrenched, the principle that racial groups were actors. The government was able to claim that the reforms increased the equitable distribution of power between groups, but they could not claim to increase equality. There are two points here. The reforms sought to distribute power among the three population groups involved, based on their relative size in the population. So while groups were the units, power was not distributed *equally* among groups, but *equitably* based on the number of individuals in each group.

Group power was therefore dependent upon individuals *within* the new dispensation. But secondly, across the whole society, individuals were not eligible to be considered for equity; only their groups were. Groups, not individuals, had politically important characteristics. The number of individuals in a group became a group characteristic. Therefore the equitable distribution of power was based on group characteristics—except, of course, for Africans. The anti-apartheid discourse attacked this logic at its most basic ontological assumption—that characteristics of political importance varied with race.

THE ANTI-APARTHEID STORY—PEOPLE'S POWER

The anti-apartheid opposition to the constitution focused on two related issues. The first was perhaps the proposal's most obvious feature—the constitution excluded Africans. What the government framed as "multiracial" or "healthy" power sharing, those disinclined to believe the government saw simply as a cynical trick designed to placate opposition. Bernard Magubane compared it to Orwellian newspeak—"far from reforming anything, it only strengthens white minority rule in South Africa."[78] Overseas, editors at the *Economist, Financial Times, Wall Street Journal,* and *Washington Post* all criticized the new constitution for continuing to exclude Africans.[79] The proposals received support from the Reagan and Thatcher administrations as a movement toward nonracial democracy, but each noted publicly that the majority was excluded.[80] At home, every major African leader except the president of the Ciskei homeland, Lennox Sebe, opposed the new constitution. Even high profile moderates like KwaZulu leader Mongosothu Gatsha Buthelezi expressed their opposition. Oscar Dhlomo, Secretary General of Buthelezi's Zulu cultural organization, Inkatha, described the reforms as an evolution in oppression.

> The proposed constitution purports to lure coloured and Indian fellow-countrymen into the role of co-oppressors of black [African] people. Indians and coloureds who accept participation in the proposed tricameral Parliament will accept the status of partners in propping up white supremacy and they will be rightly regarded as co-oppressors.[81]

At a slightly more subtle level, the constitution was criticized for entrenching racism even further into the formal structures of governance, contradicting the government's claim that the constitution was a "step in the right direction."

> [T]he Bill retains all the undesirable features of Westminster and, by enshrining division and discrimination in its very essence, it ensures that consensual politics will be well-nigh impossible to obtain. The new constitution is an exercise in co-optation: it seeks to incorporate the coloured and Indian categories into the white-controlled structure so that their incorporation will strengthen that structure, but without jeopardizing white power.[82]

This rhetoric of entrenchment was particularly strong during the lead up to the White referendum. Frederik van Zyl Slabbert, leader of the Progressive Federalist Party, told a rally the night before the voting that "those voting Yes tomorrow would vote for racist legislation to become a cornerstone of the constitution."[83] Allan Boesak characterized a vote for the constitution as a vote for "the entrenchment of racism and the continuation of violence inherent in apartheid . . . for the break-up of family life, the erosion of human dignity and security laws which had placed South Africa 'firmly in the infamous role of a totalitarian regime.'"[84] Oscar Dhlomo said "the establishment of three ethnic chambers also entrenches racism as a fundamental political principle in South African politics."[85] Another commentator summarized the campaign against the proposals.

> Founded on the rock of apartheid, in which group identities and segregated lives will be enshrined from the basement up, the new constitution is a whited sepulcher which uneasily disguises the ugly face of white supremacy. Because it is based on group identity, the cross-racial affiliations which are essential if South Africa is to avoid conflict become impossible.[86]

Not only was the constitution racist, the argument went, but it actually legitimated apartheid's particular vision of race by giving Coloureds and Indians political standing as racial groups.

Casting the constitution as a legitimation and entrenchment of racism helped the opposition movement not only demonize the constitution, but also raise awareness about apartheid and the implications of racism in general. Focusing on racism made the distinction between the government and the Charterist ideology of nonracism became even more stark. As a general sense that the constitution was bad spread among Blacks, this antinomy simplified the process of winning people over to the unofficial UDF (and official ANC) philosophy that race was an inappropriate determinant of political rights and responsibilities. In this way the rhetoric of the discourse helped opposition movements solidify, clarify, and distribute both their vision of the political identity of apartheid and their alternative philosophies.

One of the mechanisms that subtly spread the idea of political participation was the UDF's 1984 "Million Signatures Campaign" in opposition to the constitution. The organization did not reach its goal, but the campaign got the UDF out into neighborhoods talking to ordinary South Africans. The UDF selected a different township every weekend and sent well-trained canvassers to talk to each household, ideally spending about twenty minutes at each home talking about politics and collecting signatures. Aside from the consciousness-raising function, the UDF treated these people, perhaps for the first time, as if their opinions and actions mattered in the political arena. Through these and other tactics like large public rallies, often with popular music stars, the UDF did reach an increasing number of South Africans. "In a sense the UDF appeared to fall squarely in a well-established South African populist tradition in which large and excited gatherings, powerful oratory, and strong, attractive leaders substituted for systematically structured organizations, carefully elaborated ideologies and well-coordinated programs."[87] This style of politics was particularly well suited to the decentralized and grassroots nature of the resistance movement of the early 1980s. The movement needed to motivate people into action rather than indoctrinate them with an intricate ideology. Instead the ideological discourse began from below. As it did, resistance expanded beyond the stages of noticing, questioning, and causing others to question, and many South Africans began to work for a specific alternative to apartheid. Given the localized nature of politics, these alternatives were dispersed and diverse, but as the resistance movement continued, they began to coalesce into specific beliefs and institutions.

One of the notions that helped to consolidate the anti-apartheid movement inside South Africa was "the people." Through the UDF, "the people" became a powerful rhetorical device that depersonalized the struggle (by turning resistance into a contest between "the people" and "the system"), asserted a society-wide constituency, and argued that the government was invested in narrow partisan interests. The UDF used the term to refer to the appropriation of duties normally reserved for the state by alternative, grassroots movements. As township residents responded to the ANC's call to make the townships ungovernable, "the people" began to invent their own systems of governance to solve the problems of everyday social life.

> There is a growing tendency for ungovernability to be transformed into elementary forms of people's power. . . . [The security forces] couldn't stop the people in some townships from taking power under their very noses, by starting to run those townships in different ways. . . . [T]he struggles which people had fought, and the resulting situation of ungovernability, created the possibilities for the exercise of people's power.[88]

The idea of "people's power" represented the appropriation of administrative, judicial, welfare and cultural functions by local civic and youth organizations. Often these took the form of modest concrete projects like street cleaning, park construction, and curriculum alternatives, but there were also activities that directly challenged state authority, such as people's courts. Tom Lodge suggests that these courts were "part of a deliberate effort to replace the organs of the state and in so doing transform political relationships."[89] The UDF laid out this strategy in a confidential discussion paper in May 1985.

> Having established the illegitimacy of the S. African regime, it is necessary to project a popular alternative. . . . Where the apartheid puppets are no longer able to effectively function, a stage could be reached where the people's organization assumed responsibility for organising the community to govern itself in a variety of ways from setting up health clinics to crime prevention. This will make people fully understand our vision of a future democratic South Africa. As long as utopian illusions aren't created amongst the people (leading to inevitable disillusionment), what these embryos of democracy will give birth to is a vision of a totally alternative society.[90]

People's power flowed up from grassroots organizations and respected the contributions of each individual, making the democracy of the alternative governance almost Athenian. The basic unit of governance was the street committee, a small cell formed as a means of quickly communicating with large numbers of people. Gugile Nkwinti, organizer of the Port Alfred civic, explained:

> We make decisions at the central committee on issues brought up by various organizations. When a decision goes out to the people, it goes through the street and area committees. It's not one-way traffic, though. It's a two-way thing. Sometimes a street committee itself will decide on an issue and it will be taken to the central committee. It's very very beautiful. Marvelous.[91]

Through a process called "report-backs," the UDF was able to claim to speak for "the people" in a way that excluded the government from consideration. The collective term itself helped to delegitimize the government and empower regular South Africans to resist and to creatively approach the problems of their own communities. It was very easy for individuals to see themselves as members of "the people."

Resistance to apartheid relied on both the inventions of South Africans at the grassroots level and systems of justification imported from outside that validated those inventions and gave them power against apartheid. These alternative systems challenged the apartheid assertion that political agency was naturally distributed according to racial groupings. For resistance, politics became rooted in a variety of other social divisions and personas. People whose relationship to politics had previously been solely based on their race found organizations that emphasized that political interests could be aligned according to identities of pensioners, workers, students, youth. Others, including Allan Boesak and the South African Catholic Bishops Conference, anchored their resistance to apartheid in religion.[92] Acts of resistance require the actor to step outside the trajectory of the existing social order. In South Africa in the early 1980s, resistors found a wide variety of places to stand once they made that leap. By the time the era of reform ended in June of 1986, that multitude of standpoints had begun to coalesce into a decreasing number of increasingly coherent platforms, from which resistors began to negotiate the shape of post-apartheid reality.

CONSTITUTIONAL REFORM AND POLITICAL IDENTITY

Alterations to Political Agency

Under apartheid, political agency, like all other characteristics of political importance, was subordinated to race. Apartheid was designed around the concept of self-determination for White South Africans, and its rhetorical justifications meant that only Whites were capable of the kind of rational, civilized decision-making that would characterize participation in South Africa's Western-style or first-world democracy. Under the flag of self-determination, Africans were granted limited agency within the homelands. Apartheid had granted Indians and Coloureds somewhat greater economic rights (especially property rights), but they were still deemed to be political objects within the Republic, racially incapable of participation in a White system of governance.

After Soweto, the government's control over political agency was loosened. In the process of letting go to get a better grip, President Botha launched a discourse that resulted in questions about not only the parts of the social order that he wanted to change, but others as well. Because the reforms were, in many ways, meant to placate a foreign audience, an audience with overwhelmingly liberal values, Botha needed the reform discourse to have an air of liberal legitimacy, and that required the possibility of expressing real dissent. This created opportunities for discursive conflicts that the state chose not to control. The resulting freedom of expression inspired opposition groups and produced an atmosphere of fluidity that encouraged new social cleavages and strategic groupings within apartheid reality. The existing literature often uses the metaphor of discursive space to explain these opportunities for action, but another way to think about them is as newly normalized behaviors that people began linking to previously disempowered identities. Coloureds, Indians, and Africans were suddenly participating in changes to the politics of South Africa as Coloureds and Indians and Africans.

In the early 1980s, apartheid's opponents mobilized action on a very local level, with consumer boycotts and other activities directed at influencing local issues. Those shut out of the nation's formal political process cut their teeth on mundane issues, but their experiences demonstrated, not least to themselves, that they had the power to alter the social order. Matthew Goniwe, a pioneering UDF activist, wrote in his private notes, "We are instruments of change, agents of change. Change will NOT come if we DON'T stand up. Change will NOT come if we expect other people to bring it—each and every one of us has a contribution to make."[93] Enlivened by this action-oriented philosophy, regular South Africans found opportunities within the system to break out of the small and subordinate spheres of political activity to which they had been confined. Black South Africans increasingly rejected the image of themselves as political objects. They came to believe that they could act in situations in which apartheid's norms and rules prohibited them from acting. Once the issues they were addressing began to be redefined as national and even global problems, agency also shifted to a much wider scope of contexts, and people began to think of their actions at the local level as working against not just their own personal injustice, but also against a kind of transcendental injustice.

This redefinition of the problems faced by South Africans from personal and local to national and global was facilitated by the government's constitutional reforms. The norms against Black agency were cast as constitutional rules, which put them under the control of the state. Because the reforms continued to deal with South Africans in terms of their race, and because they evoked a largely negative response from the global guardians of the liberal ideal they were designed to appease, South Africans opposed to apartheid were able to draw strength and rhetorical support from a global discourse about the immorality of racism. The opportunity was organic to the process of reform. The government's admission that changes were needed politicized apartheid and invited consideration of alternatives. The sudden promotion of Coloureds and Indians to a new status as politically responsible agents and the continued exclusion of Africans placed under scrutiny not only the limited nature of the expansion, but the entire ontological assertion that agency was somehow linked to race. At the grassroots level, the campaigns of the UDF encouraged South Africans to approach the political arena as agents capable of resistance, to consider how things might be different, and to participate in trying to institute those changes. The result was increased disorder and rebellion in a highly politicized atmosphere. Apartheid and resistance struck each person differently, but as daily life became politicized and people became convinced that their hardships could be blamed on apartheid, apartheid's rules were increasingly challenged. Steven Mufson tells of youths in Soweto purposefully running red traffic lights to demonstrate reclaiming authority from the government's social order. "The signals, they said, had no legitimacy because no one had consulted the youngsters about the placement of the lights."[94] The depth to which the social order was politicized meant that people began to become agents with respect to more and more aspects of their lives.

Key to the translation of frustration into action was the belief that things could be different. The unevenness of this belief and the localized contexts into which it was translated and adapted created a great variety of new models for political action. Through the use of newly accessible and globally legitimated understandings of agency and governance, South Africans began not only to dismantle apartheid authority, but also to construct alternatives.

> In the middle of 1985, however, a critical change in black strategy began to take place, arising principally from within the country rather than from the ANC in exile. Instead of making urban black townships ungovernable for the white-sanctioned administration, anti-apartheid leaders started tightening their own ability to orchestrate events in the black areas. Instead of simply thwarting government initiatives, black community organizations (generally affiliates of the UDF) tried to seize the initiative.[95]

People's power rejected the apartheid scheme for distributing political agency. "People" here is not a category but a universal, symbolizing a modern liberal assumption about how politics should be structured. People are political agents by dint of their rationality and thus deserve a say in their governance. This imported theme became the widely resonant core for a set of principles that justified the movement for a nonracialist, post-apartheid order in globally dominant understandings of justice and equity. The worldwide appeal of modern antiracism overpowered the group-oriented, racial ideology of apartheid. Thinking globally thus gave those opposed to apartheid strength.

The expansion of political agency in the first half of the 1980s, both orchestrated and spontaneous, constitutes a critical juncture in the transformation of the apartheid social order. As more people felt empowered to act, and act creatively, in contexts in which they never had before, the ability of formal social structures to control behavior shifted. As newly diverse behaviors coalesced around sets of justifications from outside of and opposed to the apartheid order, the creation of competing systems of governance became possible. These changes in agency necessitated alterations to the social discourse and more specifically to the identity labels that were used to organize action in the political realm.

Political Identity of the Constitutional Discourse

The conflict over the new constitution, and over reforms in general, was a battle over the politics of agency, cast as changes to the political power of apartheid's identity groups and thus accessible through the identity labels each side used to present their positions. Focusing on identity aids in the study of agency because labels are how people understand their relative social position and hence their *power* to act, but identity labels are also how people sort and organize descriptions of themselves and hence their *capabilities* to act. Capabilities are descriptions; identity labels are codes for descriptions. Shifts in agency are accompanied by changes to the systems of identity labels that agents use to organize their relationships and interactions. New labels are coined and old ones redefined. In a very real sense, therefore, the battle for the future of apartheid was waged through identity labels.

The essence of the government's reforms was an expansion in the scope of political agency through official decree. From the government's perspective, the new constitution changed the meaning of two of apartheid's defining identity labels—"Coloured" and "Indian"—in a profound way. The labels had been used to exclude people from the political arena and as a result had become a focus for resistance. The extension of the franchise and, thereby, political agency was seen as a partial solution to international critics' main complaint—that apartheid excluded some from the political arena based solely on their race. Because the reforms were created by and had to be sold to people who had been raised on apartheid's rhetoric of radical racial difference, the reforms were still built around the fundamental importance of racial groups. Indeed, the reforms were an attempt to reinvigorate Coloured and Indian as separate racial categories after the Black Consciousness Movement had some success in redefining the label "Black" to include all those oppressed by apartheid, effectively uniting groups the government wanted to keep separate. The assertion that these groups were suddenly worthy of political participation represented a public acknowledgement of the cracks in the system that justified White privilege, cracks that a newly reinvigorated resistance movement was able to exploit effectively.

Typical of the apartheid perspective, the government's side of the discourse was directed almost exclusively at White audiences, either at home or abroad. Soweto had inflicted significant stress on the identity of White South Africans.

While South Africa had been out of favor with the international community for decades, the events of 1976 refocused international attention, renewed international disapprobation and turned the country into an international pariah. The unwelcome global interest added both material and psychological costs to being a White South African, threatening the persona of civilized, Western, benevolent leader that rationalized White power and privilege. The constitutional reforms were the government's attempt to counteract this threat.

For a significant portion of the population who justified their apartheid identities through the Bible, tradition, or other rationales unaffected by the changing global norms against racism, the reforms were anathema. Botha's struggles against the verkrampte faction of the NP in the 1970s conditioned him to direct the campaign for reforms at this group. He deftly sidelined these conservatives, aided by the internal dynamics of apartheid's political economy. Apartheid began as an Afrikaner nationalist ideology, but its function was mostly as a kind of Afrikaner affirmative action, pulling poor, rural farmers into civil service jobs and giving them an advantage in competing with the urban, wealthy, English-speaking Whites. The success of this goal had significant implications for how Afrikaners thought about themselves.

> Some twenty-five years of increasing National Party domination of every aspect of the state apparatus, the related transformation of the Afrikaner proletariat into a solid bureaucratic middle class, and the concomitant penetration of the industrial and commercial economy by the Afrikaner community, had served to reduce the sense of economic and cultural insecurity that gave rise to the obsession with identity. . . . In sum, the effects of extended National Party rule had laid the sociocultural foundation for the NP leadership to, in effect, draw a distinction between apartheid and white supremacy and to attend to the latter by abandoning significant aspects of the former.[96]

As the rhetoric surrounding the constitutional referendum demonstrated, the National Party moved in the early 1980s to reposition its social divisions along an economic rather than an ideological continuum. The government was able to create a constituency for reform among those who wanted to see themselves as members of a modern, Western, democratic, and capitalist elite.

The international audience proved to be more difficult to convince. As the global discourse about apartheid solidified an international norm against racism, the apartheid government tried its best to distance itself from the rhetoric of race. The rhetoric of reform sought to recalibrate how observers understood the South African social order by tying into global discourses of economics, civilization, and internationally accepted models of democracy. South Africa's disparities were presented as the same ones that existed between Western and non-Western societies all over the world. Apartheid's rhetorical momentum made this very difficult. The primary goal of protecting White privilege produced a scheme of political identity as convoluted and confusing as apartheid's had been.

Since 1948 all of South Africa's black groups were supposedly different nations, yet after 1983 two of these groups—the Indians and the Coloureds—were to be given rights as races within a common (if structurally separated) central government. Henceforward there would be rights for some based on their identity as workers and for others based on the racial category to which they had been assigned. The majority, however, were to remain rightless altogether. Lacking any sound historical or contemporary rationale, the incorporation of a supposedly alien people like the Indians undermined the possible case for continuing to exclude the alien (i.e. nonemployed by whites) Africans. A new outbreak of mass unrest within a year of the promulgation of the new constitution was the somewhat predictable result.[97]

While the arguments made for the new constitution proved at least acceptable to a majority of Whites, the government had lost too much credibility, and the reforms were too obviously window dressing for it to win over a critical mass of all South Africans or the international community. The argument was even rejected by majorities of the two groups to which the power of political agency was extended. As a result, political identity in South Africa in the mid-1980s was a multifaceted and confused site of significant resistance.

From a resistance perspective, the expansion of the political attributes attached to the Coloured and Indian identity labels had little impact on the character of the political system. Critics argued that the reforms were not designed to distribute real political power but to placate dissent and appease foreigners. From this perspective, the reforms further entrenched the heart of apartheid, the idea that racial distinctions were politically important, and the reforms were seen as a defense of the overall scheme of categorizing South Africans.

While the government was tinkering with apartheid's institutional bureaucracy, however, an increasing number of Africans (and Coloureds and Indians who considered themselves unaffected by the reform efforts) began to think of themselves as effective political agents outside of the formal political system. Their efforts to solve local daily challenges, fathoms below the national government's level of attention, had begun to change the labels that many Blacks used to describe themselves. The government's reforms provided the incentive for Blacks to organize these identities into systems of agency and to mobilize the power of these new identity labels on a national level. The rise of civic associations and the boycott movement of the early 1980s began to create new labels and redefine meanings that were proactive and creative rather than reactive and primarily destructive, as "Black" and "student" and "protester" had been following Soweto. In the mid-1980s, because of the dynamics of the government's discourse about formal political participation, resistance leaders were able to gain a certain degree of control over the discourse of alternative political identity that had been gaining momentum since Soweto.

In the early 1980s, anti-apartheid activities were widely dispersed and uncoordinated. The international anti-apartheid movement centered in America and Western Europe was largely rooted in postcolonial interpretations of liberalism, which posited a philosophy of individualism and basic human equality that contradicted apartheid's differentiation along group-based identities. Some organizations, including the Pan-Africanist Congress, kept apartheid's race-based categories, but sought to invert the hierarchy to make Black identities dominant over White ones. The Inkatha movement generally sought to use apartheid's ethnic categories to secure a kind of federalist autonomy, but this changed several times at the whim of its leader. Religious systems such as the Roman Catholic and Anglican churches based their alternatives on a more transcendental understanding of justice, power, and identity. For labor unions and communists, Marxist classes and Cold War ideologies were motivating cleavages. Many other more practical anti-apartheid frameworks of identity sprang up in townships and homelands all over South Africa during the course of the struggle. Each of these alternative ideologies provided actors with a ontological ground from which to resist the state's interpretation of order. These diverse experiences and understandings of both problems and solutions were brought into the public arena by the debate over the constitution. Through the discourse, the diversity of alternative rules began to coalesce into systems of ideas that then formed a referent that individuals could use to justify their acts of resistance.

Perhaps the most important part of this discourse was sorting out the role of race in the positive ideology that would be put forward as an alternative to apartheid. At this point in the transition, this struggle took place between the Charterist ideology, the driving force behind the United Democratic Front (unofficially, however, until 1987), and Black Consciousness, the philosophy behind the National Front and the Azanian Peoples Organization (AZAPO).

> Both opposition camps [UDF and BC] sought the high ground of denying the ultimate necessity of racial or national division, in order to prevent the state from using such tools for domination and to present the people a vision of life without such division. They disagreed on whether racially exclusive or inclusive struggle could more effectively achieve this goal. Both movements saw how powerful these identities could be, especially as they were used to the state's advantage, and they tried to use the same forces for their opposite ends. BC rhetoric rejected the scientific existence of race but used racial identity to define itself and to justify opposition by all blacks. Charterists also rejected race but sought to organize all population groups into a national opposition to systematic domination.[98]

The label "Black" became an axis of contention. The Black Consciousness movement used Black as a symbol of oppression rather than race in an effort to change the psychology of apartheid and to demonstrate the socially constructed nature of race. After Soweto, the government responded with laws that made Black the official identity label for Africans, changing the references in all its legislation from Bantu. The move was an attempt to reclaim Coloured, Indian, and Black as distinct categories. A few years later in the constitutional discourses, the categories of Coloured and Indian became the primary battleground for apartheid. The UDF allowed race-based organizations to be affiliates, but vigorously promoted a nonracial perspective on politics. In the end, most people were convinced that Charterism's multi- and/or nonracialism represented their perspectives in a politically feasible way. The context for this decision was the tradition of multiracialism from the ANC legacy of the 1950s as exemplified in the person of Nelson Mandela, and the global liberal norm of antiracism that lent significant support to those suffering the consequences of resistance.

Most important for the rise of an alternative to apartheid social order, however, was the rejection of all of the government's categories of identity. The clear and deep rejection of racism in any form ultimately helped the nonracialism of the UDF and the ANC win out over other philosophies. Eventually, most antiapartheid political activity within South Africa became nonracial, albeit not completely and not overnight. Although the UDF officially had no governing philosophy other than opposition to apartheid, the practicalities of its organization and mobilization meant that nonracialism had become an organizational reality within South Africa. The movement characterized the government's reforms as racist and itself as nonracist, and used the antinomy to anchor its campaign to raise consciousness and praxis among the Black population. That philosophy became the anchor for an alternative social order that would rise in fits and starts to take the place of apartheid.

> In rendering the townships ungovernable, the insurrection of 1984–86 operated not just at the level of physical control (fighting the police and army, eliminating informers, disrupting community council administration, and the like), but also on the level of political psychology. Insurrectionary activity produced a transformation in political identity and orientation; a liberation of political consciousness as well as territory. Two closely related processes were at work, that of radicalization and that of legitimation.[99]

The UDF was able to convince people that apartheid was responsible for what was wrong with their lives, linking a national issue to local and even personal problems. At the same time, it gave them mechanisms to change it and inspired them to invent others.

As the power of the labels used by the UDF to organize its resistance became important in the political arena, political identity in South Africa became much more varied and interesting. The practical and philosophical dispersion of agency seemed to have the biggest impact on the youth of the townships. Politically centered groups of "comrades" took up the responsibility for policing many of the boycotts.[100] A former student leader and current Member of Parliament explained the power of this label.

> Once you regard yourself or you are regarded as a comrade, you would then adjust your mind and you behave accordingly. So I am a comrade, I have to fight against the government and must support all activities that are related to that and I must be seen to be participating. In the course of participating I am also becoming a comrade. And if you are labeled a traitor or a sell out, in the end you will want to be involved in some anti-[apartheid] activity.[101]

Comrades were by no means a uniform group. Some liked the thrill of fighting the police; others were idealistic youths dedicated to ending apartheid. "The phrase [comrade] was popularized by ANC documents, Radio Freedom, and prisoners on Robben Island. But black youths were the ones brazen enough to call each other comrades in daily conversation and the word became their label."[102] But "comrade" became more inclusive over time.

> As the number of people involved in township organizations soared, 'comrade' became an inclusive term, extended to anyone who joined the struggle against apartheid. Members of anti-apartheid organizations, whether young or old would call themselves comrades, as casually as one might call someone 'mister' or 'old boy.' Black trade union members called each other comrades. Even those seen as sympathizing with blacks could be called comrade.[103]

One comrade from the mid-1980s told me that comrades served as a kind of family: "Wherever we are, we are a group of comrades." He said it did not matter with which organization you were affiliated, "just as long as you were resisting and fighting for freedom."[104] In part this solidarity came from their mutual suffering. The comrades of the 1980s endured all manner of excruciating torture at the hands of the police. A member of the resistance movement from the 1950s described the difference. "In our day, when policemen kicked in the doors and kicked people around we all said 'baas [boss], please baas.' Today the police might have to kill the boy before he said 'baas.'"[105]

Similar connotations were attached to the word "youth." Since Soweto, it had been young people who had led the way in resistance. This was especially true in the mid-1980s. As the resistance movement evolved, "youth" came to have less to do with age than a mind-set. "It connotes the most energetic, volatile and impatient elements of the black communities."[106] A former activist told me that "youth" could refer to anyone up to thirty-five years old, making it a broad category.[107] "Students" were a specific subset of youth, according to the first president of the Congress of South African Students (COSAS), a nationwide group set up to organize secondary school students. "Student" was reserved for those in, just out of, or boycotting secondary school. "Youth" referred to age, and COSAS set up a separate organization called the Youth League to organize them.[108]

In general, the youth proved confident and bold enough to actualize their agency in the confines of Black living space and in the process reversed the prevailing image of several different power structures.

> The momentum for action came from the bottom levels of the organization and from its youngest members. It was children who built the roadblocks, children who led the crowd to the administrative buildings, children who delegated spokespersons, and children who in 1984 told the older folk that things would be different, that people would not run away as they had in 1960.[109]

Their leadership, though sometimes overzealous, did change the minds of older Blacks, who were alternately shamed and inspired into action by their children. The mother of one young activist killed by the police in 1988 is quoted at length by Anthony Marx.

> Under the state of emergency in 1986 . . . [my son, Sicelo] was taken to Krugersdorp Prison. That was the beginning of the change in me. I asked myself if I was doing enough, not only for Sicelo, but also for my people. I saw that he was right in all that he was doing and told myself that I would always stand by him. . . . I saw that I had been living with my eyes closed. It was my son who opened my eyes to the real world.
>
> My advice to all the mothers and fathers who have lost their loved ones like me is that they must try and understand their children. They must not tell them to stop going to meetings, but they must go with them to these meetings and stand with them, side by side. That is what Sicelo taught me.[110]

As helpful to the dismantling of apartheid as the youthful enthusiasm was, many of these youth later suffered from the tactics, especially the boycotts of Bantu education, which produced an entire sector of the population with no education at all, often referred to today as the "lost generation."

"Youth" and other labels became politically important in the era of apartheid's decline because they presented actors with a different set of rules, patterns, and expectations than the actor would have found under a strict apartheid system. What made these labels political is the fact that their power came from outside the apartheid universe and hence gave actors a position from which resistance could take place. Soweto's "students" and "protesters" provoked the noticing, questioning, and causing trouble that were necessary to get to the creative action implied by the rhetorical contexts of "comrade" and "youth." As these alternative identities were actualized through the structures of "people's power" under the auspices of the UDF, a temporary shift in control over the townships occurred, during which time the Charterist philosophy was able to establish a foothold that the government was never able to pry loose. The States of Emergency and the accompanying force and threat of force therefore had to be renewed annually until de Klerk's announcement of much more drastic changes in February of 1990. The UDF used the antinomy to clarify its opposition and eventually was able to prevail in the contest to determine the shape of the post-apartheid order.

CONCLUSION

This chapter presented the era of apartheid reform as a political conflict and a site where the transformation of the South African social order was negotiated. As Prime Minister (later State President) P. W. Botha tried to adapt the rules and arrangements that made up the formal political process, he provoked, indeed invited, a discourse over the value of the proposed reforms. This discourse is an artifact of the transformation of apartheid. The state presented the constitution as a necessary, practical, and safe adaptation of the existing social order, and succeeded in convincing a majority of Whites to adopt it. On the other side, the anti-apartheid movement was able to use the widespread illegitimacy of the constitutional proposals as a lever to nudge South Africans into political action.

As the strategies and rhetoric of opposition were adapted to changing circumstances, and as government responses took on more violent characteristics, an increasing number of South Africans found reasons to resist apartheid and work for change. Apartheid elites responded to the rising tide of opposition through a combination of heavy-handed force, enticements to a few, and ideological dike-plugging. Meanwhile, the United Democratic Front was able to unite a vast spectrum of localized, grass-roots organizations under a vague umbrella whose only requirement was being *against* some aspect of the apartheid system. But increasingly the UDF found that if it stood *for* anything, it was a nonracialism that meshed fairly well with the ANC philosophy expressed in the Freedom Charter. The only solid national-level ideological power base for opposition to apartheid became a nonracial, nonethnic, social welfare system of governance, the same philosophy that was driving a post-Cold War liberal "New World Order." The coherence of grassroots and global visions of a liberal future was not a coincidence, but the practical implication was that there was plenty to recommend such a system for post-apartheid governance.

This era of reform represents a crucial point in both processes that frame the transformation of apartheid—dismantling and reconstruction. The reforms not only failed to placate resistance to apartheid, they increased it. While Botha was able to hammer together a two-thirds majority of Whites who were willing to validate his reforms, Black South Africans registered their disapproval with the longest and most widely distributed spasm of unrest in South African history. This violence exploded on the same day that the new Coloured and Indian legislators were sworn in, and it continued for almost two years. In the end, Botha had to impose two draconian States of Emergency to regain a semblance of order in the townships. Apartheid, however, became an increasingly inefficient way of structuring social life. The protests that coalesced around the reform discourse therefore were instrumental in the dismantling of apartheid as a social order.

At the same time, but much more slowly, the reforms also provided the impetus for several frameworks of resistance to come together. This process is even now incomplete, but the broad outlines of the post-apartheid social order were evident in the success of the United Democratic Front's resistance. What began as creative grassroots problem solving in a multitude of small contexts around the country seemed to find a common bond in the idea of nonracialism, which gained added resonance from the antinomy with apartheid. Charterist nonracialism was not the only alternative to apartheid that coalesced in this period, and the grassroots nature of practical resistance produced a wide variety of rules for behavior. As the number of different rules increased, so did conflict, as people were forced to negotiate definitions of social contexts in many more interactions than had been previously been the case. This is the conflict of the "legitimacy gap." As the worth of apartheid as a set of arrangements used to orient behavior declined, and as the number of at least marginally legitimated alternative sets of rules increased, it became increasingly difficult to organize and keep track of the variety of possible social situations. For a society of people used to dealing with the simplicity of racism, the number of diverse and conflicting sets of rules with which any socially competent person had to be conversant was overwhelming.

As the aggregate amount of social legitimacy in the system decreased, and as the remaining coherence became dispersed among a number of different sets of rules, conflict, often violent, became characteristic of South African society. Whites had an entire state security apparatus designed to protect them. Blacks were not so lucky. Over the four years between the 1986 State of Emergency and de Klerk's 1990 speech to Parliament, Blacks suffered the full force of conflict and repression necessary to maintain order in White communities. Repression is never as efficient as hegemony, however, and the continued, but more muted, resistance chipped away at the value of the apartheid order and eventually produced the conditions that made the transition to a new social order possible.

From 1990 to 1994, South Africans engaged in explicit negotiations about the shape of a post-apartheid social order. As the major parties slowly coalesced into a solid central consensus, confidence rose that the transition would be successful, and South Africans became not only invested, but proud of their country and of their courage, forgiveness, and determination to make their society better. South Africans are still in the process of constructing and legitimating their post-apartheid social order, and there are still plenty of conflicts that need to be addressed. The next chapter examines perhaps the central problem that the New South Africa has had to solve—crime.

Chapter Six

POST-APARTHEID CRIME

While contemporary South African crime certainly carries the baggage of apartheid, in this chapter it is cast predominantly as a conflict about order in the New South Africa. As apartheid was dismantled, order declined significantly. Simply in the course of daily life, South Africans found more and more contexts in which no widely accepted patterns or procedures existed to guide their social interactions with others. In the absence of a working consensus, people were forced to negotiate new and, to some degree, mutually acceptable standards to govern their relationships. These negotiations continue to produce new social patterns and are an important mechanism by which South Africans collectively are building a new social order.

In many respects, crime is the social conflict most central to these negotiations over the shape and direction of contemporary South African society. As a political issue, crime is an explicit, public discourse about order. This discourse manifests both White fears about the end of minority governance and assertions by relatively powerless Blacks about standards of material equity. Crime dominates the news in this media-rich society, and every South African seems to have both a personal story of crime and an opinion about the impact of crime on society as a whole.

As such, the politics of crime provide a useful mechanism to explore the power of social identities in post-apartheid South Africa. People find it easy to talk about crime, and their opinions and explanations are windows into how they understand broader aspects of contemporary South African social reality. This chapter focuses on the discourse surrounding crime as a site where the politics of post-apartheid identity are negotiated and implemented. It begins with an overview of crime in recent history, discusses crime as a sociopolitical discourse, and then presents several arguments about the intersection of identity and crime based on the identity labels South Africans use to talk about and understand the issue. It concludes by fitting crime as an issue into the trajectory of South Africa's broader social transformation.

CRIME IN SOUTH AFRICA

Crime and Apartheid

In the heyday of apartheid, when its rules and interpretations held sway among the great bulk of the South African population, Whites defined what constituted a crime. Apartheid's racism was manifested as a system of laws, and the state was very careful to maintain a philosophically defensible relationship between those laws and the public order. While increasingly out of step with globally dominant paradigms of governance, this system was consistent with an understanding of reality in which races were fundamentally different. South Africans, regardless of race, inhabited a world in which it was not only normal but also rational to behave as racists in everyday interactions. The discriminatory, repressive, and often violent practices that apartheid laws authorized made sense in that world. This internal consistency helped sustain the system for decades in the face of determined resistance.

Within that system, law was more than just a tool for enforcing social consensus. A particularly powerful part of the White self-image was the label "civilized," and one of the most important standards of civilization was the public promulgation of and strict adherence to law. As a powerful delineation between the modern and the primitive, law commanded homage in White practice and demanded justification in its violation.[1] Even at the height of international condemnation of apartheid, South Africa's western system of law helped elites frame themselves as Western, civilized, and democratic. Law was the protector of White privilege, but it was also a safeguard for racial reality and, perhaps more important, White identity. Law was so integral to their understanding of the nature of self and other that Whites, and especially elites, had to obey the law, at least in the abstract. So they wrote racist laws that turned nonracial behavior into crimes.

Apartheid reality allowed Whites to objectify Blacks, to treat them as important only for the potential impact they could have on White lives. Aside from the labor they supplied, Blacks registered as important because of the risks they were perceived to pose to White security, including not only threats to identity, but also the danger of physical injury, economic crime, rape, and employment loss, among others. The social order was designed to provide security for Whites, which often meant turning institutions of governance against Blacks. As a result, White South Africans experienced everyday life as essentially law-governed and orderly. Encased in the high, strong, and opaque boxes of apartheid's separate development and protected by a paranoid police state, Whites were practically incapable of thinking about or even noticing the insecurity of daily life in Black living areas. However, the threat of economic and violent crime was an integral part of the urban Black experience in South Africa. Tsotsis, young, gangster-like criminals, were a ubiquitous part of Black township life, mugging, burgling, raping, and murdering fellow township residents. A 1975 survey found that Soweto residents saw crime as their biggest problem, outweighing even poverty and unemployment.²

Because the state mechanisms of law enforcement and order were designed to victimize Blacks as threats to White society, they paid little or no attention when Blacks were victimized. The police were completely implicated in apartheid, leaving Black communities with no official recourse to the plague of regular economic crime.

> The South African police clearly was not primarily in the business of catching criminals and preventing crime, at least not as those concepts are defined in most countries in the world. In 1968 the police's official historian noted that only one officer in ten was actually engaged in the detection and investigation of crime, and thereafter the proportion can only have declined. Rather, the police's job was overwhelmingly the maintenance of public order, as defined by the police themselves.³

The South African Police (SAP) was a national organization structured as a parallel, internally focused army.⁴ Whether through self-selection in career choice or as a justification for the repressive actions they performed on regular basis, White police officers were considered to be among the most racist and malicious members of the minority. In the mid-1980s, quickly recruited and inadequately trained Black "auxiliary policing units" began to serve as proxies for the police and the army in the townships. Not surprisingly, these officers were seen as collaborators and often harassed, tortured, and even killed.⁵ Compared with the White image of police as public servants, for Blacks the SAP was a blunt instrument of repression. It was the face of the government in the townships, and the vast majority of the racial violence experienced by Blacks came at the hands of SAP officers. For a Black South African to report a crime to the police was often a larger offense in Black communities than whatever was being reported. For Blacks, "even to enter a police station was to be a sell-out."⁶

The role of the police, therefore, was to implement the White order and contain the Black menace. Blacks generally registered as potential threats, not as victims. Beyond just ignoring crime, the police often promoted it in Black communities, supporting criminal gangs as a balance against more politically motivated groups of comrades.⁷ While economic crime in Black areas was against the law, it was not against the order the state was determined to police. The legal apparatus of apartheid was set up to control the far more dangerous crimes of "extra-systemic" acts of politics and resistance.

CRIME AND RESISTANCE

In social theory, crime (as the violation of certain formalized rules) is the antinomy of order (the coordination of behavior around a set of patterns and rules);

normal citizens and the public at large must be protected against crime and criminals. The institutions of the state are designed to define and maintain order by entrenching rules into the flow of everyday life and enforcing penalties if crimes occur.[8] Beginning with Soweto, many South Africans experienced a concurrent shift in the legitimacy of apartheid rules and the kinds of activities that they considered to be criminal. The definition of crime and the implications of committing a crime thus became part of the rhetorical battleground for the fight over the apartheid social order. From the perspective of resistors, much of the government's definition of crime was no longer compelling. The resistance movement successfully redefined many crimes so that they became part of "the struggle." Murder, for example, attained a certain level of acceptability when the victims were police, police informers, or White officials. Government buildings in the townships, especially schools and liquor stores, became legitimate targets for vandalism, arson, and looting because they were perceived to be instruments of apartheid's strategies against Blacks. Sporadic bombings and acts of sabotage carried out by exiled organizations were celebrated in the townships. These and other more mundane crimes like nonpayment of rent and utility bills, illegal marches, general strikes, and throwing rocks at police invested regular South Africans in acts of resistance. Even when the government was successful in preventing these activities from occurring, a growing sector of the population came to think of them as legitimate rather than criminal. For many, they were even heroic.

The cumulative effect of these various attacks was a decline in the legitimacy of apartheid's social arrangements. In the increasingly politicized atmosphere, the kinds of activities the state most wanted to be thought of as criminal instead became framed as resistance, a category of activity that more and more Blacks found worthy of esteem rather than condemnation. The authoritarian interpretation of order promulgated by the government made this change in thinking remarkably easy. The purposefully ambiguous and sweeping nature of laws like the Suppression of Communism Act and various States of Emergency turned everyday acts performed for the purpose of resistance into crimes in a legal, prosecutable sense. As a philosophical stance resistance legitimated committing these acts because they were considered crimes by the state. The distinction between crime and civil disobedience became open to personal interpretation.

In the mid-1980s, the rhetoric of localized resistance encouraged Blacks to think of themselves as powerful, as able to take control of their own living conditions. One of the first things that these newly empowered people did was to create their own systems of justice and punishment. In the 1980s, "people's courts" sprang up in many Black townships, often based on models of tribal authority, to punish the criminals that the state ignored. These courts were an attempt to balance a general strategy that embraced the disruption of everyday life with a desire for order, albeit not the kind the state wanted to impose. The diffuse nature of resistance leadership and the absence of any unifying ideology meant that there was often a large gray area between political activism and mere economic violence. The distinction was serviced by the difference between the identity labels "comrade" and "tsotsi." Comrades were politically conscious and activist youth who saw their activities as contributing to the struggle against apartheid. Groups of comrades enforced boycotts of White-owned businesses by searching the shopping bags of people returning home to the townships. They would loot and burn delivery trucks, distributing the contents to "the people."[9] In contrast, economic crime was carried out largely by tsotsis, gangsters, and other assorted parasites of apartheid's urban Black landscape. As the transition progressed, however, the key factors that made comrades and their actions political were sometimes lost.

> The degeneration of self-styled political vanguardism into the more mundane pursuit of self-aggrandizement prompted activists on the ground to coin the term comtsotsis as a way of describing the unseemly mixture of former 'comrades' who turned to gansterism and common crime.[10]

For most individuals, the fight against apartheid was ultimately more about a better material existence—better houses, cars, jobs—than about getting the vote. For those lacking education and experience doing anything besides sowing disorder, crime against those who benefited from apartheid appeared not only practical but also completely justifiable.

As this atmosphere of ungovernability and disorder spread, the calculus of efficiency that balances all social orders made apartheid increasingly costly for Whites. The culture of justifiably contravening the law helped opposition movements encourage behavior that eventually made apartheid unworkable. This decline in efficiency, projected into the future, contributed to F. W. de Klerk's decision to begin negotiations with the opposition in 1990. Those negotiations eventually resulted in the inauguration of Nelson Mandela as State President on May 10, 1994. While this transition was quite violent, the violence maintained a certain legitimacy reflected in the label "political." After the transition, that label and the claim of legitimacy it entailed were no longer viable.

THE ERA OF NEGOTIATION

The fifty-one months of the formal political transition were characterized by uncertainty and disorder. The trajectory of that disorder alternated between the bloody civil war that had been perennially associated with the idea of political change in South Africa and the hopeful embodiment of esoteric theories of nonviolent conflict resolution. In the end, South Africans careened between the two possibilities. The formal process was enough removed from the dire predictions to be classified by some as a miracle, but the years were also marked by the kind of tumultuous conflict that one would expect from people renegotiating their social order. From February 1990 to April 1994, fifteen thousand people were killed in political violence.[11] But rather than the frontal assault on White society promised by years of apartheid rhetoric about *die Swaart gevaar* and the total onslaught, this violence was almost exclusively contained within Black communities. Despite the efforts of the media and politicians to simplify the story for their respective audiences, the violence that was often represented as either ideological or tribal battles was actually much more complex, driven by local issues, petty feuds, perceived interests, and unconscious fears.

This violence provided the backdrop against which many of the issues of the transition were sorted out. As political parties negotiated with each other in a variety of formal settings, they were also competing with each other in the court of public opinion on the topic of disorder. Each side proffered interpretations, explanations, and solutions that they hoped would resonate both with their core constituencies and the widest possible range of undecided South Africans. In the newly expanded political atmosphere, suddenly the opinions of many more citizens mattered, not only to contemporary social stability, but to the electoral success that would provide the mandate to mold the congealing social order. While the parties' identities were largely established, to the degree that parties dealt with issues, the issues were those of economic and physical security.

Momentum in the multifaceted negotiations over the future social order seemed to coalesce in three broad phases. For the first eighteen months after Mandela's release, the government was in a much stronger position than the internally disorganized ANC. In July of 1991, the ANC held its first national convention since being unbanned and the party emerged unified and invigorated. As the forums for negotiations shifted to the National Peace Accord in September and the first Convention for a Democratic South Africa (CODESA) in December of 1991, momentum also shifted to the ANC. After two-thirds of the voters in an all-White referendum voted in favor of the negotiation process in March 1992, the government became more intransigent and negotiations broke down for six months. Finally, in September 1992, the negotiations entered a third phase, one in which the government and the ANC began to see their fates tied to each other and formed a contentious but sturdy center that they proceeded to defend against potential disruptions. Any one of a long list of events could easily have derailed the negotiation process, but once the formal transition hit the third phase and a political center became defined (in fits and starts) as whatever could function as a consensus among the ANC and the government, each attack from the margins produced only greater incentives for the center to push forward. Mandela and De Klerk turned a variety of tragedies into justification for continuing the process. After a three-day election in late April declared substantially free and fair by an army of international observers, on May 10, 1994, Nelson Mandela was inaugurated as State President and head of the transitional Government of National Unity (GNU).[12] The GNU consisted of all the major parties that had won more than five percent of the popular vote, and the cabinet positions were divided up between the leaders of these parties.

During the politicized atmosphere of the negotiation years, it was not just the fundamentals of formal governance that seemed open for reinterpretation, but many of the social mores that had justified the distribution of wealth and the proper methods for settling disputes. In addition to the disorder more readily associated with politics, therefore, the incidents of common economic crime also dramatically rose. In 1990, serious crime rose by a record 8.5 percent, and South Africa had a murder rate five times that of the United States.[13] These trends continued throughout the early 1990s, and most South Africans watched them with trepidation. There were, however, factors that helped mitigate perceptions of crime during the negotiations. First, other events diverted society's attention. Second, economic violence was still largely contained to Black areas, thanks to the continued strength and outlook of the apartheid police forces. Third, and as a result of the first two reasons, such common economic violence was more easily lumped together with all the political violence, and thus was labeled as part of the larger process of changing the structures of politics.

Only after the formal political changes were ceremonially sealed did these three factors change. The elections and inauguration were cathartic symbols that completed the transformation of the most politically charged aspects of apartheid. Then, contrary to centuries of South African political history, the Government of National Unity began making decisions by consensus. In a society saturated with domestic and international media intent on gauging the success of the "miracle," something else needed to become newsworthy. At the same time, the police force underwent a variety of changes, the immediate transfer of material wealth that many expected failed to materialize, and the formerly tight controls on where people could live, work, and even walk were relaxed. This was the backdrop for the 1994 "explosion" of crime. Inherent in the post-apartheid discourse on crime is a tribute to the legitimacy of the formal political negotiations, for after Mandela's inauguration the acts of violence and disorder that had been labeled political lost that implied justification and became simply crime.

CRIME IN THE POST-APARTHEID ERA

In September 1996, State President Nelson Mandela admitted for the first time that crime in South Africa was "out of control."[14] This assessment was long sought by many South Africans who had been expressing the same sentiments since soon after the elections in 1994 and were looking for some indication that the government was committed to solving the problem. The ascendance of crime to the position of South Africa's most important social problem is in part attributable to the elimination of the larger problem of formal apartheid, but crime, and especially violent crime, had been increasing since the 1980s and had manifested a "relentless upward trend" in the early and mid-1990s.[15] In the years since, the amount of crime in South Africa has become a site of some disagreement, with government crime statistics often showing rates of crime to be stable or declining and critics pointing out that such generalizations seem to contradict daily experience.[16]

Statistics are one perspective in the discourse on crime, and the politics of their use will be examined later. At this point it is sufficient to note that disparities between various sets of statistics suggest that they are best read as components of larger arguments about crime. However, statistics are useful in providing a sense of the social conflict that crime represents. For example, in the year 2000, South Africa had a murder rate of 49.3 per 100,000 in population.[17] This was nine times the international average of 5.5 per 100,000 and almost eight times the United States' 1999 rate of 6.3.[18] In the categories of burglary and motor vehicle theft, however, U.S. rates outpaced South Africa's by a large margin.[19] Between 1994 and 2000, reported crime increased by 24 percent.[20] Of the 2.4 million crimes police recorded in 1999, only 200,000 resulted in convictions.[21]

Such statistics do not adequately convey the effect that fear of crime has had on post-apartheid society, nor do they explain the ways in which crime has become a political issue. Newspapers and television newscasts are filled with sensational stories of heinous crimes, and general public perception is that crime, and particularly violent crime, has become one of the defining characteristics of post-apartheid life. Surveys indicate that crime outpaces even unemployment as a perceived problem.[22] While public perceptions of crime fluctuate to some degree, the specter of crime affects the daily life of every South African, altering established patterns, imposing restrictions on movement, and adding both material and psychological costs to a range of activities that used to be significantly more free, even for those who were oppressed in so many other ways. This loss of everyday freedom is ironic in that the struggle against apartheid was couched in terms of a wider distribution of freedom, rights, and liberties.

In my interviews, personal stories of victimization involved mostly muggings, burglaries, and experiences that would seem unremarkable, even mundane, to denizens of any large urban area in the West. Such experiences are unfortunately endemic to life in any atmosphere charged with the kind of vast disparities in wealth and lifestyle that characterize contemporary South Africa. For many of the more jaded foreign tourists, Cape Town, Durban, and even Johannesburg may seem no more dangerous than New York, Mexico City, or Washington, D.C. But in South Africa, such experiences and the stories of them must be interpreted through a social context heavy with years of apartheid sediment. Remnants of apartheid common sense have helped produced a fear that is both pervasive and resilient among all South Africans. In the years immediately following the transition of power, this fear was perhaps a bigger problem than crime itself. A Human Sciences Research Council survey from the mid-1990s found that only 28% of respondents felt that the government had crime under control and 44% felt safe in South Africa, but only 10% of the respondents indicated that they had in fact been victims of crime.[23] Certainly the percentage of South Africans who have been victims of crime has gone up in the years since, but it is still useful to separate the impact of fear from the economic impacts of crime.

While all South Africans have some reason to be fearful, fear seems particularly powerful among Whites, in part because Whites had become accustomed to having the enforcement apparatus of the state attuned to their particular security concerns. The dispersion of crime out from Black areas has forced Whites to adapt to a new situation of insecurity. This is not to suggest that the *feeling* of insecurity is new for most Whites. The apartheid social order was maintained in part by programming into Whites a deep-seated fear of what would happen if the state were not there to mediate their relationships with other groups. The White situation had always been presented as significantly tenuous, but anxiety about the future accumulated rapidly through the 1980s and early 1990s. "They had an election that was cathartic, but anxiety is not released in the few days of an election and a rugby victory. You either work through it or you displace it. Crime is the issue that gets all that anxiety about the place of Whites when Blacks take over."[24] While a small portion of the Whites to whom I spoke still believed that a civil war would take place in South Africa, more were worried about how Whites would be made to pay for apartheid. For many, crime seemed to be a way for Blacks to carry out what the formal process of negotiation denied them.

> Imbedded in whites' anxieties about South Africa's "crime wave" is a related, racist subtext: a sense of siege and insecurity effected by criminals who, almost by definition in this discourse, are black. In this sense, the "crime wave" serves as an informal validation of whites' fears of post-liberation retribution.[25]

These fears, and especially White fears, have ramifications for how South Africans organize their spaces, economics, and politics in the post-apartheid era.

Already a high art under apartheid, post-apartheid crime has both refined and diffused the ubiquitous battlements behind which urban and suburban South Africans hide. This "siege architecture" now includes electrified fences, razor wire (invented in South Africa), and wrought iron fencing that allows neighbors and police to see suspicious activities inside your fortress.[26] Behind the walls, windows sport burglar bars welded in place and passages to sleeping areas regularly have steel "rape gates" which can quickly be closed to present another barrier to anyone determined enough to actually get into the house. Other homeowners rely on big vicious-looking dogs. For those frightened enough to move, another option is presented by the trend to "cluster homes."[27] These small, walled communities have their own conspicuous, heavily armed guards who check the credentials of everyone entering the gates and stand ready to respond to any emergency within.

Beyond these physical deterrents, nearly every suburban home is also protected by a private alarm company of some kind. The security industry has its roots in the apartheid era, when the state "encouraged its growth so that state resources could concentrate on policing political dissent."[28] In post-apartheid society, security businesses are booming.[29] The ratio of private security guards to state police is around 5 to 1, compared with 2 or 3 to 1 in the U.S.[30] Increasingly home protection features an "armed response," which promises that an armed guard, trained and ready to fire upon intruders, will arrive within seconds of an alarm. These private guards are often stationed in trailers or patrol cars in each neighborhood, ready to speed to their clients' defense. For added peace of mind, many services offer guards trained as paramedics.

As security becomes a more illusive feeling, people without access to these legitimate security companies often turn to some of the very people responsible for those feelings in the first place. In the case of the townships of the Cape Flats, this often means gangs. The Firm, a cartel of major drug dealers in the Western Cape who organized themselves to divide market share and reduce conflict among the gangs, even introduced the Community Outreach Forum (CORE), a public relations vehicle designed to help replace the government as the guarantor of social stability in some communities. The Firm even applied to organize the security for the Olympics as part of Cape Town's bid for the 2004 summer games.[31] After some consideration, the committee chose not to accept the organization as an official bidder.

Vigilante groups are another controversial source of security. High profile vigilante movements include People Against Gangsterism and Drugs (PAGAD) in the Western Cape and Mapogo a Mathamaga (Mapogo) in the Northern Province and Mpumalanga. PAGAD was begun in the Coloured townships around Cape Town, where gangs were a large part of the criminal and social scene.[32] Mapogo a Mathamaga was started by a group of Black businessmen in 1996 and in 1999 claimed a membership of thirty thousand.[33] Both groups are widely known for the harsh punishment meted out to alleged criminals. A newspaper quoted a Mapogo member describing the group's philosophy as "an eye for an eye. If you kill somebody in a hijacking, you will be tracked down and killed. Punishment is inflicted in public. The world must know what happens to those who turn to crime."[34] After a spate of negative publicity and criminal charges against its members, Mapogo warned its members that the corporal punishments administered to criminals should stop short of execution.[35] The campaigns have lowered crime rates, which has helped the movements recruit people from all racial groups.[36] These vigilante movements are manifestations of a lack of faith in the power of the state to fulfill its traditional responsibilities over justice and equity issues and the perception that prison is an insufficient punishment to provide deterrence. From the state's perspective, these movements are closely related to the criminals they battle, in that both groups pursue their interests outside the government's vision of the social order.

Other grassroots movements against crime have coalesced around positions that value the state and reflect a desire to regulate social interactions through its institutions. In a sense, these groups epitomize civil society as it is widely understood. Like the vigilante movements, these nonviolent, grassroots demonstrations were built on the perception that the government was not taking the problem of crime seriously enough. Instead of challenging the authority of the state by taking actions normally reserved for it, however, these groups have focused frustrations and energy into demands that it take those actions. The specifics of these movements are analyzed below as part of the social discourse on crime.

Crime has provided South Africans with opportunities to negotiate their emerging social order. Arguing and acting about crime are some of the primary ways that South Africans participate in the solidification of order in a visceral way. Crime is one of a very few issues in a public sphere still dominated by the momentum of loyalties and party affiliations forged during apartheid. The public discourse on crime is very rich, and its many layers provide insights into the force and trajectory of the New South Africa's emerging arrangement of rules, patterns, and, most important for this study, identities. The next section presents an impression of the discourse, which is then analyzed with the constructivist theory of political identity in mind.

THE DISCOURSE ON CRIME

The issue of crime arises almost inevitably when South Africans gather. Stories of crime flow easily into casual conversation, and increasingly those stories are not just recountings of urban legends, but personal accounts of victimization. Many factors complicate the public discourse about crime, including acute media attention, the residue of apartheid's rhetoric, and the reclassification of many violent activities from political to just plain criminal. But for most South Africans, everyday life seems more dangerous since the country's first multiracial election in April 1994. This section presents analysis of the continuing discourse on crime as represented by the media, the government, and anticrime social movements.

THE MEDIA—FRAMING THE DISCOURSE

Crime has been the most consistently important news story in post-apartheid South Africa. University of Cape Town criminologist Wilfred Scharf blamed this in part on the nonadversarial style of politics that characterized the first several years of the Government of National Unity, whose consensus politics suddenly ended the spate of reliable headline stories about political conflict. To fill the gap, the media elevated crime to "public enemy number one" as "the political issue that sells papers."[37] As a result, Superintendent Renate Bellkingham of the Witswatersrand Police Psychology Services was able to argue that "[t]he media is playing a major role in heightening the public's feelings of paranoia."[38] Professor Beaty Naude, head of the University of South Africa's Criminology Department, agreed, blaming the media for a feeling of fear out of proportion to the situation. "The government really has to prove it is in control and the media has to start focusing on the positives. It is not as bad as people think. . . . Everyone is concentrating only on the negatives. The media is creating the perception that it's all bad. This heightens the feeling of fear."[39] At the same time, the issue was acceptable as news because it "generated a sense of unity, a false unity, sort of we're all in it together. It affects rich and poor nearly similarly."[40] Crime united political factions and became South Africa's modern "folk devil." Scharf claimed that news outlets reveled in "skewering the folk devil" and creating moral panics by accentuating dramatic crime scenes, turning them into "the icons of the moral abyss into which South Africans stared."[41]

The practicalities of creating this folk devil hang in the nuances. Everyone seems to agree that South Africa has a significant problem with crime. Many have argued, however, that it is only geographically different from the common economic crime that apartheid (and the struggle against it) did such a good job of hiding. Many of those aware of the extent of crime in Black areas under apartheid argue that White South Africans are finally experiencing the detrimental side effects of the kind of multiclass society that apartheid created. From this perspective, the sudden media interest in crime appears to arise from the fact that Whites are now victims as well. "That criminality is so much more a central issue in the debates within South African life than it ever was in the past is, of course, a consequence of changing perspectives on and within the country, not of the daily reality which the mass of South Africans have had to face."[42] This perception is widespread. A woman from Gugulethu told me that the only reason the ("New" National Party) provincial government of the Western Cape finally stepped in to do something about taxi violence was because an innocent White was killed during a shoot-out on a highway.[43] A retired professor and government official reflected the same cynicism in his analysis of newspaper coverage.

> A gang related murder would never get the same exposure from the media as if a White doctor gets hijacked and murdered. So crimes against Whites would be something that's very high on the list of things that people are upset about. . . . Newspapers try to be politically correct so they don't report the race of criminals. But some highlight [White criminals] to try to balance out the predominance of obviously Black criminals in the stories they report. If you compare violent criminals according to race, they are proportionally equivalent. Nobody does that.[44]

This consciousness has consequences in the formal political arena. A self-identified formerly-Black-now-Coloured activist told me that many Coloured people used the hype about crime to justify their votes for the National Party in 1994. "I don't know why we are suddenly more conscious of crime because it has been there all along. It is now more obvious, I guess."[45]

Race often has been a part of discourse on crime and the media. In a speech in September of 1998, President Mandela criticized the media for blowing the crime problem out of proportion, and he did so in racial terms. While he admitted that crime levels were unacceptable, he claimed that crime was "mainly a white preoccupation fomented by a white-owned press."[46] In response, the *Citizen* criticized the "ANC-controlled" South African Broadcasting Corporation (SABC) for what it called a "habit of playing down violence" and essentially lying to the public. "The subtext is that the government does not approve of continual reporting and comment on crime. This puts pressure on the media to distort reality."[47] The *Natal Witness* framed the two perspectives largely in terms of class differences.

> Among the poor, [the debate over crime] will be seen as just another example of the hypocritical and unpatriotic behaviour of the formerly privileged, forever whining about their loss of racist advantages. For the upper and middle classes, it will confirm their view of a society in terminal decline run by an incompetent government. Such divisive perceptions are singularly unhelpful to all South Africans. There needs rather to be a broad recognition that it is not only the wealthy and the racists who want a life free of crime, or schools which actually function, or streets free of litter.[48]

The newspapers with a heavy Black readership have tended to evoke race in their criticisms of the police. After one successful police raid on Hillbrow, a notoriously crime-ridden section of Johannesburg, that resulted in the capture of many illegal immigrants from African countries, one paper asked why areas of the city where illegal immigrants from Asia and Eastern Europe were not targeted. "Combating crime is one thing, perpetuating xenophobia and racism is another."[49] Another celebrated the appointment of Jackie Selebi as the first Black police commissioner by arguing that Selebi "is absolutely correct when he says he would serve the whole of SA and not only blacks. But we want him to treat our townships as a priority. It's about time that black people feel protected by their own kith and kin. SA is a black country and it must be seen as such."[50]

The media's relationship to the government with respect to crime has been, quite predictably, varied. In the days after apartheid, a vibrant free press in South Africa arose quite quickly, with many editorial boards generally supporting the government and others more inclined to criticism. The entire spectrum, however, could generally be counted on to comment loudly on the crime issue. The desire to fulfill the expectations of a modern democracy encouraged many newspapers to cast themselves as watchdogs for the public and the persistence of crime was an easy target. For example, the press was in the forefront of skeptics criticizing the government's crime statistics, and the comments were quite effective. One survey found that 70 percent of Whites and 50 percent of Blacks did not believe government reports about reduced levels of crime.[51] Bureaucratic ineptitude, police corruption, and the use of excessive force have also been prevalent themes in both stories and editorials. The papers were increasingly critical of the Government of National Unity for what was perceived to be a lack of action during the latter years of its tenure.

After the turnover in government in 1999, however, most newspapers expressed optimism at the prospects for addressing the scourge. From President Mbeki's first speech to open parliament two weeks after his inauguration, papers responded positively to the priority that Mbeki seemed to be putting on crime. The announcement during the same week of the formation of a special crime-fighting unit, the Scorpions, was heralded as evidence that the government intended to back up its words with action. The press cast the new department as a way to reinvent crime fighting in South Africa. New Minister of Safety and Security Steve Tshwete was received with similar enthusiasm, as was Director of Public Prosecutions Bulelani Ngcuka. Tshwete, in particular, seemed to have the passion the editors were looking for, calling criminals "human scum" and "subhuman" and promising to be "ruthless and aggressive" in his tasks. Tshwete's "tough profile" was given credit for a March 2000 HSRC survey that found that 60% of South Africans believed the government has some control over crime, compared to 49% in December 1998.[52] The esteem with which the press held Jackie Selebi, appointed as National Police Commissioner in January 2000, was so great that he was held up as a moral example for readers.

> But the reality is that we ourselves are chipping away at our country's moral edifice every time we don't stick to the straight and narrow. If we don't allow our own consciences to be heard, and we don't make an effort to clean up our acts, SA is heading for the moral cesspit, from which no number of Jackie Selebis could extract us.[53]

The new personnel, the establishment of the Scorpions unit, and several successful, highly publicized operations increased confidence in the criminal justice system and had, *Business Day* suggested, "a sobering effect on the sometimes panic stricken overstatement of SA's crime problem," encouraging citizens "to convey a less doom laden picture of the country to the outside world."[54] As confidence in the law-enforcement institutions increased and South Africa was faced with the possibility that crime might ruin their (ultimately unsuccessful) bid to host the 2006 Soccer World Cup, there was a renewed emphasis on the public's contribution to the anti-crime effort. While the effect of the press on either government or the public at large is nearly impossible to measure with respect to crime, clearly the media will continue to contribute to the discourse with both interpretations of the issues and formulations that will provide South Africans with words to express their positions.

Government—Constructing Authority

From its position as guarantor of social order, the government contributes significantly to the discourse on crime. However, because it has a vested interest in portraying the situation as improving, speeches, press releases, and statistics need to be treated not as facts about the state of crime in South Africa, but as part of the discourse over it.

As explored above, statistics have proven only marginally successful in convincing the public that government efforts at crime reduction are effective, despite several independent reports that found that public skepticism over SAPS statistics was misplaced.[55] In July of 2000, however, Minister Tshwete placed a ten-month moratorium on the release of crime statistics to allow time for the statistical process to be brought into line with accepted scientific standards. These new procedures were to provide more accurate numbers beginning in the third quarter of 2001. Even with the new procedures, the statistics only include crimes reported to the police, but the government claims that levels of reporting were substantially higher than in most other developing countries and only marginally lower than in the United Kingdom. Even with these assurances, however, people in the general population are more likely to rely on their own personal experience and that of those around them to inform their opinions about their safety and security.

During the years of the GNU, government officials generally blamed their inability to reduce crime on the momentum of the apartheid order that it inherited, implying that time and a certain amount of trial and error were inevitable ingredients to an eventual solution. For example, in a 1997 speech, President Mandela sought to defend his government against what he considered to be unrealistic expectations.

> A mind-set creeps into our discourse that suggests that some of us are given to throwing up our hands in despair at the slightest of problems, as if fundamental transformation would come overnight. Thus we have suggestions on the vexed issue of crime, that the President can wave a magic wand and the problems will disappear. Thus we have exaggerated statements that we are failing to uphold, defend and respect the constitution.[56]

The transformation of the police from a tool of repression into a "police service," one of the explicit goals of the transition, requires more than just new police cars and evocative names. Under apartheid, police were not trained as public servants, but as the repressive arm of the state. And more general problems persist. A study in early 1997 found that 70 percent of staff time was devoted to administration and only 30 percent to policing.[57] Corruption is widespread and the number of police officers convicted of crimes nearly doubled from 1998 to 1999.[58] Police statistics show that in 1997, police were three times more likely to be involved in criminal activities than members of the general population.[59] In 1999, Commissioner Fivaz revealed that 30,000 or nearly one quarter of South Africa's 127,000 police officers were functionally illiterate.[60]

After some delays as the tricky project of transforming the police gained momentum, funding for police and crime prevention went up steadily in the late 1990s, reaching 15.5 billion rand for fiscal year 2000.[61] The money funded some innovative projects—cameras in the Johannesburg Central Business District, watchtowers in Port Alfred, geographic information system technology, helicopters equipped with satellite tracking equipment—as well as more regular requirements of police work. Drastic changes such as the consolidation of a variety of existing special units into the new Scorpion division required officials who inspired confidence both among the police officers and among the population generally. Tshwete and Selebi seemed to hold such confidence. In addition, the government presented the changes as improvements by evoking models of crime fighting from the United States—the Scorpions were continuously referred to as the South African FBI and U.S. racketeering laws were held up as an example of how unconventional crime-fighting methods were compatible with a strong bill of rights.

Another issue that has plagued post-apartheid governments is the death penalty. Capital punishment was widely used under apartheid, but the ANC leadership demanded that it be outlawed in the post-apartheid constitution. For many South Africans, the contemporaneous explosion of crime levels suggests that the death penalty may have indeed been a deterrent to violent crime, and the push for the revival of the death penalty has been one of the most vociferous social movements in the post-apartheid era. Nelson Mandela and now Thabo Mbeki have repeatedly declared their opposition to reconsidering the ban, but there is a widespread perception that the experience of the ANC leadership as prisoners has caused them to overextend the rights of prisoners to the detriment of the rights of victims. This perception that too many rights have been extended to criminals was one of the factors that "put people in an advocacy type of role" for the death penalty.[62] Indeed, I interviewed wealthy conservatives, poor street people, an ANC Member of Parliament, Whites and Blacks who supported a return to the death penalty.

> The decision on the death penalty was a mistake and it will come back. We were trying to conform to others' expectations in our constitution. Eventually our toughness will come back and we need it. [Life here] is incompatible with the human rights thing—the complexity of life in South Africa is not dealt with. The ban on capital punishment erects a new apartheid of human rights, not a practice of human rights by individuals—so all the traps of apartheid rights are there again.[63]

Even an official in the Ministry of Safety and Security told me, "The longer we are in government, the more we say that we want bad guys to go to jail and keep them off the streets for a while, not to rehabilitate them. That may not be possible."[64] In a speech a mere two weeks before the 1999 election, Defense Minister Joe Modise told a gathering in Mpumalanga that the ANC needed to win a two-thirds majority so that it could amend the constitution to reduce the rights of criminals. Prisoners, he said, had "unfortunately" been given too many rights when the constitution was drafted.[65] As an ANC Member of Parliament told me, criminals are no longer afraid of going to jail.

> The criminal is afraid of the darkness, but once he goes through that darkness many times, he is not afraid of that darkness anymore. Because the apartheid system arrested people for very minor offenses, no [Black] man our age has not gone through that system. So a deterrent was overused and people got used to it. . . . The increase in violence after the end of apartheid is because there is a system of rights and people are no longer afraid of being beaten. Jail saves you from responsibility—you don't have to work to provide for your family when you are in jail and you get everything you want.[66]

It was only in 2000 that a law allowing the confiscation of the benefits of alleged crimes came (haltingly and with court challenges) into effect.

For many South Africans, the government's efforts at and success in controlling crime is the most important standard by which the legitimacy of the post-apartheid state and its claims to authority will be judged in the future. The vast majority of South Africans have accepted the legitimacy of South Africa's governance structures, and the success of the second round of post-apartheid elections held in June 1999 demonstrates that the system is continuing to coalesce into a new set of social arrangements. However, the inability of the government to provide a feeling of security to its citizens has produced social movements that do or could challenge the state's control over portions of the social sphere. Other social movements are challenging the state to expand its influence further into that sphere and meet its implicit obligations to provide security.

ANTICRIME SOCIAL MOVEMENTS

Most of the public discourse about crime has focused on policy issues and hence on the government. For some, the prevalence of crime demonstrates either incompetence or serious flaws in the government's approach or both. For others, the causes of crime rest more in a lack of effort, which demands public action to change governmental priorities. Most of these policy efforts have been focused on the police. An official in the Ministry of Safety and Security told me that the population at large had a fair amount of faith in the police in 1994. By 1997 that confidence was gone because of corruption and lack of delivery. "The floor has dropped out," he said.[67] The perception of government ineptitude produced a variety of social movements, movements that can be analyzed as contributions to the public discourse about crime.

For those convinced of the government's incompetence to deal with (or even its collusion in) post-apartheid crime, social movements have centered around the provision of extra-governmental security and sometimes justice. The strategy is an application of the "people's power" philosophy of apartheid resistance, not to negate a state control that exists, but to fill a perceived void of such authority. The zeal with which vigilante movements like PAGAD and Mapogo have pursued their war against gangs and crime appears from the government's perspective as a threat to social order in several ways. The most immediate threat is violence. A police spokesperson claimed that there were 667 violent attacks in Cape Town in 1998, and PAGAD was blamed for 188 of them.[68] This included over seventy bombs, some against purely civilian targets.[69] Underlying this visible threat is the concern that the state is no longer that guarantor of the safety of its citizens. Governmental authority that came at such a high price is weakened when citizens turn to resources outside the state to attempt to alleviate their insecurities. Therefore, in the rhetorical battle for control over the trajectory of the post-apartheid social order, the state paints both crime and vigilantism as antidemocratic. Another, less dramatic threat comes from the booming private security industry. Compared to vigilante movements, the legitimacy of private security is more widely accepted, but it also has the potential to accentuate divisions that the government has set out to try to alleviate. As security is taken out of the hands of the state, it becomes converted into a commodity, a redefinition that risks "eroding a fundamental norm of democratic societies—that policing should be uniformly available to all, its powers exercised through universally applicable laws."[70] From the perspective of the state, both of these movements reduce the government's power to dictate the terms and conditions of social order.

Other movements, however, were directed at encouraging the state to fill the perceived gap in security. Many of these movements were rather ambiguous public demonstrations demanding that the government simply act against crime. For example, among the free postcards and advertisements available in a variety of South African bars and restaurants appeared one with the South African flag punctured by three bullet holes. On the back was a plea to President Mandela to "make crime your priority today!" People were encouraged to sign the postcard and return it to a slot in the rack. After several months, three hundred thousand postcards from all across the country were dropped from a helicopter on the grounds of the Union Buildings in Pretoria. Hundreds of children from a nearby township then collected the postcards and presented them to the Minister of Safety and Security who made a speech acknowledging the outpouring of concern and citing all the government was doing to combat the scourge.

One widely publicized social movement of the late 1990s was a World Wide Web site dedicated to the story of Robby Kaplan. After Kaplan was brutally attacked, robbed, and left for dead in his own home, his brothers constructed a web page to tell people about the attack and their brother, who miraculously survived and became a vocal symbol of the anticrime movement. The web site evolved into a place for people to tell their own stories of victimization.

> This web site is dedicated to all those citizens of South Africa who have suffered the trauma of a violent crime. Please support it. Share your unique tragedies and offer your suggestions by submitting them on the discussion forums. Not only will this allow you to network with others that have experienced the trauma of a violent crime, but your input will also be used when we meet with President Nelson Mandela to demand a REAL SOLUTION to the tragic crime problem all South Africans have to face day in and day out.[71]

The site accumulated over a million hits in its first few weeks. By February 1999, 1,264 "tragedies" had been posted on the site for all to read.

While the expressed purpose of these kinds of movements was often to provoke government action or raise awareness, they also functioned as psychological venting of the fear and frustration associated with seemingly random victimization and as an opportunity to empathize with other victims and to grieve publicly for the losses associated with crime. One weekend, relatives and friends brought victims' shoes to a park and laid them out on a hill in silent tribute to their humanity and their numbers. A newspaper organized a mural along the walls of its downtown building and allowed friends and relatives to commemorate victims through art. From the government's perspective such movements functioned mostly as opportunities to empathize publicly with the plight of its citizens. It stretches the imagination to suggest that government officials were unaware of the problem or its resulting frustrations before colorful paper littered the government's lawn.

In fact, the tenor of some of these movements seemed to shift in the late 1990s. Significantly, they became focused on not only state action, but citizen participation in these efforts. For example, soon after the postcards were delivered, another postcard appeared in the racks. This time the bullet holes in the flag were covered with bandages, and the reverse side contained a pledge for each citizen to take to encourage a culture of lawfulness and order. In 1998, the National Institute for Crime Prevention and Rehabilitation of Offenders (NICRO) organized Whistle Week with events encouraging greater public participation in fighting crime. For three rand, people could buy a whistle to use to attract attention to crime. A newspaper editorial encouraged people to take action. "People do not have to be reminded of how prevalent crime is. They have to be focused rather on the opportunity to change attitudes and start believing that they can as individuals do a lot about it. So don't just stand their wailing and complaining, do something about beating it."[72] Lyndhurst, a suburb of Johannesburg, took the message to heart by funding and staffing its own police station, a move welcomed by the SAPS. The community raised 500,000 rand for the building, vehicles, and equipment and provided 151 police reservists and 64 civilian volunteers in addition to 12 permanent SAPS staff members.[73]

As the topic that dominates the social conversation about the present, crime is the issue that most defines post-apartheid South African society and mobilizes people to action. This public consciousness means that most people have opinions about crime and criminals, opinions that must be molded to evolving social arrangements. The ideas that have currency in the crime debate provide insights into the direction and momentum of those arrangements. Crime as a political issue is a site where the post-apartheid social order is being negotiated, and, therefore, the politics of crime provide a useful mechanism to explore dominant perceptions of identity categories in post-apartheid South Africa.

CRIME AND POLITICAL IDENTITY

From a theoretical perspective, crime can be seen as one of the common symptoms of the loss of social order, of the dissolution of a broad social agreement on rules. A dearth of commonly acceptable standards of interaction, let alone shared understandings of justice or morality, provides few disincentives for crime, especially when laws exist mainly on paper and then only tenuously. In such a period of transition, crime becomes one of the only ways that less powerful members of society can assert their claims and perspectives in the broader negotiations over new social rules. The discourse over crime, therefore, has become part of the complex process by which South Africa is solidifying an alternative to apartheid.

Definitions

This discourse is wrapped up in the meanings of the words members of a society use to interact with each other. Part of the problem of analyzing a political discourse as wide-ranging as the one surrounding crime in South Africa is that often meanings are neither constant nor shared. Even though "crime" has what could be considered a definitional core, people use the term to mean a variety of things. Technically a crime is something prohibited by an official statute, but in practice not every contravention of the law is treated as a crime. Societies, like individuals, develop layers of justification and even in the most stable social order there is a continuous process of negotiation that adapts laws and practices to changing circumstances. In situations of social transition, much more of the body of rules and norms becomes subject to this process of negotiation. The line dividing crime from acceptable, although technically illegal, activities (jaywalking, for example) is often very fluid, especially in a case such as apartheid, where newly unacceptable behavior had been previously entrenched in the legal structure of the state.

Apartheid failed, in part, because social movements succeeded in politicizing everyday life and redefining many crimes as resistance, thereby altering their social value. The end of "the struggle" in 1994 also ended popular support for justifying criminal activity as politics. The public nature of the transition meant that South Africans were invested as a nation in the perception that political violence had ended. There was a prevailing pride in the transition and a sense that political violence would demonstrate failure, while the same violence would be more compatible with success if it were portrayed as crime. "Everyone was invested in a peace process so crime took over for violence."[74] This largely unconscious redefinition makes it difficult to assess whether crime in the broadest sense increased after 1994.

The degree to which an assessment at such a broad level would be politically relevant is debatable. For most of the people I spoke to, crime meant theft or physical violence. When I asked my interviewees the kinds of crime they thought most concerned South Africans, 50 percent included mugging or robbery in their answer, 34 percent mentioned vehicle hijacking, 20 percent included rape, and 17 percent spoke of drugs. Another 21 percent and 30 percent mentioned violent crimes and theft generally, and 17 percent talked about gangs. An underlying theme, rarely broached explicitly, was that the more violent crimes, described several times as acts of "barbarism," were "Black crimes," meaning that they were most often perpetrated by Blacks. When it was expressed, this "fact" was often immediately mitigated by reference to the "food chain" of the crime "industry."[75] Whites, I was told, were the kingpins behind much of the more organized crimes. The example most often cited was carjacking. While Blacks were the ones stealing the cars, White businessmen "in big fancy houses" were said to get the profit.

This prevailing focus on violent crimes like carjacking, burglaries, bank robberies, and murder disguises the full complexity of illegal activity in society, especially neglecting the prevalence of government and private sector corruption. By most accounts, corruption was a normal part of both the government and business community under apartheid.[76] One person said that corruption during apartheid was "accepted as a symbol of civilization."[77] The government's top anti-corruption investigator, Justice Willem Heath, said that while corruption is indeed prevalent in post-apartheid society, under apartheid it was rife, even at the cabinet level.[78] Corruption was such a normal part of doing business that it was rarely prosecuted. In contrast to the apartheid era when corruption was ignored or even celebrated as a means to circumvent sanctions, today government corruption is a cause of serious concern. One woman, after complaining about corruption in the current government, said, "They say there was a lot of corruption in the old government but you certainly didn't see as much of it."[79] Another woman told me that the failure of the police made her suspicious that people "at the top" were benefiting from crime.[80] Such criticisms "strike some blacks here as racist attacks on black rule itself."[81] Racism also plays an important role in perceptions of the counterpart to government corruption, white-collar crime. The level of white-collar crime is very difficult to pinpoint for several reasons. For one thing, many companies decide to deal with the problem internally.[82] One survey found that nearly 77 percent of employee theft, more than 70 percent of employee fraud, and nearly half the incidents of customer theft are not reported. The common perception is that, like corruption, the roots of contemporary white-collar crime lay in the apartheid era, when such activities were sanctioned by the state and could be passed off as political.[83] In the discourse on crime, commercial crime seems to be most important because it is perceived to be White crime, that is, perpetrated by White criminals. Many South Africans use it as a counterbalance to the perceived "Blackness" of violent crime.

As a society in transition, the relationship of order to crime is still solidifying in South Africa. The definition of a criminal and the relation of such a label to other parts of an individual's identity are still being sorted out. The spectacle of the transition helped to establish a new basis for state legitimacy, but the project of disorder that brought down apartheid has left residues in popular attitudes, and attaching allegiance to a new social order will take time. This process of remaking social order takes place through social discourse in which members of society find explanations, patterns, and rules that resonate with their evolving understanding of reality. The discourse surrounding crime has been perhaps the most important opportunity for a new social order to take hold in South Africa.

CRIME AS A CATALYST

The relationship between crime and the social structures of identity is complex, especially in light of the highly charged political nature of identity inherited from both apartheid and the struggle against it. As a political issue, crime has provided many South Africans with their first practical opportunity to actualize their commitment to nonracialism. For many Blacks, the struggle against apartheid was about improving their everyday lives, and the ideological justifications for that process were left to political and community leaders. For many Whites, the decision to abandon apartheid was not a moral choice, but a pragmatic decision about efficiency and alignment with dominant international norms of justice, equity, and governance. Because the norms that South Africans sought to approximate were in effect imported from outside apartheid social reality, many South Africans, both Black and White, lack a visceral connection to their underlying philosophy. Crime is an issue around which such a connection can begin to coalesce.

There is a litany of reasons to expect that the discourse on crime would be dominated by racial ways of thinking. Most of the criminals who perpetrate visible and violent crime are Black. Ninety-six percent of those in prison would fall under the apartheid categories of African, Coloured, or Indian.[84] For most Whites, crime seemed to explode almost spontaneously with the demise of apartheid. The expectations of disaster that were programmed into the White psyche by decades of apartheid rhetoric can make crime appear as some kind of strategy to pay them back for Black suffering. Additionally, apartheid categories are deeply ingrained in common sense, and for many in South Africa the simplicity of racism is still the framework through which they interpret social events. While the number of people who proudly declare their "racialism" is declining, even those who claim to have transformed their consciousness often seem unconsciously restricted by apartheid's interpretation of reality.

In my 1997 survey, some respondents described crime in strongly racial terms. One young White woman in Cape Town told me that one hundred percent of criminals were Black.[85] A very wealthy, middle-aged White man in Port Elizabeth told me that the ANC government was deliberately not arresting criminals because they did not want to anger their constituency prior to the elections in 1999 (while describing in intimate detail how he got around paying taxes and the restrictions against foreign investment).[86] One Coloured activist told me that many Coloureds have begun to embrace their once-hated apartheid racial category partially in response to what is perceived as Black (now apparently meaning African) crime.[87] One Indian man told me that he had "heard or read somewhere" that crime was being coordinated by a right-wing White "syndicate" in an attempt to sow chaos and discredit the government.[88] Several others made references to violence being in Blacks' "nature."[89] Given the recent demise of legal racism, however, these explicitly racial explanations were surprisingly rare.

Most South Africans with whom I spoke explicitly rejected racism. Perhaps this had something to do with the fact that they were speaking to a foreigner, but contemporary society is clearly structured to reward the abandonment of racist principles. However, individuals in society do not all experience such deep change in the same way, and as a political issue, crime has become an acceptable repository for White fears about the end of apartheid. Defining social disorder as crime allowed people to discuss those fears using a politically acceptable vocabulary. Crime is consistent with the globally dominant image of a democratic society; political violence is not. Because most South Africans were invested in the success of the transition, fears that at one time had been integrally linked to race instead got foisted onto and encoded into the discourse on crime. Most of the opinions I heard, even theoretically complex ones, were expressed in subtly racial terms. To each interviewee, I eventually asked, "Who are the criminals?" Regardless of what their answer was, nearly every person assumed I was asking the question, "From which racial group(s) do criminals come?" The most common answer was that criminals "come from all of apartheid's racial groups," or even that they are "not just Blacks." For these respondents, race was so intimately woven into identities in the public arena that questions of a political nature immediately evoked it.

And yet these answers also demonstrate that simplistic racial generalizations are now understood to be wrong. South Africans know that the post-apartheid world is supposed to be nonracial, even if they do not fully appreciate the incumbent implications for their daily activities. Questions of identity are still so explicitly political that people feel pressure to present certain answers, even if they merely represent politically correct rhetoric. The dominant tenor of society is forcing people to reject racialism in a purposeful, almost defensive way. Even rhetoric, however, can help to solidify nonracial attitudes. The complex understandings of identity that frame crime give even those who simply repeat them experience justifying nonracialism to themselves and others.

Nonracialism is, however, a negative concept; its primary purpose is to convey what an attitude or philosophy is not. While such ideas can be very helpful in challenging and dismantling systems of thought, they are less useful in consolidating new social arrangements. South Africans are keenly aware that they are building a new South Africa, and the discourse around crime as a public and political issue provides people the opportunity to build new frameworks of understanding. A variety of possible substitutes spring to mind: nationalism, class, culture, geography, ethnicity, even gender. My research was designed to explore these options and the possibility of other organic systems of classification by studying how South Africans discuss crime.

What I found was a widely dispersed, sophisticated, and nuanced understanding of who criminals are. No single category of identity has the authority and legitimacy to dominate how people describe those involved in crime. Post-apartheid crime has unfocused the former categories of "criminal" and "victim," and those identities have yet to be refocused. As important public issues are interpreted through frameworks of social difference other than race, the usefulness of race as a code for determining rules of behavior in social interactions decreases. The belief that race can be used as a simple indicator of all important characteristics is challenged when labels that are clearly important to society, like "criminal" and "victim," cannot be neatly squeezed into racial boundaries. As such, crime is becoming a force for a new system of social identity that rejects apartheid's simplicity and embraces a complex and shifting identity. The next sections explore several competing categorizations through which South Africans explain crime. The competition between these assertions has important implications for the arrangement of social reality in the post-apartheid era.

Criminal and Victim

Fear of crime has imposed upon South Africans of all stripes a sense of victimization that has effectively redrawn some of the boundaries between "us" and "them." This fear of becoming a victim of violent crime is both prevalent and unsettling.

> One of the identities that I think is very interesting today is that of victim and potential victim and how that is articulated to citizen and rich and car driver and house owner and those sorts of thing. If you are a car owner in Johannesburg, there is a notion of potential victimhood that there was not three years ago. Now every time you get in your car, you are a potential victim. Your daughter is a potential victim. That identity is very explicit in our heads.[90]

This victim identity is established in opposition to that of the criminal. As the demise of apartheid has eliminated the political justification for crime, people re-adapted the meaning of the term "criminal" by reclaiming its negative implications. Crime is no longer an acceptable method for political mobilization, and being a victim of crime has become one.

The kind of social movements that crime has produced in South Africa provide an opportunity to experience the shift away from racial reality at both a visceral and practical level. Mobilization around "victimhood" has given people the chance to interact across not only racial boundaries, but ideological, class, gender, and geographic boundaries as well. In response to this victimization, South Africans have been encouraged to come together across racial boundaries and mobilize as noncriminals.

> So, how do we move beyond the racial categories imposed on us by apartheid? The first priority is to build a sense of community that will freeze out the criminals and empower law-abiding citizens. Yes, crime is a daunting thing, but fighting it is not a task for the government or for the South African police alone. We all need to pull together—black and white—in the fight against crime.[91]

The vigilante and protest movements demonstrate how crime has become a mobilizer of activity, and there are many other examples. The Western Cape Anti-Crime Forum was started in 1993 as a Coloured organization, but by 1994 was drawing people from Cape Town's African townships and increasingly from White suburbs too, resulting in a multiracial social alliance against crime with no ideological agenda.[92] The perception that the government was too worried about protecting the rights of criminals even legitimated an alliance between liberal anti-apartheid workers and old style hard-liners. "Crime [became] the confluence of left and right agendas."[93] A city official in Port Elizabeth cited a survey in one of the city's townships and another across the road in one of its richest areas. Crime was rated the biggest social problem in both. "This is something the whole community is facing together. And slowly it will bind them together until eventually the institutions to bring the problem into the public domain are created."[94]

The full impact of this interaction may be lost on those without a grasp of how well apartheid succeeded in its goal of racial separation. Crime has unified people who had been programmed for years to believe they had very little in common. "Civil disobedience campaigns being generated in Gauteng and other areas are across the board—they are race-, class-, and gender-blind in many respects whereas those distinctions could have been a lot more pronounced under other circumstances."[95] Common victimization by crime has mobilized people to enter the political arena as agents whose race is irrelevant and to coalesce into politically motivated, issue-centered groups that act and are seen to act in society. These activities and groups are organized using personas that privilege identity categories other than race. This move from race- to issue-centered politics has helped solidify a much more complex understanding of how politics and identity interact and has helped dislodge South Africans from their deeply racial realities. Once loose, people are forced to cast about for an alternate system of categorizing their fellow South Africans, a set of criteria by which similarity and difference can be organized for the rigors of daily life. Among the most prevalent systems are nationalism, class, gender, and geography.

CRIME AS NATIONALISM

While it is nearly impossible to measure such things accurately, it would be fair to guess that the apex of New South African nationalism came in the South African victory over New Zealand in the 1995 Rugby World Cup.[96] In their celebrations, South Africans chose to interpret the victory through the categories of national identity, relegating race to at least the second tier of importance. Many South Africans took the opportunity to try on nonracialism, demonstrating that something besides race could serve as the governing framework for public interaction and that it was possible to unite South Africans in national, nonracial terms. For many individuals who had lived their entire lives as primarily members of a race, this was a startling and hopeful experience. The nationalism of rugby demonstrated that issues could cross racial lines. Crime, in a less celebrated context, has done the same thing, providing an opportunity to characterize illegal immigrants as petty criminals, foreigners from specific countries as responsible for organized crime, and émigrés as false South Africans.

In 1998, the Department of Home Affairs (the government agency responsible for immigration) put the number of illegal immigrants living in South

Africa at 2.54 million, up drastically from the 1996 census that counted 500,000.[97] Other sources have placed the figure at anywhere from 1.5 million to a nearly inconceivable twelve million.[98] This influx of people, mostly from poorer African countries to the north, has resulted in xenophobia and violent attacks against foreigners perceived to be stealing jobs from South Africans and thus perpetuating the county's social ills, including crime. In 1996, for example, the National Party's Gauteng legislature spokesman estimated that illegal aliens cause fourteen percent of all crime in South Africa.[99] The combination of xenophobia and the reality of the economic and employment climate in poor urban areas has fostered the belief that those illegal immigrants who have not stolen jobs from South Africans must be stealing other things in order to survive. The nationalistic implication is that if the foreigners were expelled, there would be more jobs for South Africans and fewer would be forced to survive at the margins of society.

It is not only the unskilled and destitute foreigners that are linked with crime, however. Some of the crimes that seem to have exploded in the wake of apartheid are attributed to the exploitation of South Africa's perceived ultra-fluid borders. With the most developed system of ports in Africa, a regional economic hegemony that facilitates the movement of cargo into the rest of Africa, overwhelmed customs police, and a history of busting sanctions, South Africa has a reputation as a smuggler's haven. This smuggling and the secondary crimes it encourages are often blamed on specific nationalities. "Crime is becoming increasingly organized and internationalized, with Russians, Colombians and Nigerians believed to be involved in smuggling drugs and guns into South Africa and diamonds and luxury cars out."[100] Captain Giacomo Bondesio of the South African Police Service's Alien Investigation Unit alleged that "as many as 90 per cent of the Nigerians who applied for Section 41 permits—which grant temporary residence to political asylum applicants—were drug dealers."[101] Many people specifically brought up drugs when I asked them to specify crimes. Several made a distinction between "local drugs"—marijuana ("dagga") and mandrax—which had been prevalent and available for years, and "harder" drugs like cocaine and heroin that they blamed on foreigners.[102] The media often accentuate the nationality of non-South Africans in drug crimes. Carjacking rings are also perceived to be run by the Russian or East European mafia and stolen South African Mercedes Benzes and BMWs are said to be traversing Russia and Eastern Europe.[103] Whether they are true or not, these popular beliefs serve to accentuate the divisions between people based upon their citizenship and the ultimately imaginary concept of nation.

In September 1998, while on a state visit to Mauritius, President Mandela made a speech in which he tried to force a conversion from racial to national identity labels. A *Sunday Times/Business Times* survey had found that 74 percent of South Africa's most skilled residents were considering emigrating, with 62 percent citing crime as the most important reason.[104] In response, Mandela evoked nationalism strongly and clearly.

> Indeed some of the people have been frightened by the high level of crime but we are convinced that real South Africans are being sorted out in the course of the process, who are saying: "This is my country, I am not going to run away from the troubles of my country, I am here to serve my country."[105]

The comments touched off a public battle over nationalism couched in definitions of real South Africans. The former National Party mouthpiece, the *Citizen*, was perhaps the most vitriolic.

> Crime is a shockingly real problem for millions of South Africans, who do not have to prove their own "reality" by waiting to be murdered. People are outraged at having their life-and-death problems pooh-poohed when their leader is on yet another of his overseas trips. Real South Africans don't enjoy hearing foreign audiences being told things are not so bad here. Real South Africans would like their politicians to spend more time at home trying to help reduce crime. Real South Africans want to see their President being a stronger leader in his own cabinet, getting the ministers of justice, police and prisons working together to make sure that criminals are properly tracked down, properly tried, and properly punished.[106]

The debate thus became a competition to explain the important "national" issues of crime and emigration. Class and employability were presented in several editorials as the categories through which crime should be understood.[107] Others focused on racial divisions or the racism of the comment.[108] Several resorted to the ambiguous "communities" to describe the differential effects of crime.

What is striking is that each newspaper used the opportunity to promote nationalism as a solution to both crime and the divisions of society (whether racial, class, or party), the same thing Mandela was doing (if rather obliquely). The *Sowetan* sought answers in "civil society" and "patriotic responsibility."[109] The *Natal Witness* lumped people "regardless of their gender or colour" into the category of "our shared national resources."[110] Crime was presented as "a national problem"; it "is not a race issue and should never become one."[111] In this discourse, crime became an opportunity to move away from apartheid's racism by dealing with an important political issue in non- and in some cases antiracial terms. Crime has come to be one of the primary fulcrums across which South Africans are being pried loose from their racial reality. The hope of most national elites is that, once freed, they will adopt a more nation-based political reality, one that values those qualities and characteristics that these national elites are purported to possess, thereby increasing the power of those elites.

Class

Class was one of the most logical candidates for the scheme that would replace race as the primary set of cleavages in South Africa. South Africans altered their social arrangements in part to bring them into line with the globally dominant understanding of justice and equity, arrangements centered around the forces of market capitalism. Even though the South African Communist Party was an integral part of the ANC coalition, and the party line in exile was that the end of apartheid would lead to the implementation of anticapitalism policies including the nationalization of mines and selected industries, the ANC largely abandoned those policies during the give and take of formal negotiations. The demise of the Soviet Union contributed to an environment in which this decision made sense, but the main reason seemed to be a realization that the maintenance of a free market economy was the best way to ensure the allegiance of Whites whose skills were necessary for the continued development of the economy, an intermediate goal that would assure the uplifting of the Black population. The ANC's decision to work within the existing economic framework arguably allowed Whites to envision their lives in a post-apartheid South Africa, while also promising economic improvement for Blacks.

This strategy has allowed the continuation of the vast economic disparities that characterized South Africa under apartheid. After forty years, the apartheid policy of ethnic economic uplift had largely succeeded in making Afrikaners into an urban middle class. Meanwhile Blacks were exploited as cheap labor, and their widespread abject poverty was largely ignored. Today the categories of rich and poor are less racially pure, but no less stark. There are very rich Blacks and there are White homeless beggars, but the apartheid legacy still dominates economics and provides the context for how many South Africans interpret crime.

The portrait of crime that most of the respondents painted for me was backed by a fair measure of understanding for the economic context of post-apartheid society. One woman, who had actually shot at a burglar in her backyard several weeks before, expressed a sense of perspective by interjecting ". . . like he ever had a chance in life . . ." into the story of that night.[112] The words "privilege" and "opportunity" regularly appeared in explanations by people from all different backgrounds. These ideas were often intimately linked in the minds of South Africans with unemployment. Unemployment and the resulting poverty were the most widely cited explanations for crime, especially among admitted criminals and others who seemed most likely to commit violent crimes.[113] A retired professor and government official explained to me how poverty plays into the discourse on crime. "Crime a very complex thing. Most of the criminals would still justify themselves in terms of apartheid because of the economic discrepancies between the haves and the have-nots." By changing the focus to economics, he said, crime has the potential to redraw apartheid's social boundaries.[114]

This class-driven analysis was part of the accepted wisdom about crime, but was tempered by another distinction made between those who stole to eat and those involved in parasitic and exploitative crimes of greed. People used poverty to understand crime, even if they were not willing to go so far as to excuse or accept it. Apartheid, one man said, had destroyed the chances most Blacks had at a fair chance to earn a living. While new social systems were being developed to deal with this problem, society should expect those people to try to find some way to survive.[115] Poverty-driven crime, however, was juxtaposed against the kind of organized criminal activity that exploited the disorder of the transition in order to produce riches. The industry that had developed around carjacking was often cited as an example of this kind of parasitic activity. Increasingly, I was told, the poor are being mobilized by organized crime. The mafia-like Firm of the Western Cape was providing the poor townships with the social structures that the government had yet to set up. These structures provided support, but the cost was often participation in crime. "Today you can't be a street kid without being a member of a gang and you have to perform or you get beaten up. So poor people have become mobilized into illegal economy in an exploitative way."[116]

Unemployment is portrayed not just as a cause of crime, but also as a symptom of it. Multinational corporations have either curtailed new investment in South Africa or warned the government that they would in the future if crime rates did not begin to decline. Indeed, incidents suggest that these corporations have good reason to worry. In six months in 1996, sixteen out of the thirty chief executives of German subsidiaries were victims of violent crime, including the carjacking and murder of the financial director of the conglomerate AEG in August of 1996.[117]

> "Violent crime is a major fear among all sectors of the community and a potential deterrent to inward investment," said the rating agency Fitch IBCA recently, citing crime as one of the reasons for revoking SA's Rating Alert positive.... "The image of SA as country to invest in is diminishing as a result of its reputation for violence," said one senior European Union (EU) diplomat based in Pretoria. "It is a very big concern among the foreign investment community," said Maren Schellschmidt of the South African-German Chamber of Commerce and Industry.[118]

While the full economic impact of crime on investment will never be known, commonly repeated anecdotes about companies who curtailed or refused to invest in South Africa because of crime certainly affected the discourse about crime. Several interviewees blamed crime for their inability to get jobs and one referred to the economics of crime as "a vicious circle."[119]

This discourse about unemployment is one of the ways in which the relationship between crime and class is important, but others have made the connection between crime and the possibilities of successfully renegotiating the broad context of social relationships.

> Crime is the biggest single obstacle to Johannesburg's bid to maintain its place as Africa's leading industrial and commercial centre. But the intolerably high level of crime in the city centre and beyond has a more damaging long-term consequence for democracy and race relations generally. In spite of the popular notion that post-April 1994 SA is a rainbow nation in which colour plays only a marginal role, the fact is that SA remains a racially polarised society. The distinction between white and black is overwhelmingly one of

wealth in which whites have accumulated wealth and blacks have not. While the disparity in income between black and white is quite apparent, the emergence of a black elite in business, political life and the parastatals has been less well documented. Safe to say, that this process of enrichment has in itself driven a wedge between wealthy blacks on the one hand and a huge underclass of poverty. The new social dynamic is apparent in [patterns of] crime in Greater Johannesburg.[120]

Many of the wealthy Blacks who have successfully escaped the townships are the most disapproving of affirmative action and attempts to reduce educational standards because they feel that they have been able to overcome the obstacles to attain a middle class life.[121] Many Blacks are forced to straddle the dividing lines that still exist in living space and professional life. Accentuating class distinctions rather than racial ones is a way to separate themselves from both the stereotypes and the restrictions of apartheid. Iole, the head of a successful NGO in Durban, described the impact this process has on her children's school, saying that while the student body is very mixed racially, "they all look the same because they are all part of the middle class and they all get along fine."[122]

In the process of solidifying new social patterns, it is perhaps easiest to frame crime as a class issue because that is how it is most often understood in the West. In contemporary South Africa, class divisions are seen as much less explicitly political than racial ones, in part because the global-scale conflict over such distinctions ended with a victory for an ideology that asserted classes were a natural, normal part of human social relations. To the degree that class is employed in order to displace racial distinctions, crime appears as primarily an assault on the middle and upper classes by those in the lower. The class-based assessment of crime, however, carries an implicit definition of crime that focuses on violence and the theft of property. In contrast, a focus on white-collar crimes and corruption almost by definition implicates the middle classes as criminals.

This class-based discourse on crime emphasizes the differential interests that rich and poor have with respect to the order that is gradually solidifying in post-apartheid South Africa. The discourse values wealth and validates implicit claims by the wealthy about the legitimacy of their wealth and social status. In South Africa this seems a particularly soft kind of legitimacy, given that most of the wealth was gained through a process of exploitation that is now condemned. To the degree that wealthy South Africans can now legitimate class differences through, among other ways, the discourse on crime, most Whites will be able to adapt their identities and practices so that their privileges will remain largely intact.

In this sense, crime can be seen as one of the only mechanisms through which the economically disenfranchised can assert their interests into the negotiations over the new social order. Disruption of the dominant, or as in this case the emerging, social order has always been a tool by which those without traditional resources of power can make their opinions and ideas heard and felt. The class-based discourse over crime, its causes, and potential solutions draws attention to the plight of the poor even as it legitimates their aspirations to become part of the material economy. In this sense, crime is a site of public discourse, a way for people to remind society that the reason most Blacks fought against apartheid was because they thought its demise would bring very practical improvements in their daily lives. Criminals assert that they should have what others currently possess; victims assert that they should be able to keep what is theirs and/or that they should be protected from violence. To a certain degree, the ANC's electoral success can be attributed to the belief that they are the party who can best translate the political changes into changes in the distribution of economic privilege in the country. Whether or not they will be able to do so remains to be seen. Crime serves as a reminder that, at least in the eyes of many, they have so far failed.

OTHER DISCOURSES

One of the identity cleavages that apartheid's stress on race subsumed was gender. Under apartheid there were almost no opportunities for women of different races to come together as women, and even less incentive for that to happen.[123] All the South African cultures were heavily patriarchal, but the power of the racial divisions translated what could have been a unifying experience into an even more divisive one. White women had little or no social power within White society, but they did have power within the White household, which invariably included Black servants. Because in White society Black men were, in the words of Mamphela Ramphele, robbed of their very manhood, they closely guarded the power that tradition gave them over Black women.[124] The result was that Black women were at the very bottom of the social hierarchy. What might be called the transitive property of violence and humiliation meant that Black women often bore the brunt of apartheid.[125]

The end of apartheid freed more women to explore their gender commonalties and the result has been political movements based on women's issues. Civil rights against gender discrimination were entrenched by the new constitution, and the ANC allocated a third of its seats to women.[126] Popular attitudes, however, are another story, and plenty of social issues still attract the attention and action of women as women.[127] Because crime is such a widely acknowledged issue, it has served as a prominent site of conjuncture. Crimes that predominantly affect women include domestic violence and child abuse, but the most important motivating factor bringing women together across apartheid racial lines is rape.

Rape is both prevalent and underreported.[128] For a significant portion of the population, the idea that rape is a crime is still nascent and has spread only sporadically. Any fluctuation in the official statistics on rape, therefore, is more likely to be due to changes in reporting than changes in the practice itself. The prevalence of rape is rooted in widespread cultural attitudes that see women as objects. The unchallenged dominance of White males and the migratory and unsettled life that apartheid inflicted on Black South Africans created a culture in which sex was often more about power than anything else. Apartheid police used rape as a method of interrogation; comrades employed it to produce "comrade babies."[129] This attitude has carried over into post-apartheid society. Rape gangs still roam the townships, often with explicitly political purposes. A group calling itself SOCR—the Society of Comrades for Rape—believed that rape is a way to teach young women to behave correctly and to restore the traditional power relationship.[130]

> There is a debate, a concern that rape is so bad that one cannot legitimately attach the label of victim to it. Statistics suggest that an African woman is likely to be raped twice in a lifetime. Are those conditions where a person could consider themselves "victims"? I do not know. Police believe that rape is not as traumatic an event for a Black as for a White. That is based in fundamentally conservative notions of Black and White, but I wouldn't dismiss it out of hand because there are psychic defense mechanisms that if you regard yourself as a victim for something that is practically inevitable, then you think of yourself as a victim your whole life. "Victim" for me has a connotation of unexpected randomness about it.[131]

As if the patriarchal and other social imbalances were not enough, rape is often promoted by a horrifying myth that having sex with a virgin can cure a man of AIDS. Another myth surfaced later that sex with an elderly woman would do the same thing.

While crime in general is motivating people to action, rape as an experience provides a basis for a connection among women that has the visceral power to override other perceptions of difference. As the notion that rape is crime gains more currency, it provides an opportunity for women to act in the political arena primarily as women. "[Rape] is certainly mobilizing women. It is mobilizing women across the board. I think that what's important is that it is changing the way that our society thinks about women."[132] Unifying action is one of the explicit strategies of the anti-rape movement.[133] This movement has had a significant impact on the politics of crime.

> I think the victim lobby, and especially the anti-rape movement, has led the way to a reformulation of the rights of the victim against the perpetrator, demanding a kind of balancing out at the very least, if not going further to say that victims' rights should be paramount, and that perpetrators' rights should be subservient to victims interests and rights.[134]

Although it is impossible to attribute a quantifiable portion of the shift to crime, some anecdotal evidence suggests that the position of women in society is improving. One interviewee expressed joy over an observation he made at a conference he had attended that morning. As the conferees came back from small group discussions, the spokesperson that each group chose to present its ideas was a Black woman. "There was no instruction earlier on this and I think that is a sign of changes, an encouraging sign that if those processes are under way, despite all the barriers and the madness around us, there are things that are happening. And hopefully we will be able to divide dark and light a little bit."[135]

Another set of cleavages that have made their way into the discourse on crime is centered on geography. Many anticrime movements are community-based. Given the residue of the Group Areas Act, one would expect these movements to be largely made up of members of one race. What has been remarkable, however, is that as these movements grow, they have become regional, crossing the boundaries of apartheid's old racial communities. The Western Cape Anti-Crime Forum, for example, began in 1993 in a Coloured community. By 1994 it had drawn in people from the African townships of Khiyalitsha, Langa, and Nyanga and increasingly from White suburbs too. Eventually even lower middle class White areas were drawn in.[136] The Mapogo movement of the Northern Province and Mpumalanga has demonstrated a similar regional strategy and growth.[137]

In most people's assessments, a hierarchy exists among the most dangerous locations for violent crime. The informal "squatter camps" seem to be the worst, followed by the former African townships and, in the Western Cape, Coloured townships. The central business districts of the larger cities would come next, followed by the suburbs. In 1998, Thabo Mbeki, then Deputy President, actually used this impression to try to lure business to South Africa during a speech he gave in Hong Kong.

> Speaking at a lunch hosted by the SA Business Forum in Hong Kong and the Asia Society, he acknowledged that there was a high level of crime, but that there was a need to communicate this problem better. Referring to Cape Town, he said 75% of the city's murders occurred on the Cape Flats, a working class area. "But what gets communicated is that there is murder all over Cape Town."[138]

This focus on urban areas as the center of the crime phenomenon was disputed by a survey conducted by Statistics SA in March of 1998, which found that rural South Africans were "more vulnerable to violent crime than their urban counterparts."[139]

With the demise of the police state, crime no longer confines itself to political boundaries. The relative and artificial peace of rich White communities has been replaced by a more equitable distribution of crime. In addition, types of crime and criminals vary according to regions of the country. In Gauteng and KwaZulu Natal, the stereotypical criminal is a member of the "lost generation" of African youth whose education was sacrificed in the struggle against apartheid.[140] In the Western Cape, crime is primarily carried out by Coloured gangs.[141] In rural areas, there have been a large number of attacks on White farmers, often interpreted by them as political or retributive. These geographic differences have produced different correlations of interests and a variety in the social movements that crime has spawned.

The purpose of all these examples is to demonstrate the diverse ways that crime as a political issue has redrawn social boundaries. In addition to criminal/victim labels, nationalism, class, gender, and geography, I also found people who organized their understandings about crime around ideas of culture, age, party affiliation, and even religion.[142] Because crime is so important to South Africans, it has become a catalyst for new institutions of civil society and new alignments of interest. The variety of ways that agents have interpreted the issue and come together to seek to implement their interests demonstrates that South Africans have begun to adapt themselves to the full complexity of social life, a complexity on which apartheid attempted to impose a racial simplicity for more than a generation.

CONCLUSION

Having endured a destructive experience with racial simplification, South Africans seem to be actualizing a perspective that acknowledges and appreciates that an individual's identity is complex and socially constructed. The types of labels that are politically explanatory have proliferated beyond race and even the other categories of identity that are traditionally used to analyze politics. South Africans now think of the people involved in crime (a category that is further divided between criminals and victims) through national labels in some contexts, through class and employment distinctions in others, and through gender or geographic or cultural differences depending on the specific circumstances. Political identity is contextual and dependent upon the relationships within which the conversation is taking place. Sometimes the most important identity of a criminal or a victim is her or his gender or place of residence or occupational status. This contextuality also implies an appreciation of how individual identity can shift and change, and how the power of the identity labels that make up those individual identities can change. This complexity is a significant departure from life under apartheid, and the change is more difficult on some than others.

> Apartheid has gone but the scars and the wounds have not gone. It takes time for people to be healed. I think it will take far longer than we ever imagined to cure the cancer of apartheid that has done damage to our anatomies, not just a little part of us like a finger, which you could cut off and then be free. So the simplistic way of looking at things has gone and become complex, but within that complexity a lot of the simplistic attitudes still remain.[143]

As people in the process of explicitly rebuilding their institutions of governance and negotiating the rules that will guide their future, South Africans are in a unique position to build institutions that appreciate this diversity and to erect rules that incorporate these ideas into their political and social reality. My research suggests that they are inventing very interesting structures to do just that. In the same way that Japanese and German industries were rebuilt by adapting the world's newest technologies following the Second World War, the newest technologies of political identity may very well arise from the rubble of apartheid. As the post-apartheid social order continues to gain legitimacy, the aggregate amount of consensus will continue to rise and coalesce around new rules for society, and conflict and crime specifically should decrease. The South Africans with whom I spoke seem to sense this. In the interviews I conducted about crime, I asked people if crime was "as bad as they say it is," and every single person agreed that it was. However, I also asked them if they thought it would get better in the future. Out of over one hundred respondents, only one expressed pessimism.[144]

Chapter Seven

IDENTITY AND THE TRANSITION

Conclusions for the Political Theory of Social Change

THE ARGUMENT FOR CONSTRUCTIVIST POLITICAL IDENTITY

The transformation of a social order is an overwhelmingly complex phenomenon. While this complexity makes it nearly impossible to study the South African transition as a whole, it does make it amenable to analysis from a wide variety of perspectives. Indeed, the demise of apartheid has been studied from the viewpoint of Marxist classes, neoliberal economics, constitutional politics, elections, ethnicity, political parties, gender, biographies of individuals involved, regional politics, peace agreements, and a whole host of other heuristic positions. Each study represents an attempt to sort, organize, and understand either some aspect of the whole or, more ambitiously, the entire transformation from a particular perspective. As such, each is also an assertion of what is important about the transition. The differences in these studies reflect larger differences in the theoretical systems adopted by analysts. These systems help the analyst know which questions to ask and which aspects of the transition deserve attention in the search for answers.

The questions and the analytical criteria for this study are based in a social constructivist theory of political identity. This perspective evokes questions about the role of identity in social power. How do networks of ideas about identity mediate the relationships between members of a society and between members and their social order? Chapter 2 proposed a heuristic for organizing such ideas based on a conceptual distinction between the identity of a person (whether an individual or a corporate entity) and the identity labels that constitute that identity. This theory problematizes the dominant Western understanding of identity that fixes a person's identity as a constitutive core indicative of a nature and achieved through development. Theories of identity in Global Politics that assume this Western conceptualization tend to limit their analysis to one manifestation—nation or class or race—and to reify identity into the unit of analysis with which they are most concerned, usually either the state or the individual. While at their best these theories help explain changes to a single category of identity, they are not equipped to deal with the multiple and shifting meanings through which the often implicit negotiations of social change are carried out.

The analysis built here begins with the assumption that the power of identity flows not from any correspondence between descriptive labels and an entity's posited internal character, but rather from the labels themselves, which have power because they are imbued with meaning. The ways in which persons differ from each other become categories of political identity when members of a society act as if these differences are important. In this understanding, the descriptive identity labels that make up individual and group identities are better thought of as communal property, part of the public commons. Both the meanings of the labels and the rules by which they are applied to individuals are part of the lived consensus of the social order. Among other things, this status means that the labels are available for study through the texts that constitute social discourse.

Identity labels are methodologically important because they occupy an intermediate point in the process by which agents and structures co-constitute both each other and social reality generally. Constructivism posits that the social world is made in the recursive and power-laden interactions between agents and existing social patterns. If we choose to emphasize identity in this process, identity labels become codes that allow actors to organize their behavior; at the same time, they are the means by which behavior is systematized into the social order. As such, identity labels provide an excellent opportunity to study both the process by which social arrangements direct the actions of society's members and the way that agents change the social order. This theoretical framework can be applied to a wide variety of social phenomena. This book is my attempt to use it to understand processes of social change. I argue that this theory provides a basis for understanding not only the power of particular identity labels, but also the dynamics of labels within agents' identities and within the systems of power and resistance that produce larger social change.

This perspective is based on a number of assumptions about social change. To begin with, it assumes that societies (as well as individuals, identities, and most everything else) are continuously changing. Most of the changes are minor adaptations that preserve the integrity of the overarching themes and goals and therefore can be represented as the opposite of change—stability. Through a variety of strategies (including, often, the analysis of global politics), existing social arrangements are presented to the members of these societies as structural givens. Constructivism argues that fluidity is the normal state of social arrangements rather than an anomaly that needs to be explained. Social orders are not inert objects, but dynamic arrangements of related activities and behaviors whose power is best described as momentum. Large-scale social transformation requires altering that momentum, a change which may be more or less difficult depending on how consistently and passionately the rules of the order are being actualized. If the social order has a large amount of legitimacy with its members, even fundamental changes can be presented as preserving the trajectory of the order's most important rules. Both alterations to and the steering of social arrangements are done by actors who, temporarily and contextually, become agents.

Traditionally, theories of Global Politics treat agency as if it is an essential characteristic of either individuals or states. From a more contextual perspective, however, agency is not a continuous or inherent quality of particular entities, and how a social order organizes the distribution of agency is a matter for empirical investigation. Depending upon the context, agency can be attributed to a wide variety of entities—roles, individuals, groups, economic structures, political institutions, and many others. In addition, none of these entities is an agent all or even most of the time. In order to try to represent its conceptual and contextual fluidity, I have argued for conceiving of agency as residing not in actors, but in identity labels and personas whose meanings are determined in the recursive process of social construction. Agency-laden identity labels may be attached to those entities designated by the dominant social arrangements.

If identity labels become the unit of agency, actors are agents only in those contexts in which their personas include labels that confer agency. By charting changes to the labels that make up agents' personas in the contexts in which they are exercising their agency, the analysis of power and change gains focus and precision. At those times when the actor's persona has no labels that signify agency, or in those cases when interlocutors reject the actor's assertion of such labels, the actor cannot be considered a social agent, and actions that do not abide by existing social rules are likely to be punished. If an actor successfully asserts agency-laden labels in a particular context, actions in that context may come to be perceived by others as legitimate, authoritative, and structural, or perhaps as acceptable anomalies with no repercussions for actions outside of that highly circumscribed context. This strategy abstracts out of a social order only those representations of agency that are important for a particular study, allowing analysis to be contextualized in novel ways. Perhaps the most useful aspect of this strategy is that it permits scholars to study how social orders change over time while effectively holding personalities and group membership constant. The transformation of the apartheid social order presents an opportunity to put this perspective to work.

THE ARGUMENT ABOUT SOUTH AFRICA

On February 3, 1997, a new constitution, the product of years of negotiation between South Africa's political parties, became the country's official standard of political justice and equity, representing a successful transformation of the country's structures of governance and patterns of formal political activity. The most visible success of the transition was the expansion of the official definition of the label "voter" to roughly twenty million additional people who then became defined as agents in the political arena. The change also solidified South Africa's claim to be a full-fledged democracy. These changes to institutionalized political identity are indicative of broader changes to the allocation of power and agency in South Africa's social order. However, as the transition toward a nonracial, democratic social order continues, many of the rules and patterns of everyday life remain in a state of flux. Because the rejection of apartheid progressed in a sporadic and geographically irregular way, many of the standards by which South Africans judged the normality of social behavior (their own and others') lost their authority haphazardly and incompletely. From this perspective, apartheid appeared as a set of social arrangements in which power was manifested primarily in a hierarchical structure of racial identities, and South Africa's transition appeared as the process of trying to replace race as the characteristic of primary importance in the society's formal political discourse.

Analyzing the discourses of the transition allows the theoretical framework of constructivist political identity to be applied to the transformation of the structures of South African identity, a highly complex set of social interactions stretching over three decades. In order to organize that complexity, I chose three prominent political conflicts as sites where the meanings of identity labels were renegotiated. The discourses that surround these three conflicts represent the negotiations that constituted the transition from apartheid. Within these discourses, identity labels are the medium through which agents actualize existing social rules (they behave as "good" students would) and the medium through which they assert changes to those rules (after Soweto, "students" do indeed sometimes burn down government buildings). These labels are the codes that allow agents to organize the rules and patterns in which their everyday interactions are embedded. Conflicts are excellent opportunities to study these labels because they represent ruptures in the smooth surface of social activity. Because participants are often forced to justify rules and actions in the face of challenges, outsiders are able to view understandings of reality that are normally hidden by the fact that everyone assumes them to be natural or "just the way things are."

In chapter 3, I argued that the apartheid social order was a thoroughly modern attempt to gain control over the intricacies of social interaction by building institutions that conformed to a simple assertion—that all politically important characteristics of humans varied with race—presented as a scientific or ontotheological discovery about human nature. This principle allowed apartheid's architects to radically simplify social life by making all rights and responsibilities, and therefore behavioral rules for both self and others, dependent on race. Apartheid's four racial categories not only governed access to political privileges and responsibilities, but they also became deeply ingrained in the social order, determining the rules and expectations associated with most daily activities. Because racism made sense of the social environment, South Africans of all races behaved racially. That is, they strove to live up to the standards by which society at large judged them. For most people, and for all people most of the time, this reaction was unconscious; apartheid made racism seem natural. As a result, racial generalizations were not only acceptable, but valid predictors of behavior in social interactions. In the abstract, social order depends upon a kind of continuous active acquiescence to its rules and patterns by the members of society. During the late 1960s and early 1970s, apartheid achieved this depth of social order.

This was the context of political identity within which the transition began. The three conflicts that make up this study represent processes of that transition: its beginning, one of its primary battles, and efforts to solidify an alternative social order. In order to get at the public negotiations over political identity within each of these conflicts, I examined three types of discourses. News is primarily defined by its immediacy and by a widespread belief that the news media should do its best to present its audience with a version of events unencumbered by any particular political agenda. To the degree that news is seen as reactive, fact-driven, and independent, the discourse it presents attains a particular kind of authority. Government texts also lay claim to a certain type of authority based on the institution's mission to serve the interests of its constituency. However, government authority is tainted by an investment in the continuation of the existing social order. Government texts must generally be seen as proactively promoting the momentum of that social order. The texts that I have grouped together as symbols of resistance are also proactive, but that activity is targeted against what the actors see as the dominant momentum. Resistance is creative, raw, and often diffuse, even though it may solidify into more organized forms. These descriptions are ideal types that the particulars of the South African case complicate, but these categories of discourse are both representative and constitutive of different positions with respect to the conflicts examined. As such they can provide answers to the questions that frame this study—how did the social structures of South African identity change during the encompassing sociopolitical transformation, and what is the categorization scheme that has succeeded race as the governing identity framework of post-apartheid society?

Within apartheid reality, political agency was organized so as to exclude Blacks generally, but perhaps especially Black women and children. That the beginning of the end of apartheid came at the hands of African schoolchildren may help to explain why the events caught the government so unprepared. It was not the march against Afrikaans that planted the seeds of social revolution, although that certainly was the enabling factor. What changed the dynamics of political agency in South Africa was the Soweto students' response to the police shootings. At most, two marchers were killed in the initial confrontation on the morning of June 16, 1976, hardly deserving mention in South Africa's long history of political violence. But when the remaining students turned around and threw rocks at the police, killed White administrators, burned liquor stores, and generally rendered the entire order-keeping apparatus of the White state ineffective (even if only for a few hours), they inspired others to do the same and forever altered the relationship of South African Blacks to the apartheid state.

The stories of what happened in Soweto forced South Africans to notice (or remember) that their everyday reality was not some state of nature, but an invented system with a name and a rationale. As "uprising," Soweto demonstrated to both participants and observers that active resistance was possible and thrust forward the notion that the system was changeable. Perhaps more important was the dissemination of the belief that Blacks could act to force those changes. The government's blaming the violence on communist agitators was perfectly in tune with apartheid. It kept the power to disrupt the state contained to certain narrowly defined foreigners. The resistance story instead asserted that even African schoolchildren had both the ability and the justification to confront apartheid. Suddenly, it seemed normal for "students" and "Black youth" to commit violent acts against the state and its representatives. Because of Soweto, Blacks gained the power of disorder. Over time, Soweto took more and more people, both in South Africa and abroad, through the first three levels of resistance. They noticed the social order, they questioned its validity, and they acted in ways that caused trouble for the social order. It seems important that these acts of violence were spontaneous. This resistance was driven by actions that later needed to be woven into the explanations and justifications that helped make sense of them. Resistors even appropriated the labels the state used as weapons against them—"protester," "rioter," "comrade"—and converted them into titles worthy of honor *because* they were viewed negatively by the state. The labels of Soweto's resistance mythology empowered people to act in ways that were not possible in apartheid's reality. Now these acts became normal, even praiseworthy. These changes were encapsulated in the labels that were widely applicable and transportable to Black South Africans, altering the bank of codes available to describe and enforce standards for how people were subsequently expected to behave.

The battle lines of the 1983–1984 conflict over the constitution were drawn between those fighting a rearguard action to reestablish the hegemony of racial groupings and those seeking to undermine not only the existing power distribution, but the very categorization scheme according to which power was apportioned under apartheid. It was a battle for the structure of political identity in South African reality. It was fought, however, over the official distribution of political agency. As governmental leaders sought to redraw the line between political subject and political object, they unintentionally called into question the entire rationale upon which such categories were based. Even though this redefinition was almost exclusively rhetorical, as Whites simply shifted political power to the secure executive branch, the changes presented those opposed to apartheid with an opportunity to problematize the system in a way that struck a chord with average Black South Africans. This was necessarily an uneven and conflictual process. Changes in consciousness take place one person at a time. Apartheid lost legitimacy sporadically, with some issues and rules politicized for some and not for others. Waves of discontent ebbed and flowed at different times in different regions of the country. Many, including most Whites, continued to behave according to apartheid's rules in their interactions with others, but an increasing number of other members of society asserted entirely different patterns.

From the perspective of identity, the constitutional reforms are more easily seen as the government's attempt to expand the political scope of and further entrench apartheid identities. Even though they were pitched as an expansion of power beyond the traditional White stronghold, their purpose was to deprive the resistance movement of a portion of its potential constituency. They did not succeed. Instead, the primary result of the constitutional reforms was that the resistance movement coalesced along a broad front whose only commonality was opposition to apartheid. In the beginning, each constitutive group had its own reasons for lobbying against the reforms, but the process of battling the government fairly quickly solidified the movement around a Charterist, explicitly nonracial set of identities. The philosophical outlook encapsulated in the slogan "people's power" galvanized actors who, through the localized resistances of the early 1980s, had come to think of themselves as capable of political activity. This constituency was able to tap into an international antiracist and increasingly anti-apartheid discourse that changed the power of identity within South Africa. These labels helped organize resistance activities and later gave the ANC a receptive audience for its vision of a nonracial democracy for post-apartheid South Africa.

Following the chaos and violence of the formal political negotiations in the early 1990s, post-apartheid structures of governance have provided South Africans with "one of the world's most liberal" constitutions and a wide variety of individual rights. Many of these rights, however, should be considered exercises in social engineering, for their logic was imported from outside the existing dominant image of reality, leaving many South Africans to reconstruct for themselves the philosophical underpinnings of these adopted goals. These decisions were often influenced by global considerations, and it will take some time for the new South African reality to coalesce. Symptomatic of the continued search for a generally acceptable social order is the current conflict over crime. The discourse over crime represents both attempts to solidify a general structure of rules for privilege distribution and attempts by those disadvantaged by the congealing order to disrupt it and assert their own demands into the broader consciousness. While this solidification progresses, disorder will continue to be a part of life. However, as a new set of hegemonic rules for behavior is progressively legitimated among South Africans, as people begin to find that their assumptions about how others will behave are validated in interactions, order will return to South Africa. The more a society demonstrates functional consensus about its rules, the less conflict it will experience and the more coordinated the actions of its members will be. The rules that constitute the framework for that order are still being negotiated and will be renegotiated continuously. Crime is one of the political issues through which such functional consensus is being substantiated.

The discourse over crime is generally marked by a diverse, nuanced, and intricate portrait of both criminals and victims, which reflects the New South Africa's structures of political identity. South Africans have abandoned the apartheid identity project, the search for a single category of identity to govern all social contexts. South Africa's social transformation has been accompanied by a change from the modernist project of control over nature to an appreciation of the complexity of social reality, and crime is the primary issue around which this process of unfocusing apartheid reality is taking place. The texts of the discourse over crime demonstrate that the actions and ideas that it forces onto South Africans are dissolving old cleavages and allowing people the opportunity to invent new rules for interaction. The multiple and shifting nature of the labels and personas through which those rules are organized means that diversity is normal, that there are nearly infinite bases for individuals to make claims on each other, a range of possibilities that makes life less predictable and much more complex.

This complexity provides the opportunity for useful analysis from a variety of different perspectives. Analyses centered around themes that are explicit in the public discourse about the post-apartheid social order, such as the themes of race/ethnicity, economics, or political institutions described in chapter 3, are more likely than my abstract discussions of identity to inspire South Africans to tackle the problems of solidifying a new social order. To the degree that these kinds of analysis use more widely accepted terminology and present themselves as explanations with incumbent predictions about the future, they may even produce alterations in policy or behavior that will benefit the lives of South Africans. In contrast, if the argument made here can be said to have succeeded, it has succeeded only in problematizing the heuristic simplifications on which these more practical studies rely and perhaps in adding to the complexity of the topics that they seek to analyze.

CONCLUSIONS AND GENERALIZATIONS

The people who have inhabited the land we now call the Republic of South Africa have provided students of politics with more than their share of examples and cases through the years. Once again, a scholar has gone to South Africa's well in search of interesting phenomena and, I hope the reader will agree, has not been disappointed. Having sorted through South African discourses from the perspective of a social constructivist theory of political identity, I can now provide some answers to the questions laid out in the beginning of the project, questions about the politics of identity in the transformation of the South African social order and the end result of that process. For the purposes of drawing some final conclusions, let me restate the two questions that guided this study.

Question #1: Is race no longer the most important characteristic of South Africans, and if it is not, what is?

Question #2: In what ways have South Africans gone about undoing the social importance of race, and how have they constructed a different system for categorizing people?

While the answers to these questions are deeply rooted in empirically unique discourses and the particular politics of apartheid, I assert that the South African transition provides generalizable lessons that may be useful for assessing the relationship between political identity and social change in other contexts. Therefore, I will conclude with a series of three models that I hope may be portable beyond this context.

The first model that the South African transition provides is the answer to the first question, what has replaced race as the defining characteristic of the social order after apartheid? The shift to post-apartheid identities is, I argue, a model for the kinds of adaptations social structures generally will have to make in an increasingly globalized world. In this model, the transition is a move from the fundamentally modern simplicity of racial apartheid to a much more complicated array of possible identities in post-apartheid politics. Instead of trying to simplify human relations and tame "human nature" by cramming diversity into a set of four universalistic categories, post-apartheid politics are diffuse and based on the contexts and interests of the individuals involved. Political boundaries are increasingly drawn by social identities that depend upon the particular context. As a result, South Africans now need a more complicated system of identity labels to help them navigate social interactions. Apartheid constructed life as simple. "Rainbow nationalism" constructs it as complex. This complexity makes it more difficult to avoid conflicts because a single characteristic no longer gives actors a safe default set of assumptions and rules for social interaction.

For most South Africans the changes to the formal political structure of rights and responsibilities have not completely deflected the momentum of apartheid rules and standards in their everyday lives. It would be unrealistic to expect changes in the formal structure of power to alter the racist nature of wider reality in less than a generation, let alone to undermine the seemingly more innocuous, less politicized concept of groupness. But race, while often still important, can no longer be relied upon as a consistent predictor of attitudes and behavior. Race is now one of many types of identity labels used to organize reality, and actors have the ability to choose among a much wider variety of behavioral rules and standards.

This condition of complexity is indicative of many other contexts in an increasingly globalized world. Globalization presents more opportunities to confront diversity, to have contact and communication with people who are different in new and unexpected ways. Different societies have different identity categories and different schemes for distributing power among those categories. Interactions increase not only awareness of but experience in dealing with these differences. The diversity of identity in the politics of this interactive world means that there are many more bases for asserting power in interactions with others. Even in the international arena, the end of the Cold War has altered the scheme by which nation-states are sorted and categorized and has brought forth new interpretations of what a nation-state is and the rights and privileges associated with it. In general, more identity labels are becoming infused with agency and power is becoming more diffuse.

As more interactions are taking place outside the luxury of the shared rules and expectations of a mutual social order, interlocutors must confront differences more often, and conflict (in the broadest sense of a perception that goals are incompatible) increases. This kind of conflict is an inevitable and normal part of social interaction. It is not the existence of diversity, but rather the rules and strategies that we develop to deal with the conflicts it inevitably spawns that will determine the definition of peace that prevails and how much of it we have. Within a shared social order, conflict is often resolved quickly because the parties share understandings of the world and how it works. Intercultural conflicts are often more difficult to resolve because the parties lack this shared understanding. Negotiations become necessary to determine which party to an interaction has power over it. Exposure to diversity may increase the options parties feel they have for defining the context of the conflict. If the prevailing definition of a context puts one of the parties at a disadvantage relative to those with whom she, he, or it is interacting, the disadvantaged party may well be able to assert a different encompassing framework (encoded in and accessed through identity labels) that would alter that relative power distribution. The era of flux associated with globalization is marked by the increasing consciousness of this ability to step out of the prevailing definition of reality and challenge it with a specific alternative. In the search for means to assert their power in the world, new identities and old identities empowered in new ways may allow political actors to build constituencies and to mobilize those constituencies to action. If a society's members believe that rules and patterns are open to reinterpretation, they are more likely to accept assertions of agentic creativity. In other words, as its momentum decreases, there are more chances to steer the social order. The lesson of the South African transition is that changes to behavior that are justified, accepted, and systematized can change social arrangements.

The second model I would like to discuss has provided a framework for thinking about South Africa's social changes throughout the manuscript. It forms part of the answer to the study's second defining question concerning the process by which the transformation of apartheid identities have taken place. As a framework for thinking about social change, the transformation of apartheid has been divided into two overlapping processes—the dismantling of the social apparatus of apartheid and the construction of an alternative set of arrangements. The two processes, while simultaneous and often intersecting, can be heuristically separated for the purposes of studying the transformation. Both processes constitute resistance as it has been defined here, with the first a necessary component of the second.

Over the twenty years following Soweto, resistance to apartheid increased in fits and starts as more and more South Africans proceeded through the four stages of resistance presented in chapter two. During this time, an increasing number of South Africans found an increasing number of instances which forced them to notice their normal way of doing things and to question their lives as perhaps infected by apartheid. Whether or not governing elites used the word to describe government policies and social patterns, South Africans began blaming apartheid for the bad things that happened in their lives. As these ideas were translated into actions against apartheid life and as the government resorted to the use of force to maintain order, the efficiency of apartheid as an organizing principle for South African life eroded. The loss of apartheid's authority meant that the ordered behavior that it had once produced dissolved in the face of resistance, and with it the order that was apartheid. Without the actions of individuals to constantly remake it, the apartheid social order shriveled.

Especially in the beginning, this resistance to apartheid was extremely diffuse. While there were broadly dispersed rhetorical frameworks for understanding resistance, there was no single alternative set of patterns and arrangements to guide resisters. The result was that individuals often had to construct their own justifications for their anti-apartheid actions. For most people in the late 1970s and early 1980s, it was often enough justification simply to say that actions were against apartheid. However, slowly and unevenly, these scattered acts of resistance began to coalesce into commonly recognized patterns, and justifications were reworked from being simply against apartheid to being for a particular vision of nonracial democracy. The dominant alternative metaphysics, Charterism, gained legitimacy only very slowly and did not command enough allegiance to replace apartheid as the social standard until well into the 1990s. Charterism was by no means destined to succeed apartheid, and the story of its victory over other alternative visions of post-apartheid society is as uneven and conflictual as that of apartheid's decline. As this process of solidifying new social arrangements continues, there is certainly less order in contemporary South Africa than apartheid enjoyed in the years prior to 1976.

This "legitimacy gap" created by the decline of apartheid and the much slower rise of an alternative helps explain the high levels of conflict in South African society over the past three decades. The gradual dissolution of the practical consensus that had surrounded apartheid as a social order and its replacement by multiple and creative rules for interaction resulted in a decline in the aggregate amount of order in South African society. As members of society began to follow standards of behavior that differed in significant ways from those asserted by other South Africans, the amount of conflict in society increased. The frustration, conflict, and violence that characterized the end of apartheid are perhaps best understood as the result of the practical confusion and contestation over the choice of rules and patterns for managing social interactions. This model of conflictual social change seems as if it could very well be transferable to other situations.

The third model evident in the discourses examined here concerns the role of identity labels in the continuous negotiations of social order. This model also represents part of the answer to the second question about South Africa's process of identity transformation. The specifics of the identity discourses of the three conflicts have been laid out above, but the question of the process seems to require a more general answer based in the theory of constructivist political identity. In contrast to most modern political theory, which assumes the continuity of identity, constructivism focuses on the nearly continuous changes in the hierarchies of labels that describe actors and, less frequently, in the meanings of the labels themselves. The labels of a person's identity are constantly shifting with alterations in social context, continuously forming new personas that carry implications for behavior, social expectations, and relative power. Labels are the codes of the social arrangements, and their meanings have a momentum generated by expectations built upon past experiences and actions.

Constructivism argues that societies exist because members coordinate their actions to an evolving set of rules. These rules define the society as distinct from others, and acquaintance with the rules is what qualifies an actor to be a member of that society. The arrangements are supported by rhetorical and ideological systems of truth that create perceptions of normality and human nature consistent with the current dominant order, making it easy to present societies as largely static and consistent. Elites support this process because their status, which is dependent upon the social arrangements, bestows upon them the power (encapsulated in the experience, skills, wisdom, or other qualities associated with their identities) and incentive to convince others that the current system should continue. Additionally, the values and standards by which people judge assertions are part of the existing social order, making it very difficult for radical changes to catch on.

From a constructivist perspective, however, social orders are constantly changing. Large, explicit social changes are carried out by agents, who, in certain contexts, successfully assert labels that carry particular kinds of social power. Most changes to the social order, however, are merely adaptations needed to meet core social goals in the face of changing circumstances. While they perpetuate the distribution of privilege in the existing arrangements, even these small modifications to the system are creative interventions by members of society acting as social agents. Such changes almost always appear to be structural from the perspective of those not involved in the initial creative acts that produced them. That is, even if they notice an act as change rather than continuity, members are confronted with an alteration whose origin they are unable to pinpoint. Constructivist political identity theory argues that identity labels are the repositories of agency and that actors feel constricted in their activities by the labels they are able to assert. Under apartheid, agency was distributed according to race. Resistance was about claiming agency for labels not recognized as agentic by apartheid.

The example of the transformation of the South African social order accentuates the importance of agency in explaining change. Social orders do have momentum and trajectories, but alterations in the patterns and rules, caused by the dissemination of convincing ideas among actors who institute corresponding changes in their behavior, can slow the social order down, speed it up, or push it in different directions. In the momentum metaphor, rules constitute the mass of the social order and acts that follow the rules give this mass force and direction. If a large percentage of actions are coordinated with each other, aligned in the same direction, as it were, the order will have considerable momentum. In such situations, the rules for most interactions will be evident, the power of each persona will be clear, and interactions should take place efficiently. If, however, the context is conflictual, momentum will be diffused by actors pushing in different directions. If enough actors are convinced to change the patterns of their activities and align them with another ideal, their resulting activities will change the trajectory of the larger social order. Such changes may or may not be represented as radical.

However, to radically change social arrangements is not a simple process. Almost all actions are based on and interpreted as reinforcing the momentum of the existing social order. Each interaction in which people assert different orders and incompatible identities is a conflict in the broad sense of the perceived mutual exclusivity of means and/or ends. When a conflict arises, unless one of the parties immediately concedes to the assertions of the other, a negotiation of some sort takes place. In these often very subtle interactions, each party tries to convince the other to accede to the identity structure, and thus the rules and power distribution that she, he, or it feels will be the most beneficial. It is here that the power of the existing social momentum is most felt. If negotiations do change the social order, they will also either expand or contract the scope of an identity label, empower it in a way different than it had been (thus appropriating the label from the existing power structure), or invent new labels and make them socially important. Because human behavior constructs social arrangements, if alterations in behavioral rules become widespread enough, the social order is changed. Whether these alterations are initially perceived to be changes that challenge the existing order or simply adaptations that reinforce its continuity, as these invented rules become widely accepted, they become simply part of the social order. This continuous dual process of agents inventing rules and rules governing behavior explains the social construction of reality.

In some cases, unexpected events, like the shooting of children or the eruption of riots, force people into a situation for which they have no rules, sparking improvisation and the spontaneous creation of new patterns, which in turn require new labels to organize them. The case of Soweto demonstrates the fundamental randomness of agency as an essentially creative force, a quality that makes it impossible to theorize in any positivistic sense. For many individuals, the rupture that Soweto represented began the process of resistance to apartheid. As that process continued through other stages, represented here by the debate over the constitution and mobilization around crime, an increasing number of people became convinced that new patterns of behavior centered around an alternate set of social arrangements were justified. These meanings and power were negotiated through discourses, both public and interpersonal. All of these changes in rules were reflected in alterations to the meanings and social power of the corresponding identity labels.

Encounters with other reality systems will sometimes present people with new ideas that resonate somehow with their experience, a possibility that is increasingly likely in this globalizing world. Within South Africa's political and social transformation, this phenomenon was actualized in the ability of South Africans to tap into, gain legitimacy from, and affect global patterns of thought. Armed with the belief that racism was universally wrong and that apartheid was a "crime against humanity," the global anti-apartheid movement issued condemnations, imposed sanctions, funded organizations aimed at the overthrow of the South African government, and successfully mobilized vast numbers of average citizens around the world. As dominant global opinion solidified in opposition to apartheid, the state's identity as an international pariah gave South Africans working against apartheid strong psychological reinforcement. At the same time, the label "democratic," so sought by the South African state, was redefined to be less about being anticommunist and more about actualizing a particular set of individual rights. The existence of a broad, powerful liberal ideology of individual rights and antiracism provided a rationale for anti-apartheid activities and a way to organize ideas and actions that had legitimacy among a wider global audience. The availablity of these outside justifications gave people confidence in resisting the often overwhelming momentum of their own social order. Those who suffered under apartheid found support and power in alternative schemes of identity, in systems of thought that repudiated race and ethnicity as important determinants of political and social power. The failure of the apartheid government's counterarguments about sovereignty is indicative of a shift away from the supremacy of this principle. Indeed, the worldwide condemnation of apartheid was the first concrete, explicitly antisovereignty global movement that was able to involve individuals as world citizens. In the process, those in power in South Africa found it progressively harder to sell their claims that their state was democratic, civilized, and Western, claims that were even more integral to a burgeoning, globalizing middle class than the protections of racist groupings.

These models are the lessons of applying a social constructivist theory of political identity to the transformation of the South African social order. The theory suggests that identity labels are a valuable methodological starting point for studying the processes of social construction and change in any context. Schemes for the distribution of agency vary extensively, but in every society and in almost every social interaction, the power to act is distributed unequally. This power is one of the primary manifestations of social hierarchy. It is relative both to context (such that even under apartheid, a Black gardener may still have had relative power to act with respect to the horticulture of his White employer's grounds) and to those with whom one is interacting. In the course of normal daily life, action is limited by actors' perceptions of their ability to act in a particular context. If persons do not believe that they are capable *and* empowered to act in the public arena, they generally will not, making influence over beliefs one of the keys to the control of action within social orders. However, sometimes actors change the definition of their social power through their actions. In the process, agents can claim for themselves labels that do allow them to act, or they can alter the meanings associated with their current labels, or they can invent entirely new labels and claim that the social context has changed. As labels change, rules change, and as rules change, societies change. The actor who creates each change is an agent with respect to that change and only that change.

None of this should be read to underestimate the power of social arrangements or overemphasize the potential for radical change. Everyday activities take place within the power relations of an existing social order. In normal times, most members of a society will feel that they have very few practical choices with respect to the identities and the rules that they are able to activate in social situations, and observers are likely to punish innovations they perceive to be threatening to existing social arrangements. And yet those arrangements are adapted continuously to account for the evolution of material circumstances and to maintain a society's existing momentum. While these small, adaptive changes of everyday life appear as stability to those within the existing social arrangements, such adaptations make actors into agents in very limited contexts. The potential for any particular creative act to catch on and evolve into a larger social structure is relative to the social power of the actor to whom the act is attributed.

I also do not mean to suggest that changes in identity labels cause changes to social orders. Constructivist political identity is a methodology for tracing such changes in society. Theories of agency that locate causes of social change in one or several universal factors are artifacts of modern social science, and these have had a very difficult time locating the (sometimes random) creativity from which social changes arise. Unlike most theorizing in the contemporary mainstream, constructivism allows agents to specify through their actions which identities, interests, and aspects of the social and material environment are ontologically privileged in any particular context. However, whether a perspective privileges change or stability, social arrangements can still be understood as sorted by identity labels, and these labels constitute an opportunity to organize social analysis.

This approach should be helpful in understanding social changes in many contexts. It seems especially appropriate for analyzing conflicts that revolve explicitly around identity factors, such as the "religious" divisions in Northern Ireland and the Middle East; "ethnic" cleavages in the Balkans and Africa's Great Lakes region; "developmental" differences between "The North" and "The South"; "gender" divisions in a whole host of conflicts that usually take place on a more localized scale; relations between "Great Powers" and "Postcolonial States"; or even "national" and "class" differences. From the perspective of the theory of constructivist political identity, all of these conflicts, while irrefutably material in nature, are actualized through particular identity cleavages that define their primary opposition. Because social orders are necessarily linked to the distribution of privilege and because conflicts assume otherness, labels are always involved in how conflicts are organized in the minds of the participants. Conflicts become entrenched and difficult when categories of labels and the hierarchies that relate them to each other are represented as being static, frozen as the one cleavage within which all other distinctions are organized. The South African transition from apartheid simplicity to post-apartheid complexity offers important lessons for how to problematize this kind of static identity hierarchy. The theory of political identity offers the ontological and methodological bases for analyzing these conflicts.

In contemporary South Africa, people find themselves confronted with a complex economy of respect. Respect is due based upon parts of a fragmented identity, and the potential for persons to possess some characteristics worthy of respect (regardless of whatever other characteristics they may also possess) means that hasty generalizations are dangerous and often punished. Identities still serve as effective codes that mediate relationships between social rules and social actors, and some have more social power than others. But as the transition in South Africa shows, the attempt to impose simplicity on that system of codes will ultimately fail. On a global scale, increasing globalization demands that socially competent people understand and pay attention to a complex and shifting hierarchy of codes and assertions of identity in their interactions. The explicit abandonment of their apartheid past has provided South Africans with an opportunity to consciously adopt this complexity and build it into their society's image of the self. This revolution in political identity has so far only been realized in rhetoric and then only partially, but the South African experience of social change suggests that it may provide a model for the creation of a truly multicultural reality.

NOTES

CHAPTER ONE

1. Favorite targets include Allister Sparks, *Tomorrow Is Another Country* (Chicago, University of Chicago Press, 1995), and Patti Waldmeir, *Anatomy of a Miracle: The End of Apartheid and the Birth of the New South Africa* (London: Viking, 1997).

2. The party/hangover comparison comes from Heribert Adam, Frederick van Zyl Slabbert, and Kogila Moodley, *Comrades in Business: Post-Liberation Politics in South Africa* (Utrecht: International Books, 1998), 1. Academic targets among the earlier authors include Tim Sisk, *Democratization in South Africa: The Elusive Social Contract* (Princeton: Princeton University Press, 1995), and Andrew Reynolds, editor, *Elections '94 South Africa: The Campaign, Results and Future Prospects* (London: James Curry, 1994).

3. The phrase comes from Adrian Guelke, *South Africa in Transition: The Misunderstood Miracle* (London: I. B. Tauris, 1999). See chapter 9 for a good rehearsal of previous transition literature.

CHAPTER TWO

1. John Gerard Ruggie, "What Makes the World Hang Together? Neo-utilitarianism and the Social Constructivist Challenge," *International Organization* 52, no. 4 (Autumn 1998): 855–885.

2. Alexander Wendt, *Social Theory of International Politics* (Cambridge: Cambridge University Press, 1999). Wendt characterizes his perspective as "thin" and mine as "thick" constructivism. The distinction rests on Wendt's concessions to the epistemology of philosophical realism that grounds the positivist mainstream of the field of International Relations.

3. Jeffrey Checkel, "The Constructivist Turn in International Relations Theory," *World Politics* 50 (January 1998): 327; Emanuel Adler, "Seizing the Middle Ground: Constructivism in World Politics," *European Journal of International Relations* 3 (1997): 319–363; and with the more pretentious *via media,* Alexander Wendt, 1999. For an alternative view, see Jennifer Sterling-Folker, "Competing Paradigms or Birds of a Feather? Constructivism and Neoliberal Institutionalism Compared," *International Studies Quar-*

terly 44, no. 1 (March 2000): 97–119. I find the "middle" metaphor too one-dimensional and prefer Ted Hopf's complex characterization of multiple differences in "The Promise of Constructivism in International Relations Theory," *International Security* 23, no. 1 (Summer 1998): 171–200.

    4. Wendt acknowledges scientific realism as a strategic choice. He admits that realism does not deal well with social change (*Social Theory,* 76), but argues it is better for solving problems within an existing system (377). For Wendt's argument about theory and material constraints, see *Social Theory,* 112–113.

    5. Jurgen Habermas, *The Theory of Communicative Action—Volume One: Reason and Rationalization in Society,* translated by Thomas McCarthy (Boston: Beacon Press, 1984).

    6. Nicholas Onuf, "Constructivism: A User's Manual," in *International Relations in a Constructed World,* edited by Vendulka Kubalkova, Nicholas Onuf, and Paul Kowert (Armonk, N.Y.: M. E. Sharpe, 1998), 59. Italics in original.

    7. Peter Berger and Thomas Luckmann, *The Social Construction of Reality* (New York: Anchor Books, 1966); Anthony Giddens, *The Constitution of Society* (Berkeley and Los Angeles: University of California Press, 1984).

    8. Every so often it becomes necessary for actors to justify an action, to make the implicit purpose explicit, either because others do not understand the action or they think the action is wrong. The circumstances of these justifications are of particular interest to constructivists.

    9. Ian Burkitt, *Social Selves: Theories of the Social Formation of Personality* (London: Sage, 1991), 116.

    10. The terms do carry slightly different connotations because of their association with particular types of theories. Constructivists use a variety of terms. Giddens, for example, uses "structure." Onuf prefers "arrangement" because, he says, it better conveys the temporary and arbitrary nature of the rules and the coherence. Wendt uses "structure," but uses "holism" to refer to theories that privilege structure over agency (which is in turn privileged by "individualism").

    11. I beg the forgiveness of all those reader who know enough about comets to understand just how imprecise this heuristic is. This is a new kind of interstellar comet whose trajectory is not elliptical and whose momentum is provided by the pushing of accumulated acts rather than the gravity of some distant mass.

    12. For a somewhat underpoliticized theory of these intersubjective webs of meaning (which anthropologists call culture), see Clifford Geertz, *The Interpretation of Cultures* (New York: Basic Books, 1973).

    13. Nicholas G. Onuf, *World of Our Making: Rules and Rule in Social Theory and International Relations* (Columbia: University of South Carolina Press, 1989), 159.

    14. It is impossible to narrow Foucault's body of work into a summarizing footnote. For an example of power from his archaeology period, see *The Order of Things: An Archaeology of the Human Sciences* (New York: Vintage Books, 1994); and from his genealogical period, see *Discipline and Punishment: The Birth of the Prison,* translated by Alan Sheridan (New York: Vintage Books, 1979).

15. Wendt substitutes "individualism" for theories of agency and "holism" for structural frameworks, *Social Theory,* 26.

16. Michel Foucault, "What is an Author?" *The Foucault Reader,* edited by Paul Rabinow (New York: Pantheon, 1984), 107–108.

17. Jennifer Sterling-Folker (99–100) and Steve Smith (International Studies Association panel on *Social Theory of International Politics,* March 16, 2000, Los Angeles, California) have criticized some constructivists for turning functional outcomes into theoretical causes of agency, which, they argue, ignores constructivism's deeper implications. Nicholas Onuf's version of constructivism appreciates this random nature of agency by demanding, following Wittgenstein, that constructivist analysis begin by focusing on action, rather than on material facts (as positivists do) or ideas and arguments (as postmodernists suggest) (*World of Our Making,* chapter 1). This makes for very complex theoretical structures, but ones that more accurately represent the creativity of the constitution process.

18. Alexander Wendt, *Social Theory,* 187–188. See also 339–340.

19. Nicholas Onuf, "Constructivism: A User's Manual," 64–65.

20. This appears as a fundamentally liberal idea, but for constructivism the rationality of the process of choosing is impure, governed by actors' interpretations of the existing social arrangements and their role within them.

21. James C. Scott, *Domination and the Arts of Resistance* (New Haven: Yale University Press, 1990), chapter 6. The list comes from page 137. See also Scott's *Weapons of the Weak: Everyday Forms of Peasant Resistance* (New Haven: Yale University Press, 1985).

22. For an excellent discussion of this process with respect to scientific discoveries, see Thomas Kuhn, *The Structure of Scientific Revolutions,* 2nd edition (Chicago: University of Chicago Press, 1970).

23. See Ruggie's three categories of constructivist epistemology that divide scholars by how they treat causality and the possibility of social scientific research. John Gerard Ruggie, *Constructing the World Polity* (London: Routledge, 1998) 35–36. Alex Wendt calls any scholar a constructivist who combines holism (implying an appreciation of structure) with idealism (implying that structures are fundamentally shared knowledge), and he subdivides constructivists into four categories—English School, World Society, Postmodern International Relations, and Feminist International Relations (*Social Theory,* 31–32). As discussed above, Ted Hopf divides constructivists into conventional or critical types based on a variety of factors. Perhaps predictably, I think the theory presented here straddles this coarse cleavage. Ralph Pettman has three categories: conservative, social theory, and commonsense [*Commonsense Constructivism or the Making of World Affairs* (Armonk, N.Y.: M. E. Sharpe, 2000), 12–25].

24. By 'instrumental', I am referring to the tendency to adopt constructivist phraseology as a cover for any non-positivist or interpretive methodology. Such claims are often applied to case studies that have little or no appreciation of the implications of a constructivist ontology. See John Gerard Ruggie, *Constructing the World Polity,* 38; and Jennifer Sterling-Folker, who criticizes constructivists who "have generally not followed through on the historical indeterminacy implied by the approach itself" (98).

25. Paul Kowert, "Agency versus Structure in the Construction of National Identity," in *International Relations in a Constructed World,* edited by Vendulka Kubalkova, Nicholas Onuf, and Paul Kowert (Armonk, N.Y.: M. E. Sharpe, 1998), 106.

26. Peter Berger and Thomas Luckmann, 1966, 59.

27. Nicholas Onuf, *World of Our Making,* 84–85.

28. Nicholas Onuf, "Constructivism: A User's Manual," 64.

29. Yosef Lapid, "Culture's Ship: Returns and Departures in International Relations Theory," in *The Return of Culture and Identity in IR Theory,* edited by Yosef Lapid and Friedrich Kratochwil (Boulder: Lynne Rienner, 1996), 11.

30. Friedrich Kratochwil, "Is the Ship of Culture at Sea or Returning?" in *The Return of Culture and Identity in IR Theory,* edited by Yosef Lapid and Friedrich Kratochwil (Boulder: Lynne Rienner, 1996), 219.

31. Jeffrey Checkel, 343–344.

32. Ted Hopf, 199.

33. Ian Burkitt, 1.

34. Ronald L. Jepperson, Alexander Wendt, and Peter J. Katzenstein, "Norms, Identity, and Culture in National Security," in *The Culture of National Security: Norms and Identity in World Politics,* edited by Peter J. Katzenstein (New York: Columbia University Press, 1996), 33.

35. Friedrich Kratochwil, 208.

36. Friedrich Kratochwil, 208, citing Erik Erikson, *Childhood and Society* (New York: Norton, 1950).

37. See Rafael Moses, "Self, Self-view, and Identity," in *The Psychodynamics of International Relationships, Volume I Concepts and Theories,* edited by Vamik D. Volkan, Demetrios A. Julius, and Joseph V. Montville (Lexington, Mass.: Lexington Books, 1990), 47–55.

38. Uri Bronfenbrenner, "The Mirror Image in Soviet-American Relations: A Social Psychologist's Report," *Journal of Social Issues* 14: 45–56; and Sam Keen, *Faces of the Enemy* (San Francisco: Harper and Row, 1986).

39. David Taylor, *Theories of Intergroup Relations* (New York: Greenwood Press, 1987), 60. See also Henri Tajfel, editor, *Social Identity and Intergroup Relations* (Cambridge: Cambridge University Press, 1982).

40. Taylor refers to a study by Pettigrew, Alport, and Barnett asking Afrikaners to sort pictures of different races that demonstrated the subjectivity involved and the tendency to try to achieve intergroup distinctiveness (David Taylor, 66).

41. William Bloom, *Personal Identity, National Identity, and International Relations* (Cambridge: Cambridge University Press, 1990).

42. William Bloom, 120.

43. Benedict Anderson, *Imagined Communities,* 2nd edition (London: Verso, 1991); R. B. J. Walker, *Inside/Outside: International Relations as Political Theory* (Cambridge: Cambridge University Press, 1993); Partha Chatterjee, *The Nation and Its Fragments: Colonial and Postcolonial Histories* (Princeton: Princeton University Press, 1993).

44. Yosef Lapid, 10.

45. In addition to the authors mentioned here, my thinking has also been influenced by a variety of scholars writing on gender, ethnicity and ethnic conflict, and race, and by all those who unproblematically assert their own self-certitude.

46. William Connolly, *Identity/Difference: Democratic Negotiations of Political Paradox* (Ithaca: Cornell University Press, 1991). He turns this principle into a good critique of how traditional International Relations theorists marginalize postmodern IR scholars (49–56).

47. David Campbell, *Writing Security: United State Foreign Policy and the Politics of Identity*, 2nd edition (Minneapolis: University of Minnesota Press, 1998).

48. I argue below, for example, that the performative constitution of identity that Campbell argues for means that particular actors create identity structures to the degree that their acts strike others as worthy of repetition. If such acts become rules, they are structural for everyone else.

49. Peter J. Katzenstein, editor, *The Culture of National Security: Norms and Identity in World Politics* (New York: Columbia University Press, 1996); Yosef Lapid and Friedrich Kratochwil, editors, *The Return of Culture and Identity in IR Theory* (Boulder: Lynne Rienner, 1996); Jill Krause and Neil Renwick, editors, *Identities in International Relations* (New York: St. Martin's Press, 1996).

50. See for example Paul Kowert and Jeffrey Legro, "Norms, Identity, and Their Limits," in *The Culture of National Security: Norms and Identity in World Politics,* edited by Peter J. Katzenstein (New York: Columbia University Press, 1996), 469, and Jeffrey Checkel, 343–344.

51. Jennifer Sterling-Folker, 109.

52. Alexander Wendt, *Social Theory,* 326–335.

53. Alexander Wendt, *Social Theory,* 224.

54. Alexander Wendt, *Social Theory,* 224–230.

55. Wendt's category of personal or corporate identity assumes his ontology of philosophical realism and a modernist, Western conception of self. The ability to see the self as continuous and "auto-genetic" (225) is dependent on socially constructed images of agents' stability. Wendt seems to need this materialist platform to integrate identity into his scientific realism. He does not rely on it any further. Similar problems arise with Wendt's attempt to differentiate type identities from roles. While the meaning of type identities are socially constructed, they are based on physical qualities or "preexisting properties" intrinsic to particular actors (226–227). Wendt's basic materialism lets him claim that some properties are intrinsic, that an individual can be a teenager or a state or a democracy even if he/she/it is the only one. But this ignores the fact that the meaning of the identity label is social property, susceptible to the assertions of all who use the term. As a result, such descriptions are only important to the degree that they are actualized in society. Intrinsic qualities are only important or real in the context of relationships with others, and as such are social in the same way as role identities. While there are many instances in which the study of labels should be limited to those with entrenched academic meaning, as Wendt suggests with his example of parliamentary and democratic states (226), in the abstract scholars should be open to the possibility that any grouping and hence any label could become politically important. The distinction between role (oppo-

sitional) and collective (aligning) identity (229–230) also seems an unnecessary heuristic device. Action is still dependent upon the labels attributed to self and interlocutor. The distinction is based on the effect of the relationship rather than the processes that govern it.

56. Ted Hopf, 184.

57. For a very helpful discussion, see Marshall Singer, *Intercultural Communication: A Perceptual Approach* (Englewood Cliffs, N.J.: Prentice-Hall, 1987).

58. This difference is explored in Dorinne Kondo's ethnographic study of identity in a Japanese candy factory. *Crafting Selves: Power, Gender, and Discourses of Identity in a Japanese Workplace* (Chicago: University of Chicago Press, 1990).

59. Dorinne Kondo, 30.

60. Dorinne Kondo, 47.

61. William Connolly, *Identity Difference*, 64.

62. This example comes from Gerhard Mare, *Ethnicity and Politics in South Africa* (London: Zed Books, 1993), 7.

63. R. B. J. Walker, 117 and 176–179.

64. Ian Burkitt, 190.

65. See George Herbert Mead, *Mind, Self, and Society* (Chicago: University of Chicago Press, 1934). Alexander Wendt provides a compelling explanation of this process in *Social Theory*, 326–335, 341.

66. Jennifer Sterling-Folker criticizes Martha Finnemore for this assumption (105–106).

67. Alexander Wendt, *Social Theory*, 340.

68. "The ways in which people organize themselves for political ends evolve along with everything else, and an intellectual map that focuses only on the interaction of two hundred 'states' captures only a slice of reality." Yale Ferguson and Richard Mansbach, "The Past as Prelude to the Future? Identities and Loyalties in Global Politics," in Yosef Lapid and Friedrich Kratochwil, 34.

69. While this may not be difficult for the modern Western mind to grasp with respect to institutions, it may well be a rather new way of thinking about the human body. Ian Burkitt suggests thinking about it as removing the locus of selfhood from inside to the boundary between the body and the external, social world. "In this respect, the self is the new dimension which is created in the active relationship between human bodies and their material environment" (190).

70. Alexander Wendt, "Collective Identity Formation and the International State," *American Political Science Review* 88, no. 2 (June 1994): 385. Parenthetical reference to Wendt, 1987, has been deleted.

71. Many constructivists who have focused on identity have chosen to write about only one of the two directions of constitution. Many seem to neglect the agent-to-identity-to-structure direction generally adopted by mainstream International Relations. Jeff Checkel (325–326) also argues this. For an example of an article that uses the agency-to-identity-to-structure direction, see Roxanne Lynn Doty, "Sovereignty and the Nation: Constructing the Boundaries of National Identity," in *State Sovereignty as Social Construct*,

edited by Thomas J. Biersteker and Cynthia Weber (Cambridge: Cambridge University Press, 1996): 121–147. For a good example of the two way appreciation, see Ronald L. Jepperson, Alexander Wendt, and Peter J. Katzenstein, 54.

72. Alexander Wendt, *Social Theory*, 162.

73. Ted Hopf calls this a "cognitive explanation," arguing that it has minimal a priori expectations (175, n. 11).

74. Peter Berger and Thomas Luckmann, 59.

75. Alexander Wendt, "Collective Identity Formation," 389.

76. Roxanne Lynn Doty, 126.

77. James Scott presents numerous examples of this kind of rupture of the social fabric, what he calls a "saturnalia of power" (202).

78. Ted Hopf, 180.

79. See Nicholas Onuf, *World of Our Making*, chapter 1, especially 35–36.

80. Alexander Wendt, *Social Theory*, 342.

81. Ted Hopf, 180.

82. Roxanne Lynn Doty, 127.

CHAPTER THREE

1. See Kathryn A. Manzo, *Domination, Resistance, and Social Change in South Africa: The Local Effects of Global Power* (Westport, Conn.: Praeger, 1992). See also Leonard Thompson, *A History of South Africa,* 3rd edition (New Haven: Yale University Press, 2000).

2. For a history of the Xhosa conquest, see Les Switzer, *Power and Resistance in an African Society: The Ciskei Xhosa and the Making of South Africa* (Madison: University of Wisconsin Press, 1993). For an account of the colonization of Natal and the Zulu, including the only time a non-Western army defeated a colonizing European regiment in a pitched battle (the battle of Isandlwanda), see Donald R. Morris, *The Washing of the Spears* (New York: Simon and Schuster, 1965).

3. For the impact of these wars on the politics of racial and ethnic identity, see Hermann Giliomee, "The Beginnings of Afrikaner Ethnic Consciousness, 1850–1915," in *The Creation of Tribalism in Southern Africa,* edited by Leroy Vail (Berkeley and Los Angeles: University of California Press, 1989); and David Harrison, *The White Tribe of Africa* (Berkeley and Los Angeles: University of California Press, 1981). For a deconstruction of the title *Afrikaner,* see Kathryn Manzo, *Creating Boundaries: The Politics of Race and Nation* (Boulder: Lynne Rienner, 1996), 76–77.

4. See Anthony Marx, *Making Race and Nation* (Cambridge: Cambridge University Press, 1998), chapter 5.

5. Kathryn Manzo, *Domination, Resistance, and Social Change*. Aletta J. Norval refers to this idea as the principle of difference in "Decolonization, Demonization, and Difference: The Difficult Constitution of a Nation," *Philosophy and Social Criticism* 21, no. 3, (1995): 31–51.

6. D. C. van der Spuy, *Amnesty for Terrorism* (Pretoria: National Bureau of International Communications, 1978), 29.

7. This phrase comes from the biblical story of Ham, one of Noah's sons who sins by looking upon his father's naked body (although biblical scholars agree that this is probably a metaphor). Noah condemns Ham's son, Canaan, and all of his descendants to be slaves (Genesis 9:25). The Dutch Reformed Church used this and other biblical stories like the Tower of Babel (Genesis 11:1–9) as ontotheological foundations for apartheid.

8. Wynand Malan, interview by author, 31 July 1997, Johannesburg.

9. James C. Scott, *Domination and the Arts of Resistance* (New Haven: Yale University Press, 1990), 2. See also chapter 3.

10. Steven Mufson, *Fighting Years: Black Resistance and the Struggle for a New South Africa* (Boston: Beacon Press, 1990), 20.

11. Steve Biko, *I Write What I Like* (London: Heinemann, 1978), 28–29, quoted in Steven Mufson, *Fighting Years,* 24.

12. Robert Schrire, *Adapt or Die: White Politics in South Africa* (U.S.: Ford Foundation, 1991), 9.

13. Dr. Hilgard Muller, "Let the World Take Note," in *Progress through Separate Development: South Africa in Peaceful Transition,* 2nd edition (New York: Information Service of South Africa, 1968), 39.

14. D. C. van der Spuy, 30.

15. Transkei in 1976, Bophutatswana in 1977, Venda in 1979, and Ciskei in 1981. The other six, Gazankulu, KwaZulu, Lebowa, Qwaqwa, Ndebele, and KaNgwane, remained "self-governing" regions within the Republic.

16. Anthony Marx, *Making Race and Nation* (Cambridge: Cambridge University Press, 1998), 194–195.

17. Anthony Marx, *Making Race,* 196.

18. Anthony Marx, *Making Race,* 201.

19. James Barber, *South Africa in the Twentieth Century* (Oxford: Blackwell, 1999), 145–146.

20. Thomas Karis and Gail M. Gerhart, editors, *From Protest to Challenge: A Documentary History of African Politics in South Africa 1882–1964, Volume 3 Challenge and Violence 1953–1964* (Stanford: Hoover Institution Press, 1977), 205–208.

21. See James Barber, 150–153 for a good summary of issues surrounding the document.

22. James Barber, 154–158.

23. Joseph Lelyveld, *Move Your Shadow: South Africa, Black and White* (New York: Penguin Books, 1985), 315.

24. The first BC organization was the South African Students' Association (SASO), formed in 1969.

25. Kathryn Manzo, *Domination, Resistance, and Social Change,* 200.

26. Anthony Marx, "Contested Images and Implications of South African Nationhood," in *The Violence Within: Cultural and Political Opposition in Divided Societies,* edited by Kay Warren (Boulder: Westview Press, 1993), 157.

27. Adrian Guelke, *South Africa in Transition: The Misunderstood Miracle* (London: I. B. Tauris, 1999).

28. Adrian Guelke, 187.

29. Adrian Guelke, 183.

30. Anthony Marx, *Making Race and Nation* (Cambridge: Cambridge University Press, 1998); Grant Farred, "Bulletproof Settlers: The Politics of Offense in the New South Africa," in *Whiteness: A Critical Reader,* edited by Mike Hill (New York: New York University Press, 1997), 63–78; Heribert Adam, Frederick van Zyl Slabbert, and Kogila Moodley, *Comrades in Business: Post-Liberation Politics in South Africa* (Utrecht: International Books, 1998).

31. Sheila Croucher, "South Africa's Illegal Aliens: Constructing National Boundaries in a Post-Apartheid State," *Ethnic and Racial Studies* 21, no. 4 (July 1998): 639–660; and Alan Morris, "'Our Fellow Africans Make Our Lives Hell': The Lives of Congolese and Nigerians Living in Johannesburg," *Ethnic and Racial Studies* 21, no. 6 (November 1998): 1116–1135.

32. Hein Marais, *South Africa: Limits to Change—The Political Economy of Transformation* (London: Zed Books, 1998).

33. Hein Marais, 2.

34. Hein Marais, 2.

35. Alan Ward, "Changes in the Political Economy of the New South Africa," in *The New South Africa: Prospects for Domestic and International Security,* edited by F. H. Toase and E. J. Yorke (New York: St. Martin's Press, 1998), 37–56; Charles Simkins, "Problems of Reconstruction," *Journal of Democracy* 7 (January 1996): 82–95; Jonathan Michie and Vishnu Padayachee, "Three Years After Apartheid: Growth, Employment, and Redistribution?" *Cambridge Journal of Economics* 22, no. 5 (1998): 623–635.

36. Wilmot James and Daria Caliguire, "Renewing Civil Society," *Journal of Democracy* 7 (January 1996): 56–66.

37. Anthony Butler, *Democracy and Apartheid: Political Theory, Comparative Politics, and the Modern South African State* (New York: St. Martin's Press, 1998); Thomas Koelble, *The Global Economy and Democracy in South Africa* (New Brunswick: Rutgers University Press, 1998).

38. Vincent T. Maphai, "A Season for Power Sharing," *Journal of Democracy* 7 (January 1996): 66–81.

39. Jeffery Herbst, "Prospects for Elite-Driven Democracy in South Africa," *Political Science Quarterly* 112, no. 4 (Winter 1997–1998): 595–615.

40. Andrew Reynolds, editor, *Elections '94 South Africa: The Campaign, Results, and Future Prospects* (London: James Curry, 1994), and Reynolds, editor, *Elections '99: From Mandela to Mbeki* (New York: St. Martin's Press, 1999); Susan Collin Marks, *Watching the Wind: Conflict Resolution During South Africa's Transition to Democracy* (Washington, D.C.: U.S. Institute of Peace Press, 2000); Kadar Asmal, Louise Asmal, and Ronald Suresh Roberts, *Reconciliation through Truth,* 2nd edition (Cape Town: David Philip, 1997).

41. David R. Horwath and Aletta J. Norval, "Introduction: Changing Paradigms and the Politics of Transition in South Africa," in *South Africa in Transition: New Theoretical Perspectives* (New York: St. Martin's Press, 1998), 1.

42. See Ran Greenstein, *Genealogies of Conflict: Class, Identity, and State in Palestine/Israel and South Africa* (Hanover, N.H.: University Press of New England, 1995).

43. John Sharp, "Introduction: Constructing Social Reality," in *South African Keywords: The Uses and Abuses of Political Concepts,* edited by Emile Boonzaier and John Sharp (Cape Town: David Phillip, 1988), 1.

44. Kathryn Manzo, *Domination, Resistance, and Social Change,* 1.

45. Kathryn Manzo, *Domination, Resistance, and Social Change,* 166–167.

46. Deborah Posel, *The Making of Apartheid, 1948–1961* (Oxford: Clarendon Press, 1991), 5.

47. Emile Boonzaier and John Sharp, editors, *South African Keywords: The Uses and Abuses of Political Concepts* (Cape Town: David Phillip, 1988).

48. John Sharp, 6–7.

49. Aletta J. Norval, "Decolonization, Demonization, and Difference," 36.

50. Quoted in Gerhard Mare and Georgina Hamilton, *An Appetite for Power: Buthelezi's Inkatha and South Africa* (Johannesburg: Ravan Press, 1987), 30.

51. Leroy Vail, "Introduction," 1–19; Patrick Harries, "Exclusion, Classification, and Internal Colonialism: The Emergence of Ethnicity Among the Tsonga-Speakers of South Africa," 82–117; and Hermann Giliomee, "The Beginnings of Afrikaner Ethnic Consciousness, 1850–1915," 21–54, in Leroy Vail, editor, *The Creation of Tribalism in Southern Africa* (Berkeley and Los Angeles: University of California Press, 1989).

52. Donald Horowitz, *A Democratic South Africa? Constitutional Engineering in a Divided Society* (Berkeley and Los Angeles: University of California Press, 1991). For criticism, see Morris Szeftel, "Ethnicity and Democratization in South Africa," *Review of African Political Economy* no. 60, v. 21 (June 1994): 198–199.

53. Rupert Taylor, "The Myth of Ethnic Division: Township Conflict on the Reef," *Race and Class* 33, no. 2 (1991):1–14; Paul Forsyth, "The Real Zulu: How Political Conflict Has Forged Variants of 'Zuluness,'" *Track Two* 2, no. 1 (February 1993): 8–9; Daphna Golan, *Inventing Shaka: Using History in the Construction of Zulu Nationalism* (Boulder: Lynne Rienner, 1994).

54. Gerhard Mare, *Ethnicity and Politics in South Africa* (London: Zed Books, 1993); Morris Szeftel, 185–199.

55. Ran Greenstein, *Genealogies of Conflict: Class, Identity, and State in Palestine/Israel and South Africa* (Hanover: University Press of New England, 1995).

56. In addition to the books previously cited, *Domination, Resistance, and Social Change in South Africa* and *Creating Boundaries,* there is also a more compact version of the principal arguments (published under the name Kate Manzo) "Global Power and South African Politics: A Foucauldian Analysis," *Alternatives* 17 (1992): 23–66.

57. "Social Ambiguity and the Crisis of Apartheid," in *The Making of Political Identities,* edited by Ernesto Leclau (New York: Verso, 1994); and "Decolonization, Demonization, and Difference: The Difficult Constitution of a Nation," 31–51.

58. Charles C. Ragin, *The Comparative Method: Moving Beyond Qualitative and Quantitative Strategies* (Berkeley and Los Angeles: University of California Press, 1987), x.

59. Thomas Kuhn uses this term to help represent the contextual nature of the rules that delineate which methodologies for studying material reality are acceptable. Such rules are not a priori, but based upon assumptions that are fundamentally arbitrary. See *The Structure of Scientific Revolutions,* 2nd edition (Chicago: University of Chicago, 1970).

60. Charles C. Ragin, ix.

61. Dorinne Kondo, *Crafting Selves: Power, Gender, and Discourses of Identity in a Japanese Workplace* (Chicago: University of Chicago Press, 1990); Kathryn Manzo, *Creating Boundaries,* Ran Greenstein, *Genealogies of Conflict: Class, Identity, and State in Palestine/Israel and South Africa.*

62. Clifford Geertz, *The Interpretation of Cultures* (New York: Basic Books, 1973), 30.

63. Clifford Geertz, 15.

64. See Donal Carbaugh, "Communicative Rules in *Donahue* Discourse," in *Cultural Communication and Intercultural Contact,* edited by Donal Carbaugh (Hillside, N.J.: Lawrence Erlbaum, 1990), 119–149; Allen Grimshaw, "Data and Data Use in an Analysis of Communicative Events," in *Explorations in Ethnography of Speaking,* edited by Richard Bauman and Joel Sherzer (Cambridge: Cambridge University Press, 1974), 419–424; Muriel Saville-Troike, *The Ethnography of Communication: An Introduction,* 2nd edition (Oxford: Basil Blackwell, 1989); and Mary Jane Collier, "Cultural and Intercultural Communication Competence: Current Approaches and Directions for Future Research," *International Journal of Intercultural Relations* 13 (1989):287–302.

65. Donal Carbaugh, *Talking American: Cultural Discourses on "Donahue"* (Norwood, N.J.: Ablex Publishing, 1989).

66. Mary Jane Collier, 195.

67. Ann Levett et al., editors, *Culture, Power, and Difference: Discourse Analysis in South Africa* (London: Zed Books, 1997).

68. Erica Burman et al., "Power and Discourse: Culture and Change in South Africa," in *Culture, Power, and Difference,* 3.

69. Erica Burman et al., 3.

70. Jonathan Friedman, "The Past in the Future: History and the Politics of Identity," *American Anthropologist* 94, no. 4 (1992): 853.

71. I interviewed the main pollster for a nongovernmental organization called the Institute for Democracy in South Africa (idasa) who had conducted numerous surveys tracking changes to the labels that South Africans use to describe themselves. Robert Mattes, interview by author, 7 July 1997, Cape Town.

72. James, interview by author, 27 July 1997, Bronkhurstspruit.

CHAPTER FOUR

1. "16 June Will Never Be the Same Again," *City Press,* 13 June 1999, 6, received through the Daily News Bulletin e-mail list server from the South African Embassy in

Washington (hereafter referred to as DNB), June 1999. The DNB is also available through the embassy's web site, *www.southafrica.net,* where past issues are archived.

2. For analysis of the causes and effects of the events of June 16, 1976, see John Kane-Berman, *Soweto: Black Revolt, White Response* (Johannesburg: Ravan, 1978); Baruch Hirson, *Year of Fire, Year of Ash—The Soweto Revolt: Roots of a Revolution?* (London: Zed Press, 1979); and Alan Brooks and Jeremy Brookhill, *Whirlwind Before the Storm* (London: International Defence and Aid Fund for Southern Africa, 1980). The government's official analysis is *The Report of the Commission of Inquiry into the Riots at Soweto and Elsewhere from the 16th of June 1976 to the 28th of February 1977* (Pretoria: Republic of South Africa, 1980), hereafter referred to as the Cillie Commission Report.

3. In August, this Action Committee became the Soweto Students Representative Council (SSRC).

4. The spelling of Hector's name seems to be in doubt. On a Soweto monument recently erected it is spelled *Peterson,* but for many years his gravestone bore a spelling with an *i,* which would, ironically, be more consistent with Afrikaans than English. In a twist that is all but forgotten, the Cillie Commission found that the first to die was actually Hastings Ndlovu, 17.

5. "Automatics used on rioting mobs," *Star,* 17 June 1976, 1; also Alan Brooks and Jeremy Brickhill, 12, quote a photographer from International Union of Students, *Solidarity Mission to South Africa,* 1976, 6. For foreign journalists' eyewitness accounts of unprovoked shootings on June 19, see James Sanders, *South Africa and the International Media 1972–1979* (London: Frank Cass, 2000), 165.

6. Generally, tsotsis had little or no schooling, survived by theft, and pursued their image of a gangster lifestyle, including use of drugs (mostly dagga/marijuana), multiple sexual partners, and flashy, trendy clothes. One Soweto resident calls them "dehumanised beings," created by "the insecurity and hopelessness of apartheid." Joyce Sikakane, *A Window on Soweto* (London: International Defence and Aid Fund, 1977), 27.

7. "Die uitbarsting in Soweto," *Die Burger,* 17 June 1976, page unknown. Many of the newspaper stories in this chapter were found in bound collections of newspaper clippings in the South African National Archives in Cape Town. Because the binders are organized by themes, the original page numbers on which the stories appeared were often missing. Photocopies of these articles are available from the author upon request.

8. *Star,* 17 June 1976, 1.

9. *Star,* 18 June 1976, 5.

10. *Die Vaderland,* 23 June 1976, page unknown.

11. *Cape Times,* 18 June 1976, 1 and 3.

12. Denis Herbstein, *White Man, We Want to Talk to You* (New York: Africana, 1979), 18. Television had just been introduced to South Africa in February 1976. For an account of how the SABC handled the story, see James Sanders, 171–172.

13. *Sunday Tribune,* 20 June 1976, 27.

14. "Blacks shelter White," *Star,* 17 June 1976, 3; "African saves TV crew," *Cape Times,* 18 June 1976, 1. See also Melanie Yap, "The Blacks who saved White lives," *Sunday Times,* 20 June 1976, page unknown.

15. "Black Backlash," *Star,* 19 June 1976, 1.

16. "Day's events," *Cape Times,* 17 June 1976, page unknown.

17. The quote is from witness and reporter Sophie Tema, *Bulletin of the Union of Black Journalists* 2 (date unknown, but the publication was banned August 26, 1976): 4. See also Don Knowler, "One shell—then all hell broke loose," *Star,* 17 June 1976, 25. Harry Mashabela said he saw a policeman throw "what seemed to be a stone" into the crowd ("Clenched fist a passport," *Star,* 17 June 1976, 25). Another journalist, Willie Bokala, saw a White policeman throw a stone (cited in Baruch Hirson, 181–182).

18. Langa Skosana, "Caught between police shots and pupils' stones," *Star,* 17 June 1976, 25.

19. "How march led to fire," *Cape Times,* 18 June 1976, 3.

20. "Looting, Burning as Riots Continue," *Cape Times,* 17 June 1976, 1.

21. The story broke too late to allow any significant reporting in Wednesday's afternoon papers. Morning papers include *Cape Times* and *Rand Daily Mail. Star* and *Argus* are afternoon papers.

22. "'Minimum force used'—Kruger," *Argus,* 17 June 1976, 1.

23. Alan Brooks and Jeremy Brickhill, 25, quoted from *Financial Times,* 17 June 1976. John Kane-Berman also quotes the *Rand Daily Mail* of 17 June: a "senior police officer admitted at the time that no warning shots had been fired," 1.

24. Cillie Commission Report, 549.

25. Gillian Murray, "Police blackout—Kruger explains," *Rand Daily Mail,* 19 June 1976, 3.

26. Willie Bokala, *Bulletin of the Union of Black Journalists* 2, 1976, 7.

27. However, in August, the *Rand Daily Mail* and *Star* both printed stories obtained by Black journalists of police fomenting violence by hostel dwellers against township residents. James Sanders, 175–176.

28. "Was WRAB out of Touch?" *Rand Daily Mail,* 18 June 1976, 15.

29. "Whites involved in riots—Botha," *Argus,* 24 June 1976, page unknown.

30. "We didn't expect it—Kruger," *Rand Daily Mail,* 18 June 1976, 1.

31. Police Major General W. H. Kotze, *Cape Times,* 18 June 1976, 1.

32. Soweto's assistant police chief, Colonel J. Gerber, *Star,* 18 June 1976, 3.

33. "We didn't expect it—Kruger," *Rand Daily Mail,* 18 June, 1976, 1. As noted earlier, however, the policy had remained unenforced until late 1974.

34. "Behind the scenes planning?" *Cape Times,* 17 June 1976, 1.

35. "Vorster's tough warning over 'deliberate' riots," *Argus,* 18 June 1976, page unknown.

36. "Whites involved in riots—Botha," *Argus,* 24 June 1976, page unknown.

37. Kruger referred specifically to a published interview with ANC Secretary General Oliver Tambo that, Kruger said, linked the riots not only to the ANC but also to communism. "Soweto riots linked to ANC says Kruger," *Argus,* 30 July 1976, page unknown.

38. "Soweto riots lessons for all—Kruger," *Argus,* 21 June 1976, page unknown.

39. "Vorster in attack on UN views," *Argus,* 21 June 1976, page unknown; "Soweto riots lesson for all—Kruger," *Argus,* 21 June 1976, page unknown; "Pik speaks out," *Star,* 12 July 1976, page unknown.

40. One proponent of this theory was Colonel J. P. Visser, head of a Soweto police unit. "Soweto riots linked to ANC says Kruger," *Argus,* 30 July 1976, page unknown.

41. "'Minimum force used'—Kruger," *Argus,* 17 June 1976, page unknown.

42. "Soweto riots lessons for all—Kruger," *Argus,* 21 June 1976, page unknown.

43. Denis Herbstein, 159.

44. "Soweto riots lesson for all—Kruger," *Argus,* 21 June 1976, page unknown.

45. John Brewer, *After Soweto: An Unfinished Journey* (Oxford: Clarendon Press, 1986), 97–98.

46. South African Institute of Race Relations (SAIRR), *South Africa in Travail: The Disturbances of 1976/77: Evidence Presented by the SA Institute of Race Relations to Cillie Commission of Inquiry into the Riots at Soweto and Other Places in June 1976* (Johannesburg: SAIRR, 1978), 68.

47. Poster obtained from the Archives and Records department of the University of Cape Town. There is no author or other publication information listed.

48. John Steyn, editor, *A 'Ghetto' in South Africa* (Johannesburg: Perskor, date unknown, but sometime between 1977 and 1979).

49. John Steyn, 13–14.

50. F. R. Metrowich, *The Challenge of Soweto* (Pretoria: Foreign Affairs Association, date unknown but probably late July 1976).

51. F. R. Metrowich, 4.

52. F. R. Metrowich, 4.

53. F. R. Metrowich, 7.

54. F. R. Metrowich, 10–11.

55. F. R. Metrowich, 11.

56. F. R. Metrowich, 11.

57. *Report of the Commission of Inquiry into the Riots at Soweto and Elsewhere from the 16th of June 1976 to the 28th of February 1977* (Cillie Commission Report), cited above.

58. Cillie Commission Report, 477.

59. Cillie Commission Report, 477.

60. Cillie Commission Report, 522. John Kane-Berman (26–27) using newspapers and semi-official sources, counted 661. Alan Brooks and Jeremy Brickhill say the June to December 1976 death toll was "probably over 1,000, and may have been even more than that" and that there is credible evidence to support the "widespread belief" in the townships that people were being secretly buried by the authorities to conceal the extent of the killings (256–258)

61. Cillie Commission Report, 480.

62. John Brewer, *After Soweto*, 74.

63. "Police share blame," *Cape Times*, 1 March 1980, 4; "Police reaction 'not excessive,'" *Argus*, 29 February 1980, 1.

64. "Red report on 'uprising,'" *Cape Times*, 19 June 1976, page unknown. The paper contemptuously quotes the report as saying that the violence is growing into a "veritable uprising" and that the "resistance movement" was growing in South Africa in spite of "brutal repression."

65. "This horror—by church council," *Star*, 17 June 1976, 3.

66. "'Bloodbath'—police action condemned," *Star*, 17 June 1976, 2.

67. "Only language issue cause riots—claim," *Star*, 22 June 1976, 23.

68. "Countdown to Chaos," *Sunday Times*, 20 June 1976, 21.

69. *Spotlight on Soweto* (city unknown: World Peace Council, 1976), 22.

70. *Southern Africa in Crisis* (London: Relgocrest Ltd., date unknown, probably early 1977), 1.

71. Khehla Shubane, "Soweto," in *All Here and Now: Black Politics in South Africa in the 1980s*, edited by Tom Lodge and Bill Nasson (U.S.: The Ford Foundation, 1991), 257.

72. Romesh Chandra, "The Soweto Uprising," *Spotlight on Soweto* (city unknown: World Peace Council, 1976), 2.

73. The term *comrade* was to become very important in the urban unrest of the 1980s because of the influence of the ANC, but in 1976 it referred only to a specific "militant group of youths" near Cape Town (Cillie Commission Report, 416).

74. Jon Qwelane, "One day that changed the face of SA," *Star*, 8 June 1986, page unknown.

75. By August, social workers reported that tsotsis played no significant role. The huge drop in crime over Christmas was attributed to the students' efforts (John Kane-Berman, 125).

76. In an infamous incident, migrant workers from the Mzimphlope hostel in Orlando West, protected and armed by police, went on a rampage to protest the so-called stayaway, robbing, raping, and killing 70 township dwellers (Denis Herbstein, 176–178). A more extensive discussion of this issue is found in Archie Molefe, "Soweto and its Aftermath," *Review of African Political Economy* 11 (1978): 17–30.

77. "The Will of an entire People—forged under fire," *Sechaba* 11 (first quarter, 1977): 1.

78. In "The Uprising of 16th June," *Social Dynamics* 5, no. 1 (1979): 54, Frank Molteno says that people in "some 200 Black communities throughout the country including the Bantustans actively participated in the uprising." Anthony Marx points out that the less educated, older rural people in particular were significantly more subdued than the those in urban areas [*Lessons of Struggle* (Oxford: Oxford University Press, 1992), 69–70].

79. See an interview with Tebello Motapanyane, "Secretary-General" of SASM in March 1976 in *Sechaba* 11 (second quarter, 1977): 49–59.

80. John Kane-Berman, 218–219.

81. John Brewer, *After Soweto*, 79.

82. "Claims of greater direct ANC involvement in the uprising . . . are largely based on a strong dose of retrospective wishful thinking or a pro-ANC bias . . ." (Anthony Marx, *Lessons of Struggle*, 68).

83. Nigel Worden, *The Making of Modern South Africa: Conquest, Segregation, and Apartheid* (Oxford: Blackwell, 1994), 119. For example, the ANC claimed to have rallied people with "pamphlet bombs" [*Sechaba* 11 (first quarter 1977): 8–10].

84. William Finnegan, *Crossing the Line: A Year in the Land of Apartheid* (New York: Harper and Row, 1986), 223.

85. The cavernous Regina Mundi church was an annual site of confrontations.

86. "Cops Gas Regina," *City Press*, 19 June 1983, 1.

87. "Things *do* go better with Coke," *City Press*, 3 July 1983, page unknown.

88. "It was a milestone," *City Press*, 15 June 1986, 6.

89. "June 16 . . . all's quiet in Soweto . . . it's the people's holy day," *Sunday Times*, 19 June 1988, page unknown.

90. "June 16 . . . all's quiet in Soweto . . . it's the people's holy day," *Sunday Times*, 19 June 1988, page unknown. See also "A nation remembers with solemn dignity," *City Press*, 21 June 1987, page unknown.

91. "June 16," *Business Day*, 16 June 1987, 4.

92. Robert, interview by author, 25 June 1997, Cape Town.

93. "A generation not to be forgotten," *Sowetan*, 15 June 1987, 6.

94. "Unity plea ignored by political rivals," *Sowetan*, 18 June 1990, 2; "PAC 'responsible' for lead-up to Soweto shootings," *Argus*, 14 June 1990, page unknown;.

95. "Inkatha to join in June 16 services," *Sowetan*, 14 June 1991, 1.

96. Sekola Sello, "What's gone wrong?" *City Press*, 21 June 1992, 13.

97. Sekola Sello, 13.

98. "June 16 is important," *Lentswe*, 12 June 1992, page unknown.

99. *Upbeat* 5, 1985, 3. This tribute appears on the bottom half of the contents page. *Upbeat* was a school magazine published by the liberal SACHED Trust as supplementary reading material for Black schools.

100. *Upbeat* 4, 1986, 23.

101. *Upbeat* 4, 1987, 10–11.

102. *Upbeat* 4, 1989, 3.

103. *Upbeat* 4, 1995, 2.

104. The Study Commission on U.S. Policy Toward Southern Africa, *South Africa: Time Running Out* (Berkeley and Los Angeles: University of California Press, 1981), 183–184.

105. Even if there had been African strikes, they could be somewhat expected from "workers." Students would not have the issues or the consciousness to rally such a demonstration.

106. Philip Frankel, "Race and Counter-Revolution: South Africa's 'Total Strategy,'" *Journal of Commonwealth and Comparative Politics* 18, no. 3 (November 1980): 274.

107. "Even following the convictions in October and November of a few Whites on security charges, there was reason to believe that a White hand, possibly Marxist, was still guiding aspects of the unrest from inside South Africa" [Bob Hitchcock, *Flashpoint South Africa* (Cape Town: Don Nelson, 1977), 194, quoted in Frank Molteno, 59].

108. Denis Herbstein, 15.

109. Alan Brooks and Jeremy Brickhill, 27.

110. Denis Herbstein, 158.

111. Archie Molefe, 22.

112. Cillie Commission Report, 505.

113. Steven Mufson, *Fighting Years: Black Resistance and the Struggle for a New South Africa* (Boston: Beacon Press, 1990), 17–18.

114. Ephraim, former President of Congress of South African Students (COSAS), interview by author, 30 July 1997, Johannesburg.

115. Cillie Commission Report, 550.

116. Cillie Commission Report, 480.

117. Institute for Black Research, *Soweto—A People's Response* (Natal: SAIRR: 11 January 1978). Because of government restrictions, the results were not published for a year and a half.

118. Institute for Black Research, 2.

119. Sixty-four percent of Africans, 54% of Indians, and 69% of Coloureds (Institute for Black Research, 20–21).

120. The Study Commission on U.S. Policy Toward Southern Africa, 224.

121. Percy Qoboza, *Sunday Tribune,* June 20, 1976, 27, emphasis in original.

122. Ephraim, interview by author, 30 July 1997, Johannesburg. Moutse is small town in what used to be the homeland of KwaNdebele.

123. Peter, quoted on a pamphlet created by the National Education Crisis Committee to commemorate the tenth anniversary of Soweto in 1986.

124. "June 16: Thirteen Years After," *New Nation,* 15–22 June 1989, 6.

125. Ephraim, interview by author, 30 July 1997, Johannesburg.

126. Cillie Commission Report, 547.

127. Anthony Marx, *Lessons of Struggle,* 65.

128. Archie Molefe, 24.

129. Anthony Marx, *Lessons of Struggle,* 70; Nigel Worden, 119.

130. Mpho Mashinini, quoted in Steven Mufson, *Fighting Years,* 70.

131. Colin Bundy, quoted in "Govt lost legitimacy in '76," *South,* 18–23 June 1987, page unknown.

CHAPTER FIVE

1. "[T]he world does not remain the same, and if we as government want to act in the best interest of the country in a changing world, then we have to be prepared to adapt our policy to those things that make adjustment necessary, otherwise we die." In Robert Schrire, *Adapt or Die: White Politics in South Africa* (U.S.: Ford Foundation, 1991), 29.

2. Kathryn Manzo, *Domination, Resistance, and Social Change in South Africa: The Local Effects of Global Power* (Westport, Conn.: Praeger, 1992), tables 5.2 and 5.3, 222–223.

3. Robert Schrire, 21.

4. Robert Price, *The Apartheid State in Crisis: Political Transformation in South Africa, 1975–1990* (New York: Oxford University Press, 1991), 87.

5. Robert Price, 88.

6. Adam Ashforth, *The Politics of Official Discourse in Twentieth-Century South Africa* (Oxford: Clarendon Press, 1990), 209.

7. Martin Murray, *South Africa: Time of Agony, Time of Destiny* (London: Verso, 1987), 26.

8. There were no Africans on the Council because, the Prime Minister said, the policies were a reformulation of and not a move away from separate development. Judy Seidman, *Facelift Apartheid: South Africa After Soweto* (London: International Defense and Aid Fund, 1980), 82.

9. *Final Report of the Constitutional Committee of the President's Council on the Adaptations of Constitutional Structures in South Africa* (Cape Town: Republic of South Africa, 1984), 6 and 12, hereafter referred to as the Final Report. See also L. J. Boulle's discussion of the process in *Constitutional Reform and the Apartheid State* (New York: St. Martin's Press, 1984), 133–134.

10. Department of Foreign Affairs and Information, *Republic of South Africa Constitution Act, No. 110, 1983* (Pretoria: Government Printer, October 1983), 1.

11. *SAIRR Survey of Race Relations, 1984,* 127–128, cited in Robert Schrire, 63.

12. In practice, the government retained the existing House of Assembly with 178 White members and created a House of Representatives for 83 Coloured members and a House of Delegates for 45 Indian members.

13. Department of Foreign Affairs and Information, *Republic of South Africa Constitution Act,* 9–10. An appendix lists typical "own" affairs, such as social workers, art, culture, and education of adults at trade centers, 49–51. The distinction is explained further in a memorandum, 60–64.

14. Martin Murray, *South Africa,* 117.

15. Only the clause concerning official languages was given special protections—each house needed to vote to amend or repeal it with more than a two-thirds majority.

16. C. P. de Kock, Nic Rhoodie, and M. P. Couper, "Black views on socio-political change in South Africa," in *South Africa: A Plural Society in Transition*, edited by D. J. van Vuuren, N. E. Wiehahn, J. A. Lombard, and N. J. Rhoodie (Durban: Butterworth, 1985), 344.

17. Anthony Marx, *Lessons of Struggle*, 106.

18. Stephen Mufson, "Introduction: The Roots of Insurrection," in *All, Here and Now: Black Politics in South Africa in the 1980s*, edited by Tom Lodge and Bill Nasson (U.S.: The Ford Foundation, 1991), 8.

19. Robert Price, 159–160.

20. *Transvaal Anti-South African Indian Council Committee, Congress 1983—Speeches and Papers Delivered at the Congress* (Johannesburg: Transvaal Anti-SAICC, 1983), cited in Tom Lodge, "Rebellion: The Turning of the Tide," in *All Here and Now: Black Politics in South Africa in the 1980s*, edited by Tom Lodge and Bill Nasson (U.S.: Ford Foundation, 1991), 48.

21. Tom Lodge, 45. Robert Price also credits the explosion of civil society in Black areas after Soweto with creating momentum toward the organization. "Although Pretoria's political reforms created the situational stimulus for the formation of the UDF, its foundation had been created by the phenomenal growth of township associational life during the previous four years" (178).

22. Steven Mufson, *Fighting Years: Black Resistance and the Struggle for a New South Africa* (Boston: Beacon Press, 1990), 53–54.

23. Mr. Popo Molefe, general secretary of the UDF, quoted in *Financial Mail*, 25 November 1983, page unknown, cited in David Welsh, "Constitutional Changes in South Africa," *African Affairs* 83, no. 331 (April 1984), 160. Welsh points out that this number is impossible to verify and difficult to assess because it is membership through affiliation.

24. Martin Murray, *South Africa*, 202.

25. Steven Mufson, *Fighting Years*, 59.

26. Robert Price, 181.

27. Both Robert Price (181) and Anthony Marx, *Lessons of Struggle* (139) stress that one advantage held by the UDF's Charterist nonracialism was the ability to raise funds, for example.

28. The sanctions movement was perhaps the first truly global grassroots movement in history. By 1986, even South Africa's staunchest allies, the Reagan administration in the United States and the Thatcher administration in Britain, were forced by domestic and international pressure to implement stringent economic sanctions against the government. For an excellent study tracing how these international norms developed through the anti-apartheid sanctions movement, see Audie Klotz, *Norms in International Relations: The Struggle Against Apartheid* (Ithaca: Cornell University Press, 1995).

29. Robert Price, 207.

30. Steven Mufson, *Fighting Years*, 106–107.

31. Anthony Marx, *Lessons of Struggle*, 167.

32. Robert Price defines an insurrection as a rebellion that nullifies state power in a portion of the territory. He compares South Africa of 1984–1986 to the Paris Commune in 1987, Russia in 1905, and Hungary in 1956 (Robert Price, 190–191).

33. Steven Mufson, *Fighting Years*, 80.

34. For this time period, 504 people died and 1,599 were injured in more than 10,000 unrest-related incidents (Kate Manzo, 228, citing *Southern Africa Report*, 15 August 1986, 3).

35. Robert Price, 192.

36. Robert Price, 192–193.

37. Joseph Lelyveld, *Move Your Shadow: South Africa, Black and White* (New York: Penguin Books, 1985), 321.

38. Mark Swilling, "The Extra-Parliamentary Movement: Strategies and Prospects," in *Negotiating South Africa's Future*, edited by Hermann Giliomee and Lawrence Schlemmer (London: Macmillan Press, 1989), 64–65.

39. Quoted in Steven Mufson, *Fighting Years*, 115.

40. Mpho Mashinini, quoted in Steven Mufson, *Fighting Years*, 116.

41. Anthony Marx, *Lessons of Struggle*, 164–165.

42. Robert Price, 220.

43. Catholic Institute for International Relations (CIIR), *Now Everyone is Afraid: The Changing Face of Policing in South Africa* (London: CIIR, August 1988), 12.

44. Anthony Marx, *Lessons of Struggle*, 184.

45. Anthony Marx, *Lessons of Struggle*, 190.

46. Of the 76 percent turnout of eligible voters, 1,360, 233 voted yes and 691,577 voted no.

47. "Consider Carefully," *Star*, 25 October 1983, 1.

48. Peter Sullivan, "Now Only the Decision and Nov. 2 Remain," *Star* 28 October 1983, 6.

49. Encouraging a yes were the *Daily Dispatch* (East London), *Sunday Times, Natal Mercury, Friend* (Bloomfontein), *Citizen* and *Financial Mail*. Against the constitution were the *Argus* (Cape Town), *Pretoria News, Daily News, Diamond Fields Advertiser* (Kimberley), *Sunday Tribune, Cape Times, Rand Daily Mail, Evening Post, Eastern Province Herald* (Port Elizabeth), and *Natal Witness*.

50. Otto Krause, "Westminster is Alive—and Living Surprisingly Well in South Africa," in *Bridge or Barricade? The Constitution, A First Appraisal*, edited by Fleur de Villiers (Johannesburg: Jonathan Ball Paperbacks, 1983), 81.

51. *Final Report of the Constitutional Committee of the President's Council on the Adaptation of Constitutional Structures in South Africa* (Cape Town: Republic of South Africa, 1984).

52. Department of Foreign Affairs and Information, *Constitutional Guidelines: A New Dispensation for Whites, Coloureds, and Indians* (Johannesburg: Perskor, December 1982). Hereafter referred to as the Department of Foreign Affairs and Information.

53. Department of Foreign Affairs and Information, 2.

54. Final Report, 46.

55. Final Report, 87.

56. Final Report, 48.

57. Department of Foreign Affairs and Information, 20.

58. Quoted in David Welsh, "Constitutional Changes," 150.

59. A "Johannesburg banker," quoted in Thomas J. Bray, "South Africa: Repression and Political Reform," *Wall Street Journal,* 14 September 1982, cited by Kevin Danaher, "Government-Initiated Reforms in South Africa and Its Implications for U.S. Foreign Policy," *Politics and Society* 13, no. 2 (1984): 188.

60. Fleur de Villiers, "The End—(Or the beginning? Or . . . the end of the beginning?)," in Fleur de Villiers, 139.

61. Bhadra Ranchod, "Reform—Or Change?" in Fleur de Villiers, 75.

62. Robert Schrire, 63.

63. Final Report, 16.

64. Final Report, 148.

65. Department of Foreign Affairs and Information, 3, emphasis in original.

66. Final Report, 90.

67. Peter Collins, "The Only Way to Reject Racism: Support Reform," in Fleur de Villiers, 129.

68. Brand Fourie, "American Comments on South Africa," backgrounder by the information minister of the South African Embassy, Washington, D.C., April 1982: 2, cited in Kevin Danaher, 190.

69. Gerrit Viljoen, "South Africa's Political Options," backgrounder by the information minister of the South African Embassy, Washington, D.C., January 1983: 4, cited in Kevin Danaher, 190.

70. Final Report, 50.

71. Final Report, 140–141.

72. Department of Foreign Affairs and Information, 32–33.

73. Final Report, 91.

74. Andre Thomashausen, "Power-sharing is a Utopian Dream," in Fleur de Villiers, 104–105.

75. Andre Thomashausen, 103.

76. See Kate Manzo, *Domination, Resistance, and Social Change,* cited above, and "Global Power and South African Politics: A Foucauldian Analysis," *Alternatives* 17 (1992), 23–66.

77. See John Sharp, "Two Worlds in One Country: 'First World' and 'Third World' in South Africa," in *South African Keywords,* edited by Emile Boonzaier and John Sharp (Cape Town: David Philip, 1988): 111–121.

78. Bernard Magubane, *South Africa: From Soweto To Uitenhage—The Political Economy of the South African Revolution* (Trenton, N.J.: Africa World Press, 1989), 104.

79. See Kevin Danaher, 188, 190, 191.

80. In "Africa Beset," *Foreign Affairs,* 62 no. 3 (Spring 1984): 769, Jennifer Seymour Whitaker reported that in private conversations, Reagan administration officials indicated confidence that the Botha government had a "hidden agenda" for broadening government to eventually include urban blacks in some way. The Botha regime consistently denied this.

81. Oscar Dhlomo, "Inkatha and the Reform Proposals," in Fleur de Villiers, 126.

82. David Welsh, "How Can Coloureds Be an Ethnic Group—Or Water an Ethnic Affair?" in Fleur de Villiers, 85.

83. "Racism to be constitution's cornerstone," *Argus,* 1 November 1983, page unknown.

84. "Boesak appeals to No voters," *Argus,* 10 November 1983, page unknown.

85. Oscar Dhlomo, 123.

86. Fleur de Villiers, 139.

87. Tom Lodge, 61–62.

88. Zwelakhe Sisulu, keynote address, National Education Crisis Committee (NECC), Second National Consultative Conference, 29 March 1986, mimeo, 14–15, cited in Robert Price, 202.

89. Tom Lodge, 135.

90. Quoted in Steven Mufson, *Fighting Years,* 105.

91. Gugile Nkwinti, quoted in Steven Mufson, *Fighting Years,* 109.

92. For Allan Boesak's argument, see Steven Mufson, *Fighting Years,* 53. For the SACBC, see *Commonweal* 112, no. 8 (19 April 1985): 227–228.

93. Steven Mufson, *Fighting Years,* 326.

94. Steven Mufson, *Fighting Years,* 11.

95. Steven Mufson, *Fighting Years,* 104–105.

96. Robert Price, 84.

97. Kate Manzo, *Domination, Resistance, and Social Change,* 243.

98. Anthony Marx, *Lessons of Struggle,* 125–126.

99. Robert Price, 197.

100. See Steven Mufson, *Fighting Years,* 118–121.

101. Mighty, interview by author, 29 July 1997, Bronkhurstspruit.

102. Steven Mufson, *Fighting Years,* 118.

103. Steven Mufson, *Fighting Years,* 121.

104. George, interview by author, 29 July 1997, Johannesburg.

105. Robert Matji, interview by Steven Mufson, *Fighting Years,* 76.

106. Shaun Johnson, 'The Soldiers of Luthuli': Youth in the Politics of Resistance in South Africa," in *South Africa: No Turning Back,* edited by Shaun Johnson (Bloomington: Indian University Press, 1989), 95.

107. Clayton, interview by author, 27 June 1997, Cape Town.

108. Ephraim, interview by author, 31 July 1997, Johannesburg.

109. Tom Lodge, 76.

110. "A Mother's Memories," *Learn and Teach* 1 (1988), 8, cited in Anthony Marx, *Lessons of Struggle,* 164.

CHAPTER SIX

1. While apartheid laws like the Suppression of Communism Act validated almost any form of repression, States of Emergency were declared when the state needed to justify particularly harsh treatment or the suspension of the minor legal protections that did exist.

2. John Kane-Berman, *Soweto: Black Revolt, White Reaction* (Johannesburg: Ravan Press, 1978), 54–55. The survey was from Market Research Africa, *Today's Urban Black Household,* (Johannesburg, Fourth Quarter 1975), table 4b. It seems fair to assume that "apartheid" was not presented as an option for the biggest problem.

3. Robert Ross, "Getting to the New South Africa from the Old," *Ethnic and Racial Studies* 19, no. 2 (April 1996): 440.

4. For a great snapshot of the structure and numbers for the SAP in 1988, see Catholic Institute of International Relations, *Now Everyone Is Afraid: The Changing Face of Policing in South Africa* (London: CIIR, 1988), appendix A. For another in 1993, see *Economist* of September 11.

5. In the mid-1980s, Black police officers were among the principal victims of the brutal practice of necklacing, a form of community retribution in which mobs would jam a rubber tire down over a victim's shoulders, douse it in gasoline, and set both tire and victim alight. A 1988 survey found that 41% of Black police suffered from Post Traumatic Stress Disorder. Juan Nel and Thoe Burgers, "The South African Police Service: 'Symptom Bearer' of the New South Africa?" *Track Two* 5, no. 1 (March 1996): 17.

6. Rory, interview by author, 11 July 1997, Port Elizabeth.

7. Martin Murray, *The Revolution Deferred: The Painful Birth of Post-Apartheid South Africa* (London: Verso, 1994), 55; and "South Africa: Murder and Siege Architecture," *Economist* 336, no. 7923 (15 July 1995), 28.

8. Michel Foucault has provided perhaps the best articulation of the relationship between order, crime, and social mechanisms for enforcing behavioral standards, a discussion that underlies this study, but is beyond the scope of the current discussion. See, in particular, *Discipline and Punish: The Birth of the Prison,* translated by Alan Sheridan (New York: Vintage Books, 1979).

9. George, a former comrade, interview by author, 25 July 1997, Johannesburg.

10. Martin Murray, *The Revolution Deferred*, 54–55.

11. A SAIRR table of monthly political deaths appears in Adrian Guelke, *South Africa in Transition: The Misunderstood Miracle* (London: I. B. Tauris, 1999), 46.

12. Several academics have suggested that the results were actually too good to be true. See R. W. Johnson, "How Free? How Fair?" in *Launching Democracy in South Africa: The First Open Election, April 1994*, edited by R. W. Johnson and Lawrence Schlemmer (New Haven: Yale University Press, 1996), 323–352.

13. *Financial Mail*, 15 February 1991, and *Pretoria News*, 28 January 1991, cited in Martin Murray, *The Revolution Deferred*, 56.

14. *Sunday Independent*, 1 September 1996, quoted in Greg Mills, *War and Peace in Southern Africa: Crime, Drugs, Armies, and Trade* (Cambridge: World Peace Foundation, 1996), 1.

15. Executive Summary of Nedcor Project on Crime, Violence, and Investment [Web Page], http://www.web.co.za/bac/nedkor.htm [Accessed February 14, 1999].

16. The government's official crime statistics are distributed through two special sections of the South African Police Services (SAPS), the Crime Information Management Centre (CIMC), and the Crime Information Analysis Centre (CIAC). The Monthly Bulletin on Reported Crime in South Africa, January 99 [Web Page], http://www.saps.co.za/8_crimeinfo/bulletin/1999(1).htm [Accessed February 14, 1999]. Through these two units, the government tracks twenty-eight "crime tendencies" with statistics from 1994.

17. Media Statement by the Minister of Safety and Security [Web Page], http://www.saps.org.za/8_crimeinfo/bulletin/crime2001.htm [Accessed June 19, 2001].

18. *The US Federal Bureau of Investigation's Uniform Crime Report*, cited in "A Struggle to Control Crime," *Philadelphia Inquirer* 1 June 1999, A8.

19. *The U.S. Federal Bureau of Investigation's Uniform Crime Report*, A8.

20. Eric Presler, "South Africa's Criminal Culture," *Foreign Policy* (September/October 2001), 80.

21. Eric Presler, 81.

22. Angela Johnson, "The Real Facts on SA Crime," *Weekly Mail and Guardian* 2–8 June, 1997, 6.

23. Tom Nevin, "Anatomy of a National Menace," *African Business* 216 (December 1996): 11.

24. Official in the Ministry of Safety and Security, interview by author, 31 July 1997, Johannesburg.

25. Hein Marais, *South Africa: Limits to Change—The Political Economy of Transformation* (London: Zed Books, 1998), 269.

26. "Siege architecture" comes from *Economist* 336, no. 7923 (15 July 1995): 28. I had a very serious conversation with a retired police general and his wife about the relative merits of concrete and wrought iron ramparts. General and Marike, interview by author, 29 July 1997, Marble Hall.

27. These "high-walled and high security residential complexes" accounted for 26% of new residential buildings in 1995, compared to 15% in 1992. Tom Nevin, 12.

28. Mark Shaw, "Urban Conflict, Crime, and Policing in South African Cities," *Africa Insight* 25, no. 4 (1995): 219.

29. The South African Security Association reports that, "In 1997 South Africans spent R9bn on security measures, triple that of three years before." "'Fear Industry' Booming in an Increasingly Paranoid SA," *Pretoria News,* 14 March 1998: 6, received through the Daily News Bulletin e-mail list server from the South African Embassy in Washington (hereafter referred to as DNB), March 1998. The DNB is also available through the embassy's web site, *www.southafrica.net,* where past issues are archived. The figure had risen to 11 billion rand by 1999. "The Endless Assault," *Economist* 358, no. 8210: s7–s8, received through ProQuest online database, June 19, 2001.

30. Wilfred Scharf, criminologist at the University of Cape Town, interview by author, 7 July 1997, Cape Town. Mark Shaw suggests that the ratio varies from 3:1 to 5:1 depending on whether in-house security personnel are counted. Mark Shaw, 220, ff 41.

31. Wilfred Sharf, interview by author, 7 July 1997, Cape Town.

32. See their web site at *www.pagad.co.za.*

33. "Don't Retaliate, Says Vigilante Leader," *Star,* 9 November 1999, 5, received from the DNB list server, November 1999. A "sjambok" is a flexible rubber whip.

34. "Provinces Adopt Conflicting Stances On Mapogo Vigilantes," *Business Day,* 6 October 1998, 5, received from the DNB list server, October 1998.

35. "Don't Retaliate, Says Vigilante Leader," *Star,* 9 November 1999, 5, received through the DNB list server, November 1999.

36. "Vigilante 'Medicine' Cuts Crime," *Pretoria News,* 29 July 1998, 8, received from the DNB list server, July 1998.

37. Wilfred Scharf, interview by author, 7 July 1997, Cape Town.

38. "(Crime) 'Not So Bad'," *This Week in South Africa* 8, no. 29 (5–11 August 1997), 3, citing *Citizen,* 5 August 1997.

39. "(Crime) 'Not So Bad'," 3.

40. Wilfred Scharf, interview by author, 7 July 1997, Cape Town.

41. Wilfred Scharf, interview by author, 7 July 1997, Cape Town.

42. Robert Ross, 443.

43. Nomzi, interview by author, 7 July 1997, Cape Town.

44. Jaap, interview by author, 30 June 1997, Stellenbosch.

45. Craig, interview by author, 21 July 1997, Cape Town.

46. "Moving Beyond Fear and Loathing," *Sunday Independent,* 20 September 1998, 10, received from the DNB list server, September 1998.

47. "Real South Africans," *Citizen,* 15 September 1998, 6, received through the DNB list server, September 1998.

48. "Wake Up Call," *Natal Witness,* 14 September 1998, 8, received through the DNB list server, September 1998.

49. "Punish all Illegals," *Sowetan,* 17 March, 2000, 10, received through the DNB list server, March 2000.

50. "About Time for Selebi," *City Press,* 23 October 1999, 6, received from the DNB list server, October 1999.

51. Mark Shaw, Institute for Security Studies, cited in "Whites Skeptical about Crime Figures," *Business Day,* 9 June 1998, 6, received from the DNB list server, June 1998.

52. "The Tshwete Factor," *Business Day,* 9 March 2000, 5, received from the DNB list server, March 2000.

53. "Morality Begins at Home," *Saturday Star,* 23 October 1999, 10, received through the DNB list server, October 1999.

54. "The Tshwete Factor," *Business Day,* 9 March 2000, 5, received from the DNB list server, March 2000.

55. "Skepticism Over Crime Statistics Misplaced," *Business Day,* 29 May 1998, 2, received from the DNB list server, May 1998.

56. "There's No Magic Wand, Says President Mandela," *This Week in South Africa* 8, no. 15 (15–21 April 1997) 3, citing *Star,* 17 April 1997.

57. Hein Marais, 109, citing *SouthScan* 12, no. 14 (11 April 1997).

58. "Crimes by Police Increase," *Sowetan,* 17 April, 2000, 2, received through the DNB list server, April 2000.

59. "SAPS Bests Public in Criminal Deeds," *Citizen,* 15 April 1998, received from the DNB list server, April 1998.

60. "A Severe Handicap for Police," *Pretoria News,* 27 September 1999, 7, received through the DNB, September 1999.

61. "The Endless Assault," *Economist* 358, no. 8210 (24 February 2001): s7–s8, received from the ProQuest electronic database.

62. Wilfred Scharf, interview by author, 7 July 1997, Cape Town.

63. Wynand, interview by author, 1 August 1997, Johannesburg.

64. Official from Ministry of Safety and Security, interview by author, 31 July 1997, Johannesburg.

65. "67% Win Needed to Reduce Rights of Criminals," *Pretoria News,* 18 May 1999, 1, received through the DNB list server, May 1999.

66. ANC MP, interview by author, July 1997, South Africa.

67. Official from Ministry of Safety and Security, interview by author, 31 July 1997, Johannesburg.

68. "Crime Quickly to the Fore," *Citizen,* 4 January 1999, 6, received from the DNB list server, January 1999.

69. "Signs Of Anarchy" *Star,* 5 January 1999, 8, received from the DNB list server, January 1999.

70. Mark Shaw, 219.

71. "Join Us in Fighting Crime in SA" [Web Page], *http://www.robkaplan.org.za/* [Accessed February 14, 1999]

72. Editorial, "Blowing the Whistle on Crime," *Pretoria News,* 18 September 1998, 13, received from the DNB list server, September 1998.

73. "Lyndhurst Leads the Way in Privately Funded Police Stations," *This Week in South Africa* (October 28–November 10, 1997): 6–7, citing *Star,* 10 November 1997.

74. Anthony, interview by author, July 31, 1997, Johannesburg.

75. The food chain analogy comes from an interview with Glenda, 23 July 1997, Durban.

76. Jasmine, interview by author, 1 August 1997, Johannesburg; Wilfred Sharf, interview by author, 7 July 1997, Cape Town; see also Sampie Terreblanche, "The Brotherhood Syndrome: The Origins of Favouritism," *SASH* 33, no. 2 (September 1989): 9–10.

77. Jaap, interview by author, 30 June 1997, Stellenbosch.

78. Lynne Duke, A13. Heath is reportedly investigating two or three cabinet members from the apartheid era. He said the corruption in the current government did not reach as high.

79. Mary, interview by author, 11 July 1997, Port Elizabeth.

80. Glenda, interview by author, 23 July 1997, Durban.

81. Lynne Duke, A12.

82. Mark Shaw, *Partners in Crime? Crime, Political Transition and Changing Forms of Policing Control, Centre for Policy Studies Research Report no 39* (June 1995) 12, quoted in Mark Shaw "Urban Conflict, Crime and Policing in South African Cities," *Africa Insight* 25, no. 4 (1995): 219, ff 20.

83. Jasmine, interview by author, 1 August 1997, Johannesburg.

84. Wilfred Scharf, interview by author, 7 July 1997, Cape Town. The highest per capita incarceration rate is among Coloureds.

85. I asked her if that meant there were no White criminals and she said yes. Julie, interview by author, 21 June 1997, Cape Town.

86. Os, interview by author, 11 July 1997, Port Elizabeth.

87. "We've been having lots of burglaries, bank robberies, armed robberies, with Black people involved and so immediately Coloureds say well 'These people are supposed to govern us.' For them, it's not the ANC that's governing, it's Black people. . . . Whites still have. Blacks are getting and Coloureds THINK they have been left behind. They have integrated the victim mentality. It's completely irrational but because it's internalized and it has become part of the attitude of Coloured people. . . . Because affirmative action is targeted toward Blacks, there is a sense that we're not going to get any jobs. We need to live so the only way we can live is by robbing a bank." Craig, interview by author, 21 July 1997, Cape Town.

88. Lloyd, interview by author, 22 July 1997, Durban.

89. Mary, interview by author, 11 July 1997, Port Elizabeth; and Suzanne, interview by author, 23 July 1997, Durban.

90. Anthony, interview by author, 31 July 1997, Johannesburg.

91. "Moving Beyond Fear and Loathing," *Sunday Independent,* 20 September 1998, 10, received from the DNB list server, September 1998.

92. Wilfred Scharf, interview by author, 7 July 1997, Cape Town.

93. Wilfred Scharf, interview by author, 7 July 1997, Cape Town.

94. Rory, interview by author, 11 July 1997, Port Elizabeth.

95. Wilfred Scharf, interview by author, 7 July 1997, Cape Town.

96. David Black and John Nauright, *Rugby and the South African Nation* (Manchester: Manchester University Press, 1998).

97. "Illegal Alien Problem," *Mercury,* 11 September 1998, 16, received from the DNB list server, September 1998.

98. See Sheila Croucher, "South Africa's Illegal Aliens: Constructing National Boundaries in a Post-Apartheid State," *Ethnic and Racial Studies* 21, no. 4 (July 1998): 650.

99. Sheila Croucher, 651, citing *Citizen,* 15 April 1996, 8.

100. Michael Bratton, "After Mandela's Miracle in South Africa," *Current History* 97, no. 619, (May 1998): 218.

101. Alan Morris, "'Our Fellow Africans Make Our Lives Hell': The Lives of Congolese and Nigerians Living in Johannesburg," *Ethnic and Racial Studies* 21, no. 6 (November 1998): 1120, citing the *Sunday Independent,* 22 June 1997.

102. Joe, interview by author, 22 July 1997, Durban; Wilfred Scharf, interview by author, 7 July 1997, Cape Town.

103. Anthony, interviewed by author, 31 July 1997, Johannesburg and Richard, interviewed by author, 22 July 1997, Durban.

104. "Real South Africans," *Citizen,* 15 September 1998, 6, received from the DNB list server, September 1998. The newspapers surveyed 11,000 South Africans.

105. "True S. Africans 'Won't Run Away'," *Citizen,* 14 September 1998, 1, received from the DNB list server, September 1998.

106. "Real South Africans," *Citizen,* 15 September 1998, 6.

107. "Crime and Emigration," *Business Day,* 15 September 1998, 19; "Wake Up Call," *Natal Witness,* 14 September 1998, 8; both received from the DNB list server, September 1998.

108. "The 'White' Factor," *Eastern Province Herald,* 15 September 1998, 4; "Moving Beyond Fear and Loathing," *Sunday Independent,* 20 September 1998, 10; "Real South Africans," *Citizen,* 15 September 1998, 6; all received from the DNB list server, September 1998.

109. "Comment," *Sowetan,* 15 September 1998, 8, received from the DNB list server, September 1998.

110. "Wake Up Call," DNB, 14 September 1998.

111. "The 'White' Factor," DNB, 15 September 1998.

112. Joan, interview by author, 25 June 1997, Cape Town.

113. In contrast, an organization of South African businesses dismissed the correlation between unemployment and crime, claiming that the cause was rather "tolerance for criminal activity by the community." Wendy Lucas-Bull, interview by Anver Versi, *African Business* 216 (December 1996): 13.

114. Jaap, interview by author, 30 June 1997, Stellenbosch.

115. Rory, interview by author, 11 July 1997, Port Elizabeth.

116. Wilfred Scharf, interview by author, 7 July 1997, Cape Town.

117. Duma Gqubule, "The Hidden Cost of Crime," *South African Economist* (February 1997): 7.

118. "Crime Still Driving Off Investors," *Business Report,* 9 July 1998, 5, received through the DNB list server, July 1998.

119. Rickus, interview by author, 30 June 1997, train from Stellenbosch to Cape Town.

120. "Crime and Our Society," *Star,* 9 October 1997, 16, received through the DNB list server, October, 1997.

121. Brian, interview by author, 11 July 1997, Port Elizabeth; and Iole, interview by author, 23 July 1997, Durban.

122. Iole, interview by author, 23 July 1997, Durban.

123. One notable exception was the increasing interracial interaction that the Black Sash, an organization of liberal White women, began after a period of reorganization in 1958, but this organization maintained a membership of only about 2000 women. See *1955–1995—Anniversary Supplement to SASH* 37, no. 3 (May 1995): 3.

124. Quoted in "The Endless Assault," *Economist* 358, no. 8210 (24 February 2001): s7–s8, downloaded from the ProQuest database, June 19, 2001.

125. Even the anti-apartheid movement, which saw itself as very progressive, perpetuated "unfree attitudes toward women folk" and claimed gender issues were dangerous because they diverted attention from the primary battle against racism. Athol, interview by author, 22 July 1997, Durban.

126. Jasmine, a high ranking government official, said that women in government were often foisted off onto committees and issues perceived to be women's, frustrating many to the degree that many are leaving government "because they want to do real things and they are not being allowed to." As a result the government was having trouble finding women to fill its quotas (interview by author, 1 August 1997, Johannesburg).

127. Two women executives in an NGO talked to me about their experiences. At a conference on gender they attended with a lot of socially powerful women including Members of Parliament, the common complaint was that they all had to make dinner. They claimed that *all* men were chauvinists—across all social divisions—and that sexual harassment was commonplace. But, they said, women are often complicit, in that their self-esteem was wrapped up in men's projections of women as sex objects. Women brought up in other places find SA stifling and demeaning. Iole and Glenda, interview by author, 23 July 1997, Durban.

128. The Millennium Edition of the Guinness Book of World records lists South Africa as the country with the highest rate of rape in the world. "Rape Earns SA a New World Record," *Pretoria News,* 8 October 1999, 1, received from the DNB list server, October 1999.

129. Jasmine, interview by author, 1 August 1997, Johannesburg.

130. Jasmine, interview by author, 1 August 1997, Johannesburg.

131. Official of the Ministry of Safety and Security, interview by author, 31 July 1997, Johannesburg. Robert Ross reports the same statistic, 442.

132. Jasmine, interview by author, 1 August 1997, Johannesburg.

133. One of the suggestions in a pamphlet put out by the Natal Midlands Black Sash is to "Join a women's group or organization, or start your own. . . . Women around the world, in rich and poor countries, have used many ways to make sure their voices are heard. We need to spread the word that rape has no place in our country. Women are stronger working together than working alone." *Say No to Rape,* Black Sash pamphlet, 30–31.

134. Wilfred Scharf, interview by author, 7 July 1997, Cape Town.

135. Athol, interview by author, 22 July 1997, Durban.

136. Wilfred Scharf, 7 July 1997, Cape Town.

137. General, interview by author, 28 July 1997, Marble Hall.

138. "SA Crime Not So Bad, Mbeki Tells Business," *Citizen,* 18 April 1998, 8, received from the DNB list server, April 1998.

139. "Survey Shows Criminals Target Rich And Poor," *Business Day,* 11 December 1998, 1, received from the DNB list server, December 1998. The survey included over 4000 households.

140. Wilfred Scharf, interview by author, 7 July 1997, Cape Town.

141. Official from Ministry of Safety and Security, interview by author, 31 July 1997, Johannesburg.

142. Culture was important to Ady, 13 July 1997, Cape Town; Mary, 11 July 1997, Port Elizabeth; and Paul, 22 July 1997, Durban. Age was significant for Lengiwe, 19 July 1997, Cape Town; Andre, 20 July 1997, Cape Town; Athol, 22 July 1997, Durban; and Susan, 23 July 1997, Durban. Crime was understood according to party affiliation by Iole and Glenda, 23 July 1997, Durban. Religion was a key to crime for Ron and Hydie, 13 July 1997, Cape Town; Athol, 22 July 1997, Durban; and Vincent, 23 July 1997, Durban. All were interviewed by the author.

143. Athol, interview by author, 22 July 1997, Durban.

144. Joe, interview by author, 22 July 1997, Durban.

Bibliography

Please note: In addition to the sources listed below, I made extensive use of four categories of sources which are too numerous and intricate to be listed individually. The first is a series of newspaper clippings obtained from the newspaper archives at the South African National Library in Cape Town. These clippings have been cut and pasted into binders and, as a result, almost all lack page numbers. In addition, several key government pamphlets found in the archives give no publication date. I have either originals or photocopies of these sources and can provide photocopies on request.

The second category of source not included below is newspaper stories received through Daily News Bulletin (DNB) e-mail list server from the South African Embassy in Washington, D.C. The DNB is a daily summary of major stories and editorials in the South African press, most of which are condensed down to three or four sentences. I have archived interesting stories since 1996. The DNB is also available through the embassy's web site, *www.southafrica.net,* where past issues are archived. I have cited the original newspapers and the date of publication, but indicated in each case that it has been chosen and processed to fit into the DNB.

The third category of data is a similar summary of South African newspaper stories published weekly and, more recently, bi-weekly by the South African Consulate in New York. I have an archive of these eight- to twelve-page documents dating from July 1995. For these data, I cite the summary, *This Week in South Africa,* as well as the newspaper to which the summary attributes the story. The Newspapers covered by the summary are *Sowetan, Citizen, Business Day, Star, Natal Mercury, Pretoria News, Beeld* (Afrikaans), *Sunday Times, Sunday Star, Argus, City Press, Cape Times, Channel Africa News, Weekly Mail, Eastern Province Herald, Daily News,* and *Natal Witness.*

Finally, in June, July, and August of 1997, I conducted over 100 interviews throughout South Africa with the widest variety of people available to me. The interviews are dealt with more explicitly in the introductory chapter. Each citation consists of a first name (with two exceptions), the date of the interview, and the city in which it took place. Listing each again here seemed superfluous.

1955–1995—Anniversary Supplement to SASH 37, no. 3 (May 1995).

Adam, Heribert. "Variations of Ethnicity: Afrikaner and Black Nationalism in South Africa." In *Ethnic Identities and Prejudices: Perspectives from the Third World.* Edited by Anand C. Paranjpe. Leiden: E. J. Brill, 1986.

Adam, Heribert, Frederick van Zyl Slabbert, and Kogila Moodley. *Comrades in Business: Post-Liberation Politics in South Africa.* Utrecht: International Books, 1998.

Adam, Heribert and Hermann Giliomee, editors. *Ethnic Power Mobilized: Can South Africa Change?* New Haven: Yale University Press, 1979.

"Address by State President Nelson Mandela to Parliament, February 5, 1999" [Web Page], *http://www.mweb.co.za/parliament/madiba.html* [Accessed April 18, 1999].

Adler, Emanuel. "Seizing the Middle Ground: Constructivism in World Politics." *European Journal of International Relations* 3 (1997): 319–363.

Allen, Michael. "Bargaining Environments of a Post-Apartheid State: Market, Class, and Ethnic Dimensions." In *The Dynamics of Change in Southern Africa.* Edited by Paul Rich. New York: St. Martin's Press, 1994. 71–100.

Anderson, Benedict. *Imagined Communities.* 2nd edition. London: Verso, 1991.

Ashforth, Adam. *The Politics of Official Discourse in Twentieth-Century South Africa.* Oxford: Clarendon Press, 1990.

Asmal, Kadar, Louise Asmal, and Ronald Suresh Roberts. *Reconciliation Through Truth.* 2nd edition. Cape Town: David Philip, 1997.

Barber, James. *South Africa in the Twentieth Century.* Oxford: Blackwell, 1999.

Barth, Frederick, editor. *Ethnic Groups and Boundaries.* Boston: Little Brown, 1969.

Berg, Bruce. *Qualitative Research Methods for the Social Sciences.* 3rd edition. Boston: Allyn and Bacon, 1998.

Berger, Peter, and Thomas Luckmann. *The Social Construction of Reality: A Treatise in the Sociology of Knowledge.* New York: Anchor Books, 1966.

Bernard, H. Russell. *Research Methods in Anthropology: Qualitative and Quantitative Approaches.* 2nd edition. Walnut Creek, Cal.: Alta Mira Press, 1994.

Biko, Steve. *I Write What I Like.* London: Heinemann, 1978.

Black, David, and John Nauright. *Rugby and the South African Nation.* Manchester: Manchester University Press, 1998.

Bloom, William. *Personal Identity, National Identity, and International Relations.* Cambridge: Cambridge University Press, 1990.

Bokala, Willie. *Bulletin of the Union of Black Journalists* 2, date unknown.

Boonzaier, Emile, and John Sharp, editors. *South African Keywords: The Uses and Abuses of Political Concepts.* Cape Town: David Phillip, 1988.

Boulle, L. J. *Constitutional Reform and the Apartheid State.* New York: St. Martin's Press, 1984.

———. "The RSA Constitution: Continuity and Change." In *South Africa: A Plural Society in Transition.* Edited by D. J. van Vuuren, N. E. Wiehahn, J. A. Lombard, and N. J. Rhoodie. Durban: Butterworth, 1985. 1–27.

Bourdieu, Pierre. *Outline of a Thoery of Practice*. Translated by Richard Nice. Cambridge: Cambridge University Press, 1977.

Bratton, Michael. "After Mandela's Miracle in South Africa." *Current History* 97, no. 619 (May 1998): 214–219.

Brewer, John. *After Soweto: An Unfinished Journey*. Oxford: Clarendon Press, 1986.

———. *Black and Blue: Policing in South Africa*. Oxford: Clarendon Press, 1994.

Bronfenbrenner, Uri. "The Mirror Image in Soviet-American Relations: A Social Psychologist's Report." *Journal of Social Issues* 14:45–56.

Brooks, Alan, and Jeremy Brickhill. *Whirlwind Before the Storm*. London: International Defence and Aid Fund for Southern Africa, 1980.

Burkitt, Ian. *Social Selves: Theories of the Social Formation of Personality*. London: Sage, 1991.

Burman, Erica, Amanda Kottler, Ann Levett, and Ian Parker. "Power and Discourse: Culture and Change in South Africa." In *Culture, Power, and Difference: Discourse Analysis in South Africa*. Edited by Ann Levett, Amanda Kottler, Erica Burman, and Ian Parker. London: Zed Books, 1997. 1–14.

Butler, Anthony. *Democracy and Apartheid: Political Theory, Comparative Politics, and the Modern South African State*. New York: St. Martin's Press, 1998.

Campbell, David. *Writing Security: United States Foreign Policy and the Politics of Identity*. 2nd edition. Minneapolis: University of Minnesota Press, 1998.

Campbell, Horace. "Challenging the Apartheid Regime from Below." In *Popular Struggles for Democracy in Africa*. Edited by Peter Nyong'o. Tokyo: U.N. University, 1987. 142–169.

Carbaugh, Donal. "Communicative Rules in *Donahue* Discourse." In *Cultural Communication and Intercultural Contact*. Edited by Donal Carbaugh. Hillside, N.J.: Lawrence Erlbaum, 1990. 119–149.

———. *Talking American: Cultural Discourses on "Donahue."* Norwood, N.J.: Ablex Publishing, 1989.

Catholic Institute for International Relations (CIIR). *Now Everyone Is Afraid: The Changing Face of Policing in South Africa*. London: CIIR, August 1988.

Chandra, Romesh. "The Soweto Uprising." *Spotlight on Soweto*. City unknown: World Peace Council, 1976.

Charney, Craig. "The Politics of Changing Partners—Control and Co-option in the New South African Constitution." *Review of African Political Economy* 29 (July 1984): 122–131.

Chatterjee, Partha. *The Nation and Its Fragments: Colonial and Postcolonial Histories*. Princeton: Princeton University Press, 1993.

Checkel, Jeffrey T. "The Constructivist Turn in International Relations Theory." *World Politics* 50 (January 1998): 324–348.

Cillie Commission of Inquiry. *The Report of the Commission of Inquiry into the Riots at Soweto and Elsewhere from the 16th of June 1976 to the 28th of February 1977*. Pretoria: Republic of South Africa, 1980.

Cobbing, Julian. "The *Mfecane* as Alibi: Thoughts on Dithakong and Mbolompo." *Journal of African History* 29 (1988): 487–519.

Collier, Mary Jane. "Cultural and Intercultural Communication Competence: Current Approaches and Directions for Future Research," *International Journal of Intercultural Relations* 13 (1989): 287–302.

Collins, Peter. "The Only Way to Reject Racism: Support Reform." In *Bridge or Barricade? The Constitution, A First Appraisal.* Edited by Fleur deVilliers. Johannesburg: Jonathan Ball, 1983. 127–130.

Commonweal 112, no. 8 (19 April 1985): 227–228.

Connolly, William. *Identity/Difference: Democratic Negotiations of Political Paradox.* Ithaca: Cornell University Press, 1991.

———. *Political Theory and Modernity.* Ithaca: Cornell University Press, 1993.

Couper, M. P., N. J. Rhoodie, and C. P. de Kock. "Indian Attitudes Toward the New Constitutional Dispensation and Related Issues." In *South Africa: A Plural Society in Transition.* Edited by D. J. van Vuuren, N. E. Wiehahn, J. A. Lombard. and N. J. Rhoodie. Durban: Butterworth, 1985. 379–394.

"Crime: South Africa's New Enemy." *Christian Century* 13, no. 11 (10 April 1996): 396.

Croucher, Sheila. "South Africa's Illegal Aliens: Constructing National Boundaries in a Post-Apartheid State." *Ethnic and Racial Studies* 21, no. 4 (July 1998): 639–660.

Danaher, Kevin. "Government-Initiated Reforms in South Africa and Its Implications for U.S. Foreign Policy." *Politics and Society* 13, no. 2 (1984): 177–202.

Daily News Bulletin (DNB). A list service from the South African Embassy in Washington, D.C., that summarizes stories from most of the major newspapers in South Africa five days a week (except holidays). Archives are available at *www.southafrica.net.*

Davenport, T. R. H. *The Birth of a New South Africa.* Toronto: University of Toronto Press, 1998.

de Kock, C. P., Nic Rhoodie, and M. P. Couper. "Black views on socio-political change in South Africa." In *South Africa: A Plural Society in Transition.* Edited by D. J. van Vuuren, N. E. Wiehahn, J. A. Lombard, and N. J. Rhoodie. Durban: Butterworth, 1985. 335–363.

de St. Jorre, John. "White South Africa Circles the Wagons." In *Apartheid in Crisis.* Edited by Mark A. Uhlig. New York: Vintage Books, 1986. 61–84.

de Villiers, Fleur, editor. *Bridge or Barricade? The Constitution, A First Appraisal.* Johannesburg: Jonathan Ball, 1983.

———. "The End—(Or the beginning? Or . . . the end of the beginning?)." In *Bridge or Barricade? The Constitution, A First Appraisal.* Edited by Fleur deVilliers. Johannesburg: Jonathan Ball, 1983. 136–141.

Department of Foreign Affairs and Information. *Constitutional Guidelines: A New Dispensation for Whites, Coloureds, and Indians.* Johannesburg: Perskor, December 1982.

———. *Republic of South Africa Constitution Act, No. 110, 1983.* Pretoria: Government Printer, October 1983.

Der Darian, James, and Michael J. Shapiro, editors. *International/Intertextual Relations: Postmodern Readings of World Politics.* New York: Lexington Books, 1989.

Dhlomo, Oscar. "Inkatha and the Reform Proposals." In *Bridge or Barricade: The Constitution, A First Appraisal.* Edited by Fleur de Villiers. Johannesburg: Jonathan Ball, 1983. 122–126.

Doty, Roxanne Lynn. "Sovereignty and the Nation: Constructing the Boundaries of National Identity." In *State Sovereignty as Social Construct.* Edited by Thomas J. Biersteker and Cynthia Weber. Cambridge: Cambridge University Press, 1996. 121–147.

Duke, Lynne. "Corruption a Hot Election Issue in S. African Election." *Washington Post,* 24 April 1999, A12.

Erikson, Erik. *Childhood and Society.* New York: Norton, 1950.

Esterhuyse, Willie. "The Catch 22 Afflicting White Politics." In *Bridge or Barricade? The Constitution, A First Appraisal.* Edited by Fleur deVilliers. Johannesburg: Jonathan Ball, 1983. 67–72.

Executive Summary of Nedcor Project on Crime, Violence, and Investment [Web Page]. *http://www.web.co.za/bac/nedkor.htm* [Accessed February 14, 1999].

Executive Summary of the Quarterly Report of Incidences of Serious Crime from January to June 1998 [Web Page]. *http://www.saps.co.za/8_crimeinfo/398/executive_summary.htm* [Accessed February 14, 1999].

Farred, Grant. "Bulletproof Settlers: The Politics of Offense in the New South Africa." In *Whiteness: A Critical Reader.* Edited by Mike Hill. New York: New York University Press, 1997. 63–78.

Ferguson, Yale, and Richard Mansbach. "The Past as Prelude to the Future? Identities and Loyalties in Global Politics." In *The Return of Culture and Identity in IR Theory.* Edited by Yosef Lapid and Friedrich Kratochwil. Boulder: Lynne Rienner, 1996. 21–44.

Final Report of the Constitutional Committee of the President's Council on the Adaptations of Constitutional Structures in South Africa. Cape Town: Republic of South Africa, 1984.

Finnegan, William. *Crossing the Line: A Year in the Land of Apartheid.* New York: Harper and Row, 1986.

Forsyth, Paul. "The Real Zulu: How Political Conflict Has Forged Variants of 'Zuluness.'" *Track Two* 2, no. 1 (February 1993): 8–9.

Foucault, Michel. *Discipline and Punish: The Birth of the Prison.* Translated by Alan Sheridan. New York: Vintage Books, 1979.

———. *The Order of Things: An Archaeology of the Human Sciences.* New York: Vintage Books, 1994.

———. "What is an Author?" In *The Foucault Reader.* Edited by Paul Rabinow. New York: Pantheon, 1984. 101–120.

Frank, Jerome D. "The Face of the Enemy," *Psychology Today* 2, no. 6, (1968): 24–29.

Frankel, Phillip. "Race and Counter-Revolution: South Africa's 'Total Strategy.'" *Journal of Commonwealth and Comparative Politics* 18, no. 3 (November 1980): 272–292.

Friedman, Jonathan. "The Past in the Future: History and the Politics of Identity." *American Anthropologist* 94, no. 4 (1992): 837–859.

Gastrow, Peter. *Bargaining for Peace: South Africa and the National Peace Accord.* Washington: USIP Press, 1995.

Geertz, Clifford. *The Interpretation of Cultures.* New York: Basic Books, 1973.

Giddens, Anthony. *The Constitution of Society: Outline of the Theory of Structuration.* Berkeley and Los Angeles: University of California Press, 1984.

———. *Modernity and Self Identity: Self and Society in the Late Modern Age.* Stanford: Stanford University Press, 1991.

Giliomee, Hermann. "The Beginnings of Afrikaner Ethnic Consciousness, 1850–1915." In *The Creation of Tribalism in Southern Africa.* Edited by Leroy Vail. Berkeley and Los Angeles: University of California Press, 1989. 21–54.

———. *The Parting of the Ways: South African Politics 1976–82.* Cape Town: David Phillip, 1982.

Giliomee, Hermann, and Lawrence Schlemmer. *From Apartheid to Nation-Building.* Cape Town: Oxford University Press, 1989.

Giliomee, Hermann, and Lawrence Schlemmer, editors. *Negotiating South Africa's Future.* New York: St Martin's Press, 1989.

Glaser, Daryl. "South Africa and the Limits of Civil Society." *Journal of Southern African Studies* 23, no. 1 (March 1997): 5–25.

Golan, Daphna. *Inventing Shaka: Using History in the Construction of Zulu Nationalism.* Boulder: Lynne Reinner, 1994.

Gqubule, Duma. "The Hidden Cost of Crime." *Southern African Economist* (February 1997): 7–9.

Gramsci, Antonio. *Selections from the Prison Notebooks.* Edited by Quintin Hoare and Geoffrey Hoare Smith. New York: International, 1971.

Greenstein, Ran. *Genealogies of Conflict: Class, Identity, and State in Palestine/Israel and South Africa.* Hanover, N.H.: University Press of New England, 1995.

Grimshaw, Allen. "Data and Data Use in an Analysis of Communicative Events." In *Explorations in Ethnography of Speaking.* Edited by Richard Bauman and Joel Sherzer. Cambridge: Cambridge University Press, 1974. 419–424.

Guelke, Adrian. *South Africa in Transition: The Misunderstood Miracle.* London: I. B. Tauris Publishers, 1999.

Habermas, Jurgen. *Theory of Communicative Action, Volume One.* Translated by Thomas McCarthy. Boston: Beacon Press, 1984.

Harries, Patrick. "Exclusion, Classification, and Internal Colonialism: The Emergence of Ethnicity Among the Tsonga-Speakers of South Africa." In *The Creation of Tribalism in Southern Africa.* Edited by Leroy Vail. Berkeley and Los Angeles: University of California Press, 1989. 82–117.

Harrison, David. *The White Tribe of Africa*. Berkeley and Los Angeles: University of California Press, 1981.

Haugaard, Mark. *The Constitution of Power: A Theoretical Analysis of Power, Knowledge, and Structure*. Manchester: Manchester University Press, 1997.

Herbst, Jeffery. "Prospects for Elite-Driven Democracy in South Africa," *Political Science Quarterly* 112, no. 4 (Winter 1997–1998): 595–615.

Herbstein, Denis. *White Man, We Want to Talk to You*. New York: Africana, 1979.

Hill, Christopher. *Change in South Africa*. Totowa, N.J.: Barnes and Noble, 1983.

Hirson, Baruch. *Year of Fire, Year of Ash—The Soweto Revolt: Roots of a Revolution?* London: Zed Press, 1979.

Hitchcock, Bob. *Flashpoint South Africa*. Cape Town: Don Nelson, 1977.

Hopf, Ted. "The Promise of Constructivism in International Relations Theory." *International Security* 23, no. 1 (Summer 1998): 171–200.

Horowitz, Donald. *A Democratic South Africa? Constitutional Engineeringin a Divided Society*. Berkeley and LA: University of California Press, 1991.

———. *Ethnic Groups in Conflict*. Berkeley and LA: University of California Press, 1985.

Horwath, David R., and Aletta J. Norval. "Introduction: Changing Paradigms and the Politics of Transition in South Africa." In *South Africa in Transition: New Theoretical Perspectives*. New York: St. Martin's Press, 1998.

Institute for Black Research. *Soweto—A People's Response*. Natal: SAIRR: 11 January 1978.

Isaacs, Harold. *Idols of the Tribe: Group Identity and Political Change*. New York: Harper and Row, 1975.

James, Wilmot. "Reinforcing Ethnic Boundaries: South Africa in the 1980s." In *Competitive Ethnic Relations*. Edited by Susan Olzak and Joane Nagel. London: Academic Press, 1986.

James, Wilmot, and Daria Caliguire. "Renewing Civil Society," *Journal of Democracy* 7 (January 1996): 56–66.

Jepperson, Ronald L., Alexander Wendt, and Peter J. Katzenstein. "Norms, Identity, and Culture in National Security." In *The Culture of National Security: Norms and Identity in World Politics*. Edited by Peter J. Katzenstein. New York: Columbia University Press, 1996. 33–75.

Johnson, Angela. "The Real Facts on SA Crime." *Weekly Mail and Guardian*. 2–8 June 1997. 6.

Johnson, Janet Buttolph, and Richard A. Joslyn. *Political Science Research Methods*. 3rd edition. Washington, D.C.: Congressional Quarterly Press, 1995.

Johnson, R. W. "How Free? How Fair?" In *Launching Democracy in South Africa: The First Open Election, April 1994*. Edited by R. W. Johnson and Lawrence Schlemmer. New Haven: Yale University Press, 1996. 323–352.

Johnson, Shaun. "'The Soldiers of Luthuli': Youth in the Politics of Resistance in South Africa." In *South Africa: No Turning Back*. Edited by Shaun Johnson. Bloomington: Indiana University Press, 1989. 94–151.

"June 16," *Drum* (August 1983): 4.

Kane-Berman, John. *Soweto: Black Revolt, White Reaction.* Johannesburg: Ravan Press, 1978.

Karis, Thomas, and Gail M. Gerhart, editors. *From Protest to Challenge: A Documentary History of African Politics in South Africa 1882–1964.* Vol. 3, *Challenge and Violence 1953–1964.* Stanford: Hoover Institution Press, 1977.

Katzenstein, Peter J., editor. *The Culture of National Security: Norms and Identity in World Politics.* New York: Columbia University Press, 1996.

Keen, Sam. *Faces of the Enemy: Reflections of the Hostile Imagination.* San Francisco: Harper and Row, 1986.

Klotz, Audie. *Norms in International Relations: The Struggle Against Apartheid.* Ithaca: Cornell University Press, 1995.

Koelble, Thomas. *The Global Economy and Democracy in South Africa.* New Brunswick: Rutgers University Press, 1998.

Kondo, Dorinne. *Crafting Selves: Power, Gender, and Discourses of Identity in a Japanese Workplace.* Chicago: University of Chicago Press, 1990.

Kowert, Paul. "Agency Versus Structure in the Construction of National Identity." In *International Relations in a Constructed World.* Edited by Vendulka Kubalkova, Nicholas Onuf, and Paul Kowert. Armonk, N.Y.: M. E. Sharpe, 1998. 101–122.

Kowert, Paul, and Jeffrey Legro. "Norms, Identity, and Their Limits." In *The Culture of National Security: Norms and Identity in World Politics.* Edited by Peter J. Katzenstein. New York: Columbia University Press, 1996. 451–497.

Kratochwil, Friedrich. "Is the Ship of Culture at Sea or Returning?" In *The Return of Culture and Identity in IR Theory.* Edited by Yosef Lapid and Friedrich Kratochwil. Boulder: Lynne Rienner, 1996. 201–222.

Krause, Jill, and Neil Renwick, editors. *Identities in International Relations.* New York: St. Martin's, 1996.

Krause, Otto. "Westminster is Alive—and Living Surprisingly Well in South Africa." In *Bridge or Barricade? The Constitution, A First Appraisal.* Edited by Fleur de Villiers. Johannesburg: Jonathan Ball, 1983. 78–83.

Kuhn, Thomas. *The Structure of Scientific Revolutions.* 2nd edition. Chicago: University of Chicago Press, 1970.

Lapid, Yosef. "Culture's Ship: Returns and Departures in International Relations Theory." In *The Return of Culture and Identity in IR Theory.* Edited by Yosef Lapid and Friedrich Kratochwil. Boulder: Lynne Rienner, 1996. 3–20.

Lapid, Yosef, and Friedrich Kratochwil, editors. *The Return of Culture and Identity in IR Theory.* Boulder: Lynne Rienner, 1996.

Lash, Scott, and Jonathan Friedman. "Introduction." In *Modernity and Identity.* Edited by Scott Lash and Jonathan Friedman. Oxford: Blackwell, 1992.

Leatt, James et al., editors. *Contending Ideologies in South Africa.* Cape Town: David Phillip, 1986.

Lelyveld, Joseph. *Move Your Shadow: South Africa, Black and White.* New York: Penguin Books, 1985.

Levitt, Ann, Amanda Kottler, Erica Burman, and Ian Parker, editors. *Culture, Power, and Difference: Discourse Analysis in South Africa.* London: Zed Books, 1997.

Lipjhart, Arendt. *The Politics of Accommodation: Pluralism and Democracy in the Netherlands.* Berkeley and Los Angeles: University of California Press, 1968.

Lodge, Tom. "Rebellion: The Turning of the Tide." In *All, Here, and Now: Black Politics in South Africa in the 1980s.* Edited by Tom Lodge and Bill Nasson. U.S.: Ford Foundation, 1991. 23–204.

Lodge, Tom, and Bill Nasson, editors. *All, Here, and Now: Black Politics in South Africa in the 1980s.* U.S.: Ford Foundation, 1991.

Lucas-Bull, Wendy. *African Business* 216 (December 1996): 13.

Mack, John E. "The Enemy System." In *The Psychodynamics of International Relationships.* Vol. 1, *Concepts and Theories.* Edited by Vamik D. Volkan, Demetrios A. Julius, and Joseph V. Montville. Lexington, Mass.: Lexington Books, 1990. 57–70.

Magubane, Bernard. *The Political Economy of Race and Class in South Africa.* New York: Monthly Review Press, 1979.

———. *South Africa: From Soweto To Uitenhage—The Political Economy of the South African Revolution.* Trenton, N.J.: Africa World Press, 1989.

Manzo, Kathryn A. *Creating Boundaries: The Politics of Race and Nation.* Boulder: Lynne Rienner, 1996.

———. *Domination, Resistance, and Social Change in South Africa: The Local Effects of Global Power.* Westport, Conn.: Praeger, 1992.

———. "Global Power and South African Politics: A Foucauldian Analysis," *Alternatives* 17 (1992): 23–66.

Maphai, Vincent T. "A Season for Power Sharing." *Journal of Democracy* 7 (January 1996): 66–81.

Marais, Hein. *South Africa: Limits to Change—The Political Economy of Transformation.* London: Zed Books, 1998.

Mare, Gerhard. *Ethnicity and Politics in South Africa.* London: Zed Books, 1993.

Mare, Gerhard, and Georgina Hamilton. *An Appetite for Power: Buthelezi's Inkatha and South Africa.* Johannesburg: Ravan Press, 1987.

Marks, Susan Collin. *Watching the Wind: Conflict Resolution During South Africa's Transition to Democracy.* Washington, D.C.: U.S. Institute of Peace Press, 2000.

Marx, Anthony. *Lessons of Struggle.* New York: Oxford Press, 1992.

———. "Contested Images and Implications of South African Nationhood." In *The Violence Within: Cultural and Political Opposition in Divided Societies.* Edited by Kay Warren. Boulder: Westview Press, 1993. 157–179.

———. *Making Race and Nation.* Cambridge: Cambridge University Press, 1998.

Mashall, Leon, and Tos Wentzel. "Yes Vote Triumphant," *Argus,* 3 November 1983, 1.

Mattera, Don. *Sophiatown.* Boston: Beacon Press, 1987.

Mayer, Phillip M. "Class, Status, and Ethnicity as Perceived by Johannesburg Africans." In *Change in Contemporary South Africa.* Edited by Leonard Thompson and Jeffrey Butler. Berkeley and Los Angeles: University of California Press, 1975. 138–167.

Mead, George Herbert. *Mind, Self, and Society.* Chicago: University of Chicago Press, 1934.

Metrowich, F. R. *The Challenge of Soweto.* Pretoria: Foreign Affairs Association, date unknown.

Michie, Jonathan, and Vishnu Padayachee. "Three Years After Apartheid: Growth, Employment, and Redistribution?" *Cambridge Journal of Economics* 22, no. 5 (1998): 623–635.

Mills, Greg. *War and Peace in Southern Africa: Crime, Drugs, Armies, and Trade.* Cambridge: World Peace Foundation, 1996.

Molefe, Archie. "Soweto and its Aftermath." *Review of African Political Economy* 11 (1978): 17–30.

Molteno, Frank. "The Uprising of 16th June." *Social Dynamics* 5, no. 1 (1979): 54–59.

Monthly Bulletin on Reported Crime in South Africa, January 99 [Web Page]. http: //www.saps.co.za/8_crimeinfo/bulletin/1999(1).htm [Accessed February 14, 1999].

Morris, Alan. "'Our Fellow Africans Make Our Lives Hell': The Lives of Congolese and Nigerians Living in Johannesburg." *Ethnic and Racial Studies* 21, no. 6 (November 1998): 1116–1135.

Morris, Donald R. *The Washing of the Spears.* New York: Simon and Schuster, 1965.

Moses, Rafael. "Self, Self-view, and Identity." In *The Psychodynamics of International Relationships.* Vol. 1, *Concepts and Theories.* Edited by Vamik D. Volkan, Demetrios A. Julius, and Joseph V. Montville. Lexington, Mass.: Lexington Books, 1990. 47–55.

Motapanyane, Tebello. Interview. *Sechaba* 11 (2nd quarter, 1977):49–59.

Mufamadi, Sidney. Media statement, 13 June 1997, Pretoria, photocopy.

Mufson, Stephen. "Introduction: The Roots of Insurrection." In *All, Here and Now: Black Politics in South Africa in the 1980s.* Edited by Tom Lodge and Bill Nasson. U.S.: The Ford Foundation, 1991. 3–17.

———. *Fighting Years: Black Resistance and the Struggle for a New South Africa.* Boston: Beacon Press, 1990.

Muller, Dr. Hilgard. "Let the World Take Note." In *Progress through Separate Development: South Africa in Peaceful Transition.* 2nd edition. New York: Information Service of South Africa, 1968.

Murray, Martin. *The Revolution Deferred: The Painful Birth of Post-Apartheid South Africa.* London: Verso, 1994.

———. *South Africa: Time of Agony, Time of Destiny.* London: Verso, 1987.

Nel, Juan, and Thoe Burgers. "The South African Police Service: 'Symptom Bearer' of the New South Africa?" *Track Two* 5, no. 1 (March 1996): 17.

Nevin, Tom. "Anatomy of a National Menace." *African Business* 216 (December 1996): 11–15.

Nieuwoudt, J. M., and C. Plug. "South African Ethnic Attitudes: 1973 to 1978." *Journal of Social Psychology* 121 (December 1983): 163–171.

Norval, Aletta J. "Decolonization, Demonization, and Difference: The Difficult Constitution of a Nation." *Philosophy and Social Criticism* 21, no. 3 (1995): 31–51.

———. "Social Ambiguity and the Crisis of Apartheid." In *The Making of Political Identities.* Edited by Ernesto Leclau. New York: Verso, 1994. 115–137.

Oden, Bertil. *The South African Tripod: Studies on Economics, Politics, and Conflict.* Uppsala: Scandinavian Institute, 1994.

Omar, Dullah. "And Justice For All." *Track Two* 5, no. 1 (March 1996): 4.

Onuf, Nicholas G. "Constructivism: A User's Manual." In *International Relations in a Constructed World.* Edited by Vendulka Kubalkova, Nicholas Onuf, and Paul Kowert. Armonk, N.Y.: M. E. Sharpe, 1998. 58–78.

———. *World of Our Making: Rules and Rule in Social Theory and International Relations.* Columbia: University of South Carolina Press, 1989.

"Pamphlet Bombs." *Sechaba* 11 (first quarter 1977): 8–10.

Patten, John. "Hot potato report on Coloured new deal." *Star,* 18 June 1976, 2.

Pettman, Ralph. *Commonsense Constructivism or the Making of World Affairs.* Armonk, N.Y.: M. E. Sharpe, 2000.

Posel, Deborah. *The Making of Apartheid, 1948–1961.* Oxford: Clarendon Press, 1991.

President's Council on the Adaptation of Constitutional Structures in South Africa. *Final Report of the Constitutional Committee of the President's Council on the Adaptation of Constitutional Structures in South Africa.* Pretoria: Government Printer, 1984.

Presler, Eric. "South Africa's Criminal Culture." *Foreign Policy* (September/October 2001): 80–82.

Price, Robert. *The Apartheid State in Crisis: Political Transformation in South Africa, 1975–1990.* New York: Oxford University Press, 1991.

Prugl, Elisabeth. "Feminist Struggle as Social Construction: Changing the Gendered Rules of Home-Based Work." In *International Relations in a Constructed World.* Edited by Vendulka Kubalkova, Nicholas Onuf, and Paul Kowert. Armonk, N.Y.: M. E. Sharpe, 1998. 123–146.

Ragin, Charles C. *The Comparative Method: Moving Beyond Qualitative and Quantitative Strategies.* Berkeley and Los Angeles: University of California Press, 1987.

Ranchod, Bhadra. "Reform—Or Change?" In *Bridge or Barricade? The Constitution, A First Appraisal.* Edited by Fleur deVilliers. Johannesburg: Jonathan Ball, 1983. 73–77.

Reynolds, Andrew, editor. *Elections '94 South Africa: The Campaign, Results, and Future Prospects.* London: James Curry, 1994.

———, editor. *Elections '99: From Mandela to Mbeki.* New York: St. Martin's Press, 1999.

Rhoodie, Nic, C. P. de Kock, and M. P. Couper. "White perceptions of socio-political change in South Africa." In *South Africa: A Plural Society in Transition.* Edited by D. J. van Vuuren, N. E. Wiehahn, J. A. Lombard, and N. J. Rhoodie. Durban: Butterworth, 1985. 303–334.

Ross, Robert. "Getting to the New South Africa from the Old." *Ethnic and Racial Studies* 19, no. 2 (April 1996): 438–444.

Ruggie, John Gerard. "What Makes the World Hang Together? Neo-utilitarianism and the Social Constructivist Challenge." *International Organization* 52, no. 4 (Autumn 1998): 855–885.

———. *Constructing the World Polity.* London: Routledge, 1998.

Sanders, James. *South Africa and the International Media 1972–1979.* London: Frank Cass, 2000.

Saville-Troike, Muriel. *The Ethnography of Communication: An Introduction.* 2nd edition. Oxford: Blackwell, 1989.

Say No to Rape. Black Sash pamphlet. date unknown.

Schrire, Robert. *Adapt or Die: White Politics in South Africa.* U.S.: Ford Foundation, 1991.

Scott, James C. *Domination and the Arts of Resistance.* New Haven: Yale University Press, 1990.

———. *Weapons of the Weak: Everyday Forms of Peasant Resistance.* New Haven: Yale University Press, 1985.

Seidman, Judy. *Facelift Apartheid: South Africa After Soweto.* London: International Defense and Aid Fund, 1980.

Shannon, Vaughn P. "Norms Are What States Make of Them: The Political Psychology of Norm Violation." *International Studies Quarterly* 44, no. 2 (2000): 293–316.

Sharp, John. "Introduction: Constructing Social Reality." In *South African Keywords: The Uses and Abuses of Political Concepts.* Edited by Emile Boonzaier and John Sharp. Cape Town: David Phillip, 1988. 1–16.

———. "Two Worlds in One Country: 'First World' and 'Third World' in South Africa." In *South African Keywords: The Uses and Abuses of Political Concepts.* Edited by Emile Boonzaier and John Sharp. Cape Town: David Philip, 1988. 111–121.

Shaw, Mark. "Urban Conflict, Crime, and Policing in South African Cities." *Africa Insight* 25, no. 4 (1995): 216–220.

Shotter, John. *The Cultural Politics of Everyday Life.* Toronto: University of Toronto Press, 1993.

Shubane, Khehla. "Soweto." In *All, Here, and Now: Black Politics in South Africa in the 1980s.* U.S.: The Ford Foundation, 1991. 255–285.

Sikakane, Joyce. *A Window on Soweto.* London: International Defence and Aid Fund, 1977.

Simkins, Charles. "Problems of Reconstruction." *Journal of Democracy* 7 (January 1996): 82–95.

Simkins, Charles et al. *The Prisoners of Tradition and the Politics of Nation-Building.* Johannesburg: South African Institute of Race Relations, 1988.

Singer, Marshall R. *Intercultural Communication: A Perceptual Approach.* Englewood Cliffs, N.J.: Prentice-Hall, 1987.

Sisk, Tim. *Democratization in South Africa: The Elusive Social Contract* Princeton: Princeton University Press, 1995.

Siso, Gift Sipho. "Mandela Fails on Crime." *New African* (June 1997): 25.

South African Institute of Race Relations (SAIRR). *South Africa in Travail: The Disturbances of 1976/77: Evidence Presented by the SA Institute of Race Relations to Cillie Commission of Inquiry into the Riots at Soweto and Other Places in June 1976.* Johannesburg: SAIRR, 1978.

"South African Police Service: CIAC Table of Contents Page" [Web Page]. *http://www.saps.co.za/8_crimeinfo/bulletin/1999(1).htm* [Accessed February 16, 1999].

Southern Africa in Crisis. London: Relgocrest Ltd., date unknown.

Sparks, Allister. *Tomorrow Is Another Country.* Chicago: University of Chicago Press, 1995.

Stein, Howard F. "The Indispensable Enemy and American-Soviet Relations." In *The Psychodynamics of International Relationships.* Vol. 1, *Concepts and Theories.* Edited by Vamik D. Volkan, Demetrios A. Julius, and Joseph V. Montville. Lexington, Mass.: Lexington Books, 1990. 71–90.

Stengel, Richard. "Whites." *The New Republic,* no. 4240 (22 April 1996):13.

Sterling-Folker, Jennifer. "Competing Paradigms or Birds of a Feather? Constructivism and Neoliberal Institutionalism Compared." *International Studies Quarterly* 44, no. 1 (March 2000): 97–119.

Steyn, John, editor. *A 'Ghetto' in South Africa.* Johannesburg: Perskor, date unknown.

The Study Commission on U.S. Policy Toward Southern Africa. *South Africa: Time Running Out.* Berkeley and Los Angeles: University of California Press, 1981.

Swilling, Mark. "The Extra-Parliamentary Movement: Strategies and Prospects." In *Negotiating South Africa's Future.* Edited by Hermann Giliomee and Lawrence Schlemmer. London: Macmillan Press, 1989. 64–74.

Switzer, Les. *Power and Resistance in an African Society: The Ciskei Xhosa and the Making of South Africa.* Madison: University of Wisconsin Press, 1993.

Szeftel, Morris. "Ethnicity and Democratization in South Africa." *Review of African Political Economy,* no. 60, v. 21 (June 1994): 185–199.

Tajfel, Henri, editor. *Social Identity and Intergroup Relations.* Cambridge: Cambridge University Press, 1982.

Taylor, David. *Theories of Intergroup Relations.* New York: Greenwood Press, 1987.

Taylor, Rupert. "The Myth of Ethnic Division: Township Conflict on the Reef." *Race and Class* 33, no. 2 (1991): 1–14.

Tema, Sophie. *Bulletin of the Union of Black Journalists.* 2, date unknown.

Terreblanche, Sampie. "The Brotherhood Syndrome: The Origins of Favouritism." *SASH* 33, no. 2 (September 1989): 9–10.

Thomashausen, Andre. "Power-sharing is a Utopian Dream." In *Bridge or Barricade? The Constitution, A First Appraisal.* Edited by Fleur deVilliers. Johannesburg: Jonathan Ball, 1983. 101–106.

Thompson, Leonard. *A History of South Africa*. 3rd edition. New Haven: Yale University Press, 2000.

———. *The Political Mythology of Apartheid*. New Haven: Yale University Press, 1985.

Treurnicht, Andries. "Speech to the Conservative Party Congress of the Transvaal in August 1985." In *Apartheid in Crisis*. Edited by Mark A. Uhlig. New York: Vintage Books, 1986. 100–103.

Uhlig, Mark A., editor. *Apartheid in Crisis*. New York: Vintage Books, 1986.

Vail, Leroy, editor. *The Creation of Tribalism in Southern Africa*. Berkeley and Los Angeles: University of California Press, 1989.

———. "Introduction." In *The Creation of Tribalism in Southern Africa*. Edited by Leroy Vail. Berkeley and Los Angeles: University of California Press, 1989. 1–19.

van der Horst, Sheila T., editor. *The Theron Commission Report: A Summary of the Findings and Recommendations of the Commission of Enquiry into Matters Relating to the Coloured Population Group*. Johannesburg: SAIRR, 1976.

van der Spuy, D. C. *Amnesty for Terrorism*. Pretoria: National Bureau of International Communications, 1978.

van Wyk, C. J. Crime Information Management Centre [Web Page]. November 1997. http://www.saps.co.za/8_crimeinfo/497/intro.htm [Accessed 18 January 1998].

van Zyl Slabbert, Frederik. "Reform and Revolt: 1983 to 1988." In *Negotiating South Africa's Future*. Edited by Hermann Giliomee and Lawrence Schlemmer. London: MacMillan Press, 1989. 75–82.

Venter, Albert. "The South African Plural Society: Reflections and Musings Towards its Understanding." *Plural Societies* 19, no. 1 (September 1989): 1–20.

Waldmeir, Patti. *Anatomy of a Miracle: The End of Apartheid and the Birth of the New South Africa*. London: Viking, 1997.

Walker, R. B. J. *Inside/Outside: International Relations as Political Theory*. Cambridge: Cambridge University Press, 1993.

Ward, Alan. "Changes in the Political Economy of the New South Africa." In *The New South Africa: Prospects for Domestic and International Security*. Edited by F. H. Toase and E. J. Yorke. New York: St. Martin's Press, 1998. 37–56.

Welsh, David. "Constitutional Changes in South Africa." *African Affairs* 83, no. 331 (April 1984): 147–162.

———. "How Can Coloureds Be an Ethnic Group—Or Water an Ethnic Affair?" In *Bridge or Barricade? The Constitution, A First Appraisal*. Edited by Fleur de Villiers. Johannesburg: Jonathan Ball, 1983. 84–90.

Wendt, Alexander. "Collective Identity Formation and the International State." *American Political Science Review* 88, no. 2 (June 1994): 384–396.

———. "Identity and Structural Change in International Relations." In *The Return of Culture and Identity in IR Theory*. Edited by Yosef Lapid and Friedrich Kratochwil. Boulder: Lynne Rienner, 1996. 47–64.

———. *Social Theory of International Politics*. Cambridge: Cambridge University Press, 1999.

West, Martin. "The Apex of Subordination: The Urban African Population in South Africa." In *The Apartheid Regime: Political Power and Racial Domination*. Edited by Robert Price and Carl Rosberg. Berkeley: University of California Institute of International Studies, 1980. 127–151.

Whitaker, Jennifer Seymour. "Africa Beset." *Foreign Affairs* 62, no. 3 (Spring 1984): 769.

Wikening, Howard. *The Psychological Almanac*. Monterey, Cal.: Brooks/Cole Publishing, 1973.

"The Will of an entire People—forged under fire." *Sechaba* 11 (first quarter 1977):1.

Williams, Paul. "Reflections on the 'New' South Africa." *African Affairs* 98, no. 392 (July 1999): 417, received through ProQuest, an electronic journal service.

Worden, Nigel. *The Making of Modern South Africa: Conquest, Segregation, and Apartheid*. Oxford: Blackwell, 1994.

World Peace Council. *Spotlight on Soweto*. City unknown: World Peace Council, 1976.

Wright, John. "Political Mythology and the Making of Natal's *Mfecane*." *Canadian Journal of African Studies* 23, no. 2, (1989): 272–291.

Index

16 June, 1976. *See* Soweto
acts, primacy of, 35
African National Congress (ANC), 1, 46–47, 80, 92, 107, 127, 160, 175
  history of resistance, 46
  and Freedom Charter, 46
  UmKhonto we Sizwe, 47
  and Soweto uprisings, 71, 73, 78, 197 n. 37
  Youth League, 84
  Mass Action Campaign, 89
  and unrest in 1980s, 105
  position on the 1984 constitution, 113
  and UDF, 118, 130
  national convention in 1991, 138
  and capital punishment, 147–148
Afrikaans, 73
  language policy and Soweto, 66, 68, 69, 71, 73, 76, 77, 85, 86, 173
Afrikaners
  ethnic identity of, 1
  as possessors of SA sovereignty, 83
  and nationalism, 95
  benefits of apartheid, 124, 160
agency, 3, 15–18, 92, 187 n.17
  in liberalism, xv
  in global politics, 12
  and corporate entities, 12–13
  "person" and, 13
  and creativity, 16
  as possession, 16, 171
  as relationship, 16
  organizing using identity labels, 31, 33–35, 36–37, 123, 171, 180, 182–183
  complexity of, 37
  reification of, 37, 181
  changing South African definition, 120–123, 173–176
  unequal distribution of, 182
agents
  co-constitution with structures, xiv, 20, 22, 170
  expansion during SA reform era, 96, 104, 125
  crime as a catalyst for, 157
agent-structure problem, xiv
AIDS, 164
apartheid, 41–45, 172
  origins of, 1, 39–41, 51
  ontology of, 3
  and race, 3
  groups, 42
  resistance to, 45–48
  verkrampte visions of, 96
  verligte visions of, 97
  changes in justification for, 113
  and concepts of equality, 116–117
  as affirmative action, 124
Ashforth, Adam, 98

Bantu education, 129
behavioralism, 10
Berger, Peter, 11
Biko, Steve, 43, 47–48, 90
Black identity, 4, 126
Black Consciousness, 43–44, 46–48, 123, 126, 192 n. 24
  and Soweto, 89–91
Black Power movement, 71, 90–91

Black Sash, 79, 213 n. 123, 214 n. 133
Bloom, William, 24
bodies, xiv
Boesak, Allan, 103, 118, 120
Boiphatong massacre, 80
Botha, P.W. (Prime Minister and State President), 93, 98
 and reform, 97, 109, 121, 129
 and "total onslaught," 97
 and repression, 106–107
 and the 1984 constitution, 112, 113, 124
Botha, R.F. "Pik" (Foreign Minister), 71
boycotts, 72–73, 104, 125, 127
Brewer, John, 72, 75
Burkitt, Ian, 11, 29
Buthelezi, Mongosuthu Gatsha, 117
Buti, Sam, 76

Cambell, David, 26
Cape Town, 68, 70, 79, 102, 140
capital punishment, 147–148
capitalization of labels, 4
carjacking, 152, 158, 161
causality, 3, 16, 27, 183
change, xiii, xiv, 15–18, 35, 170
 definition, 17
 modeled, 178–179
Charterism, 46, 104, 118, 127, 130, 175, 179
Checkel, Jeff, 22
Cillie Commission, 70, 74–75, 83, 85–86, 89, 196 n. 4
civics (civic associations), 101–102, 104, 125
civil disobedience, 136, 157
civil society, xv, 102, 142, 159, 166, 203 n. 21
civilization, 51, 53, 116, 134
class identity, 3, 159–163
cognition, 10
comet, metaphor of, 14, 181
common sense, 51
Comparative Politics, 3, 4
complexity, 16, 25, 169
 of agency, 37
 of identity, 155, 166
 of South African transition, 172, 176, 177–178, 184
comrades, 84, 135, 164
 in 1980s, 106
 as political label, 127–128, 174, 199 n. 73
 and tsotsis, 137

conflict, 58, 181
 and resistance, 20
 socially defined, 20
 and identity, 58
 and methodology, 58–60
 and the South African transition, 177–178
Congress of South African Students (COSAS), 128
Connolly, William, 25, 29
Conservative Party (KP), 99, 110, 111
constitution of 1977, 99
constitution of 1984, 5–6, 59, 99–101
 referendum on, 99–100, 108–111
 governmental structure in, 100
 as impetus for UDF, 103
 media perspectives on, 109–111
 arguments for and against, 109–110
 as reform, 111–117
 and "separate development," 115
 opposition to, 117–120
 foreign perspectives on, 117
 political identity of, 123–129, 174–175
constitution of 1997, 171–172
constructivism, xiii, xiv, 9–23, 181, 187 n. 24
 epistemology, 5, 10, 20
 ontology, 5, 10–12, 20, 26
 thin and thick, 20, 185 n. 2
 critical and conventional, 27
 power, 15
 and identity, 26–38, 179–184
Convention for a Democratic South Africa (CODESA), 138
corporate entities, 12
 agency and, 12–13
 as persons, 12, 28
corruption, 153, 162
Craddock, 106
crime, 6, 133–167
 as conflict, 59
 as interview site, 61
 and apartheid, 134–135
 as resistance, 135–137
 statistics, 139–140
 fear of, 140–141
 post-apartheid, 139–143
 media's discourse on, 143–146
 as a "folk devil," 143–144
 and race, 144, 152–155
 government discourse on, 146–149
 rights of criminals, 148, 164
 social movements, 149–151, 157
 political identity of, 151–166, 175–176
 definition of, 152

and nonracialism, 153–155
   as nationalism, 157–159
   and class, 159–163
   and gender, 163–165
   and geography, 165
criminal identity, 156–157, 163, 166, 175

de Klerk, F.W., 108, 129, 130, 137–139
de Wet Nel, M.C., 52
deconstructivism, 10, 25
democracy, 172, 182
discourse analysis, 57
discursive space as metaphor, 121
Doty, Roxanne, 37
drugs, 158
Durban, 140

Eminent Persons Group (EPG), 107
ethnicity, v, xvi, 3, 182
ethnography, 56–57
everyday life, xiii, 14, 17, 18, 21, 29, 33, 152, 172, 183

Finnemore, Martha, 20
Firm, the, 142, 161
Foucault, Michel, xiii, xv, 15, 16, 53, 57
   ideas of power, 32
Freedom Charter, 46, 102, 104, 130

Garvey, Marcus, 91
Geertz, Clifford, 1
Giddens, Anthony, 11
Global Politics, xv, 3, 15, 170
   as disciplinary challenge, 4–5
globalization, 177, 178, 184
Goniwe, Matthew, 106, 121
Government of National Unity (GNU), 65, 138–139, 143, 145, 147
Gramsci, Antonio, 12, 43
Great Trek, 40
groupness, 41, 42, 177

Habermas, Jurgen, 11
Hegel, G.W.F., xv
Herbstein, Denis, 69
Herstigte Nationale Party (HNP), 111
homelands, 41, 44, 84, 192 n. 15
Hopf, Ted, 22–23, 27

identity, 23–36, 169–170
   constructivism and, xv, 26–38, 179–184, 190 n. 69
   Locke and personal, xv

collective, xvi
   South African, xvi–xvii
   as methodology, 2, 22–23
   Western definition, 23, 170
   corporate, 23
   in psychology, 23–24
   categories of group identity, 25, 170
   current theories of, 25, 29
   reification of, 25
   constructivist definition, 28
   language and, 28–29
   manifestations of, 29
   changes to, 30
   as assertion, 30
   and identity, 32
   mobilization, 53
   complexity, 155, 166
identity labels, xvi, 28, 170, 176
   creativity and, xvii
   as unit of analysis, 2, 3, 32–36, 37, 123, 170, 179–184
   practicalities of writing about, 4
   and texts, 6, 170
   construction of, 28
   changes to, 29–30, 180
   power of, 30, 170
   and agency, 31, 33–35, 36–37, 123, 171–172, 180, 182–183
   and personas, 31
   as codes, 33–34, 172, 180
   and social arrangements, 34, 35–36
   apartheid's, 50–54
   and resistance, 180
Inkatha ("cultural organization"), 117, 126
Inkatha Freedom Party (IFP), 80
institutions, xiv, 13, 14–17
   changes and stability in, 17–18
institutionalization, 12, 14–18, 21, 22
interaction
   as unit of analysis, 31, 32
International Relations, field of, xv, 3, 4, 24–26
   constructivism in, 10, 20
   units of analysis, 31

Johannesburg, 6, 70, 140, 145, 162
   protests during 1976, 68, 69, 82

Kaplan, Robbie, 150
Katzenstein, Peter, 20
Kissinger, Henry, 71, 73
Kratochwil, Friedrich, 22
Kruger, Jimmy, 69–70, 71, 72, 83

INDEX

language, uses of, 28
Lapid, Yosef, 22
law
    apartheid as, 41, 134
    enforcement. *See* South African Police and South African Police Services
Lekota, Patrick "Terror," 103
level of analysis problem, 4, 31, 170
liberalism
    image of the individual, xv, 23
lost generation, 129, 165
Luckmann, Thomas, 11

Mandela, Nelson, 1, 65, 89, 102, 107, 127
    and the transition, 137–139
    and post-apartheid crime, 139, 144, 147–148, 150, 158–159
Mandela, Winnie, 76
Manzo, Kathryn, 42, 51, 53, 116
Mapogo a Mathamaga (Mapogo), 142, 149, 165
Marx, Anthony, 45–46, 49, 102, 108, 129
Mass Action Campaign, 89
Mbeki, Thabo, 65, 145, 148, 165
methodology, 54–63
    constructivist, 20–23
    ethnographic discourse analysis, 54, 55–57
    case studies, 56
    conflict as research site, 58–60
    texts, 60–63
    interviews, 60–63
    See also identity labels, as unit of analysis,
momentum, metaphor of, 14, 181
Mufson, Steven, 106, 122

National Party (NP), 1, 40, 80, 92, 98, 109, 144
    changes to, 95, 124
    divisions within, 96–99
    New National Party (NNP), 144
National Peace Accord, 138
National Youth Day, 65, 81
nationality, 3, 157–159
Naude, Beyers, 76
necklacing, 207 n. 5
negotiation, as metaphor, 21, 34, 181
New National Party. *See* National Party
"New South Africa," 7, 65, 133, 155, 175
Ngcuka, Bulelani, 145
normality, 12, 13, 15
normalization, 17
norms, xiv, 20
Norval, Aletta, 52, 53

ontology, 9
    constructivist, 5, 10–12, 26
Onuf, Nicholas, xii–xvii, 4, 20, 22, 30
order, definitions of, 13–14
    and disorder, 54–55
    See also social arrangements and social order
Organization of African Unity (OAU), 76
"own affairs," 100, 202 n. 13

PAGAD. *See* People Against Gangsterism and Drugs
Pan Africanist Congress (PAC), 46–47, 71, 78, 90, 106, 126
people. *See* "the people"
People Against Gangsterism and Crime (PAGAD), 142, 149
"people's courts," 136
"people's power," 104–105, 117–120, 122, 149, 175
perception, 10, 13
person, 12–13, 16, 23, 27, 28, 169–170
persona, 90, 124, 176
    definition of, 31
    and agency, 34, 171
    apartheid, 36
    resistance and, 120
Petersen, Hector. *See* Pietersen, Zolile Hector
philosophical realism, 10, 185 n.2
Pietersen, Zolile Hector, 67, 79, 196 n. 4
police. *See* South African Police and South African Police Services
political identity
    as perspective, 3
    constructivist theory of, 4, 28–36
    of apartheid, 50–54
    of Soweto uprisings, 81–91
    of 1984 constitution, 120–129
    of post-apartheid crime, 151–166
    of transition, 171–176
    as methodology, 32–36, 183
    See also identity and identity labels
Political Science, 2, 4,
    and power, 15
    and identity, 25, 29
politicization, 116, 122, 152
    of Soweto 1976, 68, 89
Port Elizabeth, 102, 157
Posel, Deborah, 51
positivism, 10, 55
postmodernsim, 10
power, 15–16, 31–36
    and agency, 16–19

and resistance, 19–20
Foucault and, 32
identity and, 169–171
President's Council, 99, 100, 112
Price, Robert, 97
progress, 10
Progressive Federal Party (PFP), 109, 110, 118

race, 90–91
and apartheid, 3, 172
in this book, 4
and agency, 122
in post-apartheid society, 144–145, 152–156
rape, 69, 163–164
rationality, 187 n. 20
as component of agency, xv
definition, 17
reality, definition, 10
referendum
on 1983 constitution, 99–100, 108–111
on 1992 transition, 138
reform, 96–99
constitutional reform in the 1980s, 95–131
definition, 95
purpose, 98
repression after, 106–108
resistance, xvii, 21, 36, 48, 54
definition, 18–20, 45
four levels of, 19, 178–179
and conflict, 20
to apartheid, 45–48
in Soweto uprisings, 78–79, 87–89
in 1980s, 101–106, 119–120
and crime, 135–137
and identity, 180
Ruggie, John, 20
rules, 179, 183–184
and constructivism, xiv, 20, 180–181
in constructivist methodology, 21–22
and identity, 34, 170, 182
apartheid's, 171–173, 175
post-apartheid, 175, 177–178

sanctions, 95, 107, 182
Schlebusch Commission, 99, 114
scientific realism, 11, 186 n.4
Scorpions, 145–147
Scott, James, 19–20, 22, 43
security industries, 141–142, 149–150
Selebi, Jackie, 145–147
self-determination, 120–121

separate development, 44, 115
Shaka Zulu, 40
smuggling, 158
Sobukwe, Robert, 46, 106
social arrangements, 13, 22, 33, 186 n. 10
and identity, 34, 35–36
appearance of stability,34, 170–171
See also order and social order
social movements, 149–151, 156–157
global anti-apartheid movement, 182
social order
power of, 14
and privilege, 14–15
apparent continuity of, 17, 170–171
See also social arrangements and order
Social Identification Theory, 24
society, definition,12–13
South Africa
political history, 39–48
analytical frameworks, 48–50
transition from apartheid, 1–2, 54–55, 137–139, 171–176
See also "New South Africa"
South African Broadcast Corporation (SABC), 69, 109, 144
South African Catholic Bishops Conference, 120
South African Communist Party (SACP), 160
South African Defense Forces (SADF), 73, 91, 105
South African Police (SAP), 62, 164
and Soweto uprising, 66–67, 69–70, 71–75, 75, 77, 79, 81, 82, 83
in 1980s, 105
organization of, 135
auxiliary policing units,135
changes during 1990s, 139, 147
South African Police Services (SAPS), 147, 158
social movements and, 149–151
sovereignty, 182
Soweto, 5, 47–48, 73, 96, 101, 102, 136, 173–174
as case, 59
1976 uprisings, 65–93
Action Committee, 66, 196 n.3
news of, 68–70
as riots, 68
as conspiracy, 71–75, 88
agitators and, 72, 74, 84, 86, 91
tsotsis and, 68, 71, 72, 74, 77–78, 82, 84, 91

Soweto *(continued)*
  as uprising, 75–81, 95, 174
  spontaneity of, 78, 90, 92, 174
  anniversaries of, 79–81
  Coloureds and, 68, 74, 79
  political identity of, 81–91
  communists and, 83, 86, 91
  and level of resistance, 87–89
  and changes to identity, 89–91
  Black Consciousness and, 89–90
  and agency, 92, 181
  unrest in 1980s, 105
Soweto Students Representative Council (SSRC), 78, 196 n. 3
States of Emergency, 136, 207 n. 1
  1960, 79
  1985, 106, 107, 130
  1986, 107–108, 130, 131
State President, office of, 100
structuration, 11
structures, 15–18, 186n. 10
  co-constitution with agents, xiv, 15–16, 20–21, 22, 170
  See also order and social order and social arrangements
student identity, 84, 174
Swart gevaar, die (Black menace), 69, 82, 137–138
symbolic interactionism, 30

Tajfel, Henri, 24
"the people," 77, 78, 84, 104, 119–120, 122, 137
townships, 97, 101, 118
  and crime, 6, 135–137, 165
  and "ungovernability," 105
Total Onslaught and Total Strategy, 97–98, 137–138
transition
  two processes of, 54–55, 178–179
Treurnicht, Andries, 110

tri-cameral legislature, 100
Truth and Reconcilliation Commission (TRC), 49, 50, 62
Tshwete, Steve, 145–147
tsotsis, 67, 73, 135, 196 n. 6
  role in Soweto uprising, 68, 71, 72, 74, 77–78, 82, 84, 91
  and comrades, 137
Tutu, Desmond (Archbishop), 76, 106

unemployment, 135, 160–161, 213 n. 113
unit of analysis, 31, 32–36
  See also identity labels, as unit of analysis
United Democratic Front (UDF), 106–108, 126–127
  founding of, 103–104
  and resistance, 105
  and opposition to 1984 constitution, 118–120, 130
United Nations, 76, 81
Upbeat *magazine*, 80–81

van Zyl Slabbert, Frederick, 110, 118
victim identity, 156–157, 163–164, 166, 176
vigilantes
  during 1976 protests, 68
  and post-apartheid crime, 142, 149–150, 156–157
Vorster, John (Prime Minister), 66, 71, 73
voter identity, 172

Walker, R.B.J., 29
Wendt, Alexander, 10, 20, 31
  on identity, 27, 32, 33, 189–190 n. 55
West Rand Administrative Board (WRAB), 67, 68, 71
white-collar crime, 153
Winning Hearts and Minds (WHAM), 108

youth identity, 84, 91, 128–129

SUNY series in Global Politics
James N. Rosenau, Editor

List of Titles

American Patriotism in a Global Society—Betty Jean Craige

The Political Discourse of Anarchy: A Disciplinary History of International Relations—Brian C. Schmidt

From Pirates to Drug Lords: The Post–Cold War Caribbean Security Environment—Michael C. Desch, Jorge I. Dominguez, and Andres Serbin (eds.)

Collective Conflict Management and Changing World Politics—Joseph Lepgold and Thomas G. Weiss (eds.)

Zones of Peace in the Third World: South America and West Africa in Comparative Perspective—Arie M. Kacowicz

Private Authority and International Affairs—A. Claire Cutler, Virginia Haufler, and Tony Porter (eds.)

Harmonizing Europe: Nation-States within the Common Market—Francesco G. Duina

Economic Interdependence in Ukrainian-Russian Relations—Paul J. D'Anieri

Leapfrogging Development? The Political Economy of Telecommunications Restructuring—J. P. Singh

States, Firms, and Power: Successful Sanctions in United States Foreign Policy—George E. Shambaugh

Approaches to Global Governance Theory—Martin Hewson and Timothy J. Sinclair (eds.)

After Authority: War, Peace, and Global Politics in the Twenty-First Century—Ronnie D. Lipschutz

Pondering Postinternationalism: A Paradigm for the Twenty-First Century?—Heidi H. Hobbs (ed.)

Beyond Boundaries? Disciplines, Paradigms, and Theoretical Integration in International Studies—Rudra Sil and Eileen M. Doherty (eds.)

Why Movements Matter: The West German Peace Movement and U.S. Arms Control Policy—Steve Breyman

International Relations—Still an American Social Science? Toward Diversity in International Thought—Robert M. A. Crawford and Darryl S. L. Jarvis (eds.)

Which Lessons Matter? American Foreign Policy Decision Making in the Middle East, 1979–1987—Christopher Hemmer (ed.)

Hierarchy Amidst Anarchy: Transaction Costs and Institutional Choice—Katja Weber

Counter-Hegemony and Foreign Policy: The Dialectics of Marginalized and Global Forces in Jamaica—Randolph B. Persaud

Global Limits: Immanuel Kant, International Relations, and Critique of World Politics—Mark F. N. Franke

Power and Ideas: North-South Politics of Intellectual Property and Antitrust—Susan K. Sell

Money and Power in Europe: The Political Economy of European Monetary Cooperation—Matthias Kaelberer

Agency and Ethics: The Politics of Military Intervention—Anthony F. Lang, Jr.

Life After the Soviet Union: The Newly Independent Republics of the Transcaucasus and Central Asia—Nozar Alaolmolki

Theories of International Cooperation and the Primacy of Anarchy: Explaining U. S. International Monetary Policy-Making After Bretton Woods—Jennifer Sterling-Folker

Information Technologies and Global Politics: The Changing Scope of Power and Governance—James N. Rosenau and J. P. Singh (eds.)

Technology, Democracy, and Development: International Conflict and Cooperation in the Information Age—Juliann Emmons Allison (ed.)

The Arab-Israeli Conflict Transformed: Fifty Years of Interstate and Ethnic Crises—Hemda Ben-Yehuda and Shmuel Sandler

Systems of Violence: The Political Economy of War and Peace in Colombia—Nazih Richani

Debating the Global Financial Architecture—Leslie Elliot Armijo

Political Space: Frontiers of Change and Governance in a Globalizing World—Yale Ferguson and R. J. Barry Jones (eds.)

Crisis Theory and World Order: Heideggerian Reflections—Norman K. Swazo

Political Identity and Social Change: The Remaking of the South African Social Order—Jamie Frueh

Social Construction and the Logic of Money: Financial Predominance and International Economic Leadership—J. Samuel Barkin

What Moves Man: The Realist Theory of International Relations and Its Judgment of Human Nature—Annette Freyberg-Inan